XView Reference Manual

Books That Help People Get More Out of Computers

X Protocol Reference Manual, *516 pages*

Describes the X Network Protocol which underlies all software for Version 11 of the X Window System.

Xlib Programming Manual, *680 pages*
Xlib Reference Manual, *792 pages*

Complete programming and reference guides to the X library (Xlib), the lowest level of programming interface to X.

X Window System User's Guide

Orients the new user to window system concepts, provides detailed tutorials for many client programs, and explains how to customize the X environment.

Standard Edition, 752 pages
Motif Edition, 734 pages

X Toolkit Intrinsics Programming Manual

Complete guide to programming with Xt Intrinsics, the library of C language routines that facilitate the design of user interfaces, with reusable components called widgets.

Standard Edition, 624 pages
Motif Edition, 672 pages

X Toolkit Intrinsics Reference Manual, *776 pages*

Complete programmer's reference for the X Toolkit.

Motif Programming Manual, *1032 pages*

Complete guide to programming for the Motif graphical user interface.

XView Programming Manual, *776 pages*
XView Reference Manual, *292 pages*

Complete information on programming with XView, an easy-to-use toolkit that is widely available.

The X Window System in a Nutshell, *380 pages*

A single-volume quick reference that is an indispensable companion to the series.

Contact us for a catalog of our books, for orders, or for more information.

O'Reilly & Associates, Inc.

103 Morris Street, Suite A, Sebastopol CA 95472
(800) 338-6887 US/Canada   707-829-0515 overseas/local   707-829-0104 Fax

XView Reference Manual

Edited by Thomas Van Raalte

O'Reilly & Associates, Inc.

XView Reference Manual
Edited by Thomas Van Raalte

Copyright © 1991 O'Reilly & Associates, Inc. All rights reserved.
Printed in the United States of America.

X Series Editor: Tim O'Reilly

Printing History:

September 1991:   First Edition.
March 1992:   Second printing.

This book is printed on acid-free paper with 50% recycled content, 10-15% post-consumer waste. O'Reilly & Associates is committed to using paper with the highest recycled content available consistent with high quality.

Volume 7: ISBN 0-937175-88-9

Table of Contents

Figures

Tables

Preface

By convention, a preface introduces the book itself, while the introduction starts in on the subject matter. You should read through the preface to get an idea of how the book is organized, the conventions it follows, and so on.

In This Chapter:

Preface

This manual describes the XView attributes, callbacks, procedures, macros, data structures, as well as additional reference material. XView (**X Window-System-based Visual/Integrated Environment for Workstations**) is a user-interface toolkit to support interactive, graphics-based applications running under the X Window System. This toolkit, developed by Sun Microsystems, Inc., is derived from earlier toolkits for the SunView™ windowing system. With over 2000 SunView applications in the workstation market, there are many programmers already familiar with SunView application programmer's interface (API).

XView is based upon Xlib, the lowest level of the X Window System available to the programmer. While developing XView user interfaces does not require Xlib programming experience, there are good reasons for learning more about Xlib, especially if your application renders graphics.

How to Use This Manual

The *XView Reference Manual* includes reference material for each of the XView attributes and procedures, information about XView resources, and data structures. Within each section, reference pages are organized alphabetically.

This book is designed to be used with the *XView Programming Manual*. The *XView Programming Manual* provides an explanation of XView, including tutorial material and numerous programming examples. To get the most out of the *XView Programming Manual*, you will need the exact arguments for the attributes, and the calling sequence for the callbacks and procedures, that this reference manual provides.

The following paragraphs briefly describe the contents of this book:

Section 1, *XView Package Summary*,
> provides an introduction to XView and provides a summary of each of the XView packages.

Section 2, *Summary of Attributes*,
> provides alphabetically arranged descriptions of all attributes, and the callback procedures that are supplied by the application programmer.

Section 3, *Summary of Procedures and Macros*,
> provides alphabetically arranged descriptions of all the XView procedures and macros.

Section 4, *Data Types*,

> lists the data types defined by XView.

Section 5, *Event Codes*,

> lists the event codes in numerical order by value.

Section 6, *Command-line Arguments and XView Resources*,

> lists the XView options that can be set using command-line options. This section also lists the resources that XView uses to define certain default values when an application is initialized.

Appendix A, *Selection Compatibility Attributes*,

> provides the attributes for the old selection mechanism. A new selection package has been added in XView Version 3. The new selection package supports the standard XView API. The old selection mechanism is still supported in XView Version 3.

Appendix B, *Selection Compatibility Procedures*,

> provides the procedures and macros for the old selection mechanism. A new selection package has been added in XView Version 3. The new selection package supports the standard XView API. The old selection mechanism is still supported in XView Version 3.

Appendix C, *Textsw Action Attributes*,

> provides the `ACTION_*` attributes that are available for use with a client-supplied notify procedure. These attributes are not standard attributes and cannot be used with `xv_create()`, `xv_get()`, or `xv_set()`.

Font Conventions Used in This Manual

Italic is used for:

- UNIX® pathnames, filenames, program names, user command names, and options for user commands.

- New terms where they are introduced.

`Typewriter` Font is used for:

- Anything that would be typed verbatim into code, such as examples of source code and text on the screen.

- XView packages.*

- The contents of include files, such as structure types, structure members, symbols (defined constants and bit flags), and macros.

---

*When referring to all members of a particular package, such as CANVAS, the notation CANVAS_* will be used. This should not be interpreted as a C-language pointer construct.

- XView and Xlib functions.

- Names of subroutines of the example programs.

Italic Typewriter Font is used for:

- Arguments to XView functions, since they could be typed in code as shown but are arbitrary.

Helvetica Italics are used for:

- Titles of examples, figures, and tables.

Boldface is used for:

- Sections and headings.

Related Documents

The C Programming Language by B. W. Kernighan and D. M. Ritchie.

The following documents are included on the X11 source tape:

OPEN LOOK Graphical User Interface Functional Specification

OPEN LOOK Graphical User Interface Style Guide

The following books in the X Window System series from O'Reilly and Associates, Inc. are currently available:

Volume Zero—*X Protocol Reference Manual*
Volume One—*Xlib Programming Manual*
Volume Two—*Xlib Reference Manual*
Volume Three—*X Window System User's Guide*
Volume Four—*X Toolkit Intrinsics Programming Manual*
Volume Five—*X Toolkit Intrinsics Reference Manual*
Volume Six—*Motif Programming Manual*
Volume Seven—*XView Programming Manual*
Quick Reference—*The X Window System in a Nutshell*

Requests for Comments

Please write to tell us about any flaws you find in this manual or how you think it could be improved, to help us provide you with the best documentation possible.

Our U.S. mail address, phone numbers, and e-mail addresses are as follows:

O'Reilly and Associates, Inc.
103 Morris Street, Suite A
Sebastopol, CA 95472
in USA 1-800-338-6887,
international +1 707-829-0515

UUCP: uunet!ora!xview   Internet: xview@ora.com

Acknowledgements

The initial material for this manual was the appendices to the previous version of the *XView Programming Manual* by Dan Heller. This material has been considerably expanded and should be a helpful addition to the XView documentation.

Thanks to John Stone for all his help in preparing this manual. John dealt with formatting issues and checked and re-checked all the new attributes. Special thanks also go to Darci Chapman and Jon Lee for their assistance.

Dale Dougherty kept the big picture in sight and managed this project. Thanks to Rosanne Wagger, Lenny Meullner, Kismet McDonough, Chris Reilly, and the rest of the production and graphics team at O'Reilly and Associates who put the final manual together.

The XView developers at Sun Microsystems spent many hours going over many versions of this manual. In particular, Chris Kasso added extensively to this material and answered numerous questions. Thanks also go to Isa Hashim and Mitch Jerome for their comments and additions. Darren Austin, Sri Atreya, Shirley Joe and Shanmugh Natarajan reviewed this manual and helped in numerous ways. Thanks also go to Tony Hillman, Bhaskar Prabhala, Greg Kimura, and Stan Raichlen. Despite all the reviews, any errors that remain are my own.

– Thomas Van Raalte

1

XView Package Summary

Section 1, XView Package Summary, *provides an introduction to XView and provides a summary of each of the XView packages.*

In This Chapter:

1
XView Package Summary

This section provides a brief introduction to XView and then goes on to introduce each of the XView packages. The packages are described in alphabetical order; their order in this section does not correspond to how they are used in any particular application. Refer to the *XView Programming Manual* for a general introduction to XView and for details on creating and working with XView objects.

The last part of this section provides a description of the Notifier. The Notifier maintains the flow of control in an application. The Notifier controls XView's *notification-based* event handling using *callback procedures* supplied by application programmers. Also refer to the *XView Programming Manual* for more information on the Notifier.

1.1 XView and OPEN LOOK

XView provides a set of windows that include:

- *Canvases* on which programs can draw.

- *Text subwindows* with built-in editing capabilities.

- *Panels* containing items such as buttons, choice items, and sliders.

- *TTY subwindows* that emulate character-based terminals.

These windows are arranged as *subwindows* within *frames*, which are themselves windows. Frames can be transitory or permanent. Transient interactions with the user can also take place in *menus* which can pop up anywhere on the screen.

An important feature of the XView Toolkit is that it implements the OPEN LOOK Graphical User Interface (GUI). The OPEN LOOK GUI provides users with a simple, consistent, and efficient interface.

OPEN LOOK is supported by Sun and AT&T as the graphical user interface standard for System V Release 4. Users and developers benefit from a standard because it ensures consistent behavior across a number of diverse applications. Programmers can concentrate on the design of the application without having to "invent" a user interface for each application.

XView was built based entirely on OPEN LOOK specifications that could be mapped easily into the X Window System.

The visual design of OPEN LOOK is restrained. The design of each component in the user interface is simple and uncomplicated. The interface is based on a few simple concepts that result in a system that is easy to learn initially. And an XView application is relatively simple, and is easy to implement because many of the default values of interface components work well for most applications.

The definitive document on OPEN LOOK for application programmers is the *OPEN LOOK Graphical User Interface Style Guide*.

1.2 XView Packages

XView defines classes of objects in a tree hierarchy. For example, *frame* is a subclass of the more general class *window*, which in turn is a subclass of *drawable*. Drawable, like user interface object classes, is a subclass of the *Generic Object* class. Figure 1-1 shows the XView class hierarchy. Each class has identifying features that make it unique from other classes or packages. In XView, a class is often called a *package*, meaning a set of related functional elements. However, there are XView packages that are not members of the object class hierarchy, such as the Notifier package.

Some objects are visual and others are not. Visual objects include windows, scrollbars, frames, panels, and panel items, among others. Nonvisual objects are objects which have no appearance, per se, but they have information which aids in the display of visual objects. Examples of nonvisual objects include the server, screen, and font objects. The screen, for example, provides information such as the type of color it can display or the default foreground and background colors that objects might inherit. The display can provide information about what fonts are available for objects that display text.

All objects, both visual and nonvisual, are a part of this object classing system. The system is extensible, so you can create new classes that might or might not be based on existing classes.

XView uses static subclassing and chained inheritance as part of its object-oriented model. All objects of a particular class inherit the properties of the parent class (also known as a superclass). The Generic Object XV_OBJECT contains certain basic properties that all objects share. For example, the same object can appear in many places on the screen to optimize storage. To keep a record of this, the Generic Object maintains a reference count of its instances. Since all objects have an owner, the parent of the object is stored in a field of the generic part of the object. As the needs of an object get more specific to a particular look or functionality, lower-level classes define properties to implement it.

Each class contains properties that are shared among all instances of that object. For example, *panels* are a part of the PANEL package, which has properties that describe, among other things, its layout (horizontal or vertical) or the spacing between items (buttons) in the panel. All panels share these properties, even though the state of the properties might differ for each instance of the object.

As mentioned earlier, XView uses subclassing so that each package can inherit the properties of its superclass. The PANEL package is subclassed from the WINDOW package, which has properties specific to all windows, such as window dimensions, location on the screen, border thickness, depth, visual, and colormap information. The WINDOW package is subclassed from the root object XV_OBJECT, as are all objects, and the panel can access generic information such as the size and position of itself.

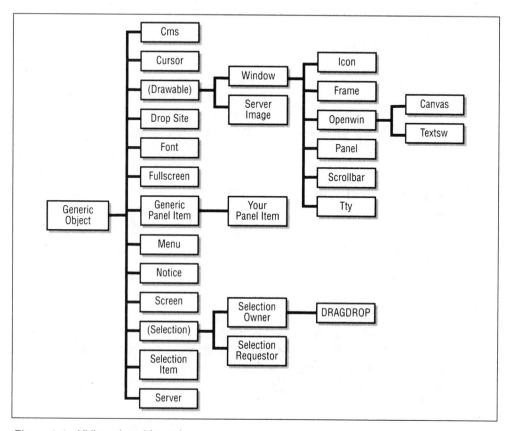

Figure 1-1. XView class hierarchy

1.2.1 Object Handles

When you create an object, an XView function returns a *handle* for the object. Later, when you wish to manipulate the object or inquire about its state, you pass its handle to the appropriate function. This reliance on object handles is a way of *information-hiding*. The handles are *opaque* in the sense that you cannot see through them to the actual data structure which represents the object.

Each object type has a corresponding type of handle. Since C does not have an opaque type, all the opaque data types mentioned above are typedef'd to the XView type Xv_opaque or Xv_object.

In addition to the opaque data types, there are several typedefs that refer not to pointers but to structures: Event, Rect, and Rectlist. Generally, pointers to these structures are passed to XView functions, so they are declared as Event *, Rect *, etc. The reason that the asterisk (*) is not included in the typedef is that the structures are publicly available.

1.2.2 Attribute-based Functions

A model such as that used by XView, which is based on complex and flexible objects, presents the problem of how the client is to manipulate the objects. The basic idea behind the XView interface is to provide a small number of functions, which take as arguments a large set of *attributes*. For a given call to create or modify an object, only a subset of the set of all applicable attributes will be of interest.

1.2.3 Creating and Manipulating Objects

There is a common set of functions that allows the programmer to manipulate any object by referencing the object handle. The functions are listed in Table 1-1.

Table 1-1. Generic Functions

Function	Role
xv_init()	Establishes the connection to the server, initializes the Notifier and the Defaults/Resource-Manager database, loads the Server Resource Manager database, and parses any generic toolkit command-line options.
xv_create()	Creates an object.
xv_destroy()	Destroys an object.
xv_find()	Finds an object that meets certain criteria; or if the object doesn't exist, creates it.
xv_get()	Gets the value of an attribute.
xv_set()	Sets the value of an attribute.

Using these six routines, objects can be created and manipulated from all packages available in XView. Table 1-2 lists the XView packages. Each of these packages is introduced in this section.

Table 1-2. XView Packages

CANVAS	NOTICE	PANEL_NUMERIC_TEXT
CMS	PANEL	PANEL_SLIDER
CURSOR	PANEL_ITEM	PANEL_TEXT
DRAGDROP	PANEL_BUTTON	SCREEN
DROP_SITE_ITEM	PANEL_CHOICE	SCROLLBAR
FONT	PANEL_CHECK_BOX	SELECTION
FRAME	PANEL_DROP_TARGET_ITEM	SERVER
FULLSCREEN	PANEL_GAUGE	TEXTSW
ICON	PANEL_LIST	TTYSW
MENU	PANEL_MESSAGE	WINDOW
MENU_ITEM	PANEL_MULTILINE_TEXT	

1.3 The CANVAS Package

A canvas is the area in which an application displays graphics and handles its input. An XView canvas object allows the user to view a graphic image that is similar to a painter's canvas. This image may be too large for the window or even too large for the display screen. The viewable portion of the graphic image is part of image's *viewport* or *view window*. Many different views of an image can use the same canvas object. While each view maintains its own idea of what it is displaying, the canvas object manages all the view windows as well as the graphic image that all views share. The ability for the canvas to maintain different views of the graphic image is a property that is inherited from the canvas's superclass, the OPENWIN package. These properties provide for *splitting* and *scrolling* views. You cannot create a canvas object with multiple views; views are split and joined generally by the user via the attached scrollbars. It is possible to programmatically split and scroll views, but OPEN LOOK's interface specification indicates that scrollbars provide the ability to split views. When a view is split, each new view may be further split into two more views, and so on. All the views are still a part of the same canvas object.

There are three types of windows involved with the canvas object:

Canvas Subwindow   Owned by a frame and manages one or more views. The canvas is subclassed from the OPENWIN package so all Openwin attributes must be set to the instance of the canvas object.

View Window   Represents the visible portion of the paint window—whenever the paint window associated with a view window changes, it is reflected in the view window. If there is more than one view window, the views are tiled. Vertical and/or horizontal scrollbars can be attached to the view subwindow to allow the user to modify which portion of the paint window is displayed for that particular view. The size of the view window can vary among all the views. Only views can be split. No graphics or user events take place in this window.

Paint Window	Graphics and events (mouse/keyboard) take place in the paint window. There is one paint window per view window. All paint windows in the canvas are the same size regardless of the size of the canvas or of the corresponding view windows. When a view is split, the old view reduces in size and a new view is created. With the new view, a new paint window is created that is identical to the paint window from the old view. This includes the same visual, width, height, depth and graphic image. However, callback functions and event masks are not inherited and must be manually installed in all new paint windows.

The CANVAS package is defined in the header file *<xview/canvas.h>* so programs that use canvases must include this file. This header file includes the OPENWIN package automatically. The owner of a canvas must be a FRAME object.

1.4 The CMS Package

The X Window System has various ways of allocating, specifying, and using colors. While all of these methods are available to applications without XView intervening, XView provides its own model for color specification that may be used as an alternative. It does not provide anything more than what is already available, but it may provide a simpler interface to request and specify colors. This model is especially useful when specifying colors for XView objects, such as panel buttons and scrollbars.

XView applications deal with color by using *colormap segments*. Window-based objects (canvases, panels, textsw, etc.) use colormap segments to get their colors. These objects get a default colormap segment when they are created, but you can assign a new one using the WIN_CMS attribute. Colormap segments must be applied to windows to assure that the window can access the color you are attempting to draw into.

A colormap segment from the CMS package is a subset of the available cells in a colormap on the X server. These are XView entities (i.e., not Xlib) that provide a veneer over the Xlib color mechanism. Colormap segments can be created as either *static* or *dynamic* and are derived from an underlying colormap of the same type.

Applications that use color must include the file *<xview/cms.h>*. The *owner* of a colormap segment is the XView screen object with which the colormap is associated. If an owner is not specified (NULL owner), the default screen of the default server is used as the owner.

1.5 The CURSOR Package

A *cursor* is an image that tracks the mouse on the display. Each window has its own cursor which you can change. There are some cursors defined by OPEN LOOK that correspond to specific window manager operations such as resizing or dragging windows. For these cases, you cannot redefine a cursor. However, for windows in your application, you can assign any cursor image you like.

To use the CURSOR package, include the header file <*xview/cursor.h*>. The owner of the cursor may be any XView object. The root window associated with the XView object is used internally by the CURSOR package. If the owner is NULL, then the root window of the default screen is used.

A number of predefined cursors are available in the CURSOR package for use as OPEN LOOK cursors. To use these cursors, you may specify the CURSOR_SRC_CHAR and CURSOR_MASK_CHAR attributes with certain predefined constants as values for these attributes. There are some OPEN LOOK cursor defines prefixed by OLC_ in <*xview/cursor.h*>.

The *hotspot* on a cursor is the location in which the cursor is located if the user generates an event like pressing a mouse button or typing at the keyboard, or if you were to query its position. For example, if a cursor is shaped like an arrow, the hotspot should be at the tip of the arrow. If the hotspot for a cursor were set to (0, 0) then the hotspot would be the upper-left corner of the image used. A cursor shaped like a bull's eye (16x16) might have its hotspot at (7, 7) to indicate that the focus for the cursor is in the middle.

1.6 The DRAGDROP and DROP_SITE_ITEM Packages

Drag and drop operations are facilitated using two packages: The DRAGDROP package and the DROP_SITE_ITEM package. DRAGDROP is subclassed from the SELECTION_OWNER package and represents the source of the drag. DROP_SITE_ITEM is subclassed from the Generic package. A drop-site item indicates a destination that is a valid drop-site. A valid drop-site is a region that may either preview a drop or receive a drop. A drag and drop operation, such as the familiar procedure of dragging a file from a folder and dropping it into another folder, allows you to easily transfer data.

Applications need to include the file <*xview/dragdrop.h*> to use these packages. Drag and drop supports *drop previewing* where the drop-site image changes to show that it is a valid drop-site and *drag feedback* where the pointer image (cursor) changes to indicate that an item is being dragged.

Attributes for DRAGDROP use a DND_ prefix. Attributes for DROP_SITE_ITEM use a DROP_SITE prefix. The owner of either a DRAGDROP object, or a DROP_SITE_ITEM object is a window.

1.7 The FONT Package

In X, a large number of fonts are provided on the server. Deciding which font to use and then trying to specify fonts by name can be difficult since there are many different styles and sizes of fonts. Most fonts are used to render text strings. So the images, or *glyphs*, represent a character set-defined language used. However, a font may be built to support glyphs for other languages or to provide a set of glyphs. Fonts are stored on the server and are associated with the display of your workstation. The *font ID* is stored in the graphics context (GC), which is used by Xlib functions like XDrawString(). Using fonts to render text is perhaps the most common application. For example, the Courier font family displays the classic typewriter or constant-width character set. This text is set in Times-Roman, a proportionally spaced font. Often within a font family, there are different styles, such as **bold** or *italic*, and different point sizes.* For example, *Helvetica bold 14* refers to the Helvetica font family; bold is the style and 14 is the point size.

Not all server fonts have a variety of styles and sizes. These special-purpose fonts are generally specified by name only—there are no corresponding styles or families for these fonts.

When accessing fonts, you typically want to specify a font either by *name* or by the *family*, *style* and *size* or *scale* of the font. In addition, XView provides an interface for determining the dimensions (in pixels) of characters and strings rendered in a specified font.

OPEN LOOK uses predefined fonts for certain items such as panel buttons and other user interface elements. These items cannot be changed, but you can assign text fonts to panel choices, text subwindows and other types of windows.

Applications that use the FONT package must include the header file, *<xview/font.h>*. In XView, when a font object is created, it loads the font from the X server. When we say, "create a font", we really mean, "load a font from the server and create an XView font object associated with that font."

While fonts can be created using `xv_create()`, it may not be necessary to create a new instance of a font. Fonts are typically cached on the server, and XView may already have a handle to a particular font. Therefore, you would obtain a handle to the font, if it already exists, rather than open another instance of the same font. `xv_find()` can be used to return the handle of an existing font. If the handle does not exist, `xv_find()` can create a new instance of the font.

The owner of the font is usually the window in which the font is going to be used. The actual X font is loaded from the server associated with the owner object. If the owner is NULL, the default server is used. Fonts may be used on any window, or in memory pixmaps, or a server image (a `Server_image` object), but these objects must have the same display (Server) associated with them as the font, or you will get an X Protocol error. What this means, is that a font can only be used on the server on which it was created.

1.8 The FRAME Package

A frame is a container for other windows. It manages the geometry and placement of *subwindows* that do not overlap and are fixed within the boundary of the frame. The OPEN LOOK specification refers to subwindows, or *panes*, as *tiled* windows because they do not overlap one another. Subwindow types include canvases, text subwindows, panels, and scrollbars. These subwindows cannot exist without a parent frame to manage them.

The FRAME package provides the following capabilities:

- A communication path between the application and the window manager.

- A mechanism to receive input for the application.

---

*Note that point sizes on workstations are based on pixels, whereas point sizes for typesetters and printers are based on inches.

- A visual container for user interface objects.

- A method to group windows with related functionality.

- A mechanism to manage footers.

A frame depends upon the window manager for its *decorations* and many basic operations. The FRAME package does *not* manage headers (title bars), resize corners, or the colors of those objects. These are all strictly functions of the window manager. The application gives hints to the window manager about some of these attributes through the FRAME package (including not to display decorations at all if so desired), but results vary depending on which window manager the user is running.

Frames do not manage events; this task is left up to the windows that the frame manages. That is, frames do not get mouse and keyboard events and propagate them to child windows. While frames are subclassed from the window package, the frame's window rarely sees any events at all, and if they do, these are not intended to be processed by the application programmer.

Basically, two types of frames are available in XView: base frames and command frames. The main frame of the application is called the *base frame*. The base frame resides on the root window; its handle is passed to xv_main_loop() to begin application processing.

A special kind of frame, called a *command frame*, is created with a panel subwindow by default. Command frames are useful as help frames, property frames, and such defined by OPEN LOOK. Programmatically, a command frame is no different from a frame with one subwindow that is a panel and a pushpin if run under the olwm (OPEN LOOK window manager).

A base frame's *parent* or owner, is the root window, whereas a subframe's parent is another frame (either a base frame or a subframe). When a frame goes away (quit or close), all of its child windows, including subframes, also go away. For example, assume you create a command subframe to display application-specific help. When this command subframe is activated, it might display explanatory text along with an OK button to dismiss the help. If you close the base frame, the help subframe also closes.

XView allows for multiple frames that are not children of the base frame. For instance, you could create a help frame that is independent of the application's base frame. The parent of this frame is the root window of the display and not the base frame. The help frame will remain visible even if the base frame goes away. The term subframe defines a relationship among frames at creation time and a slight difference in functionality.

1.9 The FULLSCREEN Package

The FULLSCREEN package is used to grab the X server, and an instance of it is considered a nonvisual object. Nonvisual objects are not viewed on the screen, but they have a place in the XView object hierarchy. Nonvisual objects are typically used internally by XView and are seldom used directly in an application. Working with FULLSCREEN objects may not be essential to all programmers.

1.10 The ICON Package

A user may *close* an application to save space on the display. The program is still running and it may even be active, but it is not receiving input from the user. In order to represent the application in its closed state, an *icon* is used. An icon is a small picture that represents the application.

The graphic image that icons use may be used for other purposes and, therefore, may be shared among other objects in the application. But the icon image should be designed to easily identify the application while in a closed state. Icons may also have text associated with them. Space is limited, so the text is usually the name of the application.

To use the ICON package, include the header file *<xview/icon.h>*. The owner of an icon is a base frame, but it may be created with a NULL owner. Once an icon is assigned to a frame, the owner of the icon is changed to that frame. This is an example of *delayed binding*.

When destroying an icon, the server image associated with the icon is not destroyed—it is the application programmer's responsibility to free the server image and the pixmap associated with the icon if needed.

1.11 The MENU and MENUITEM Packages

Menus play an important role in an application's user interface. An OPEN LOOK menu may display text or graphics. Menus may be attached to most XView objects such as *menu buttons*, *scrollbars*, or *text subwindows*, or they may exist independently from objects and be displayed on demand.

The user may cause a menu to be pinned up by selecting an optional *pushpin* in the pop-up menu. When this happens, the menu is taken down and a corresponding command frame is put up at the same location. Panel items in the pinup window correspond to the menu items in the menu. Once a menu has been pinned up, the user continues to interact with it just as if the menu were popped up each time. Menus that are used frequently are good candidates for having pushpins so the user does not have to repeat the sequence of redisplaying the menu to make selections.

OPEN LOOK requires that menus have titles. Menus or submenus that originate from *menu buttons* or *pullright* items do not need to have titles, since the name of the menu button or menu item acts as the title.

Fonts may not be specified in either menu items or menu titles; menu items follow the same constraints outlined for *panel buttons*. However, if text is not used, then menu items may contain graphic images, in which case, the font is of no concern. That is, you could specify a Server_image that has a string rendered in a particular font.

1.11.1 Menu Types

There are three different types of menus: *pop-up*, *pulldown*, and *pullright* menus. The general term *pop-up menu* may describe all three types in certain contexts since menus are *popped up*. However, pulldown and pullright menus have distinct characteristics that make them unique.

Pop-up Menus Pop-up menus are displayed when the user selects the MENU mouse button over XView objects such as *scrollbars* or *text subwindows*. An OPEN LOOK window manager also utilizes pop-up menus in the root window and from base frame title bars. XView objects handle the display of menus automatically.

Pulldown Menus Pulldown menus are attached to *menu buttons*. Menu buttons have a set of choices associated with them that the user can access only via the pulldown menu. When the user presses the MENU mouse button over a menu button, the choices are displayed in the form of a pulldown menu. If the menu button is selected using the SELECT button, the default menu item is selected.

Pullright Menus OPEN LOOK provides for items in the menu to have *pullright menus* associated with them. Also called *cascading menus*, these menus are activated from the user dragging the MENU mouse button to the right of a menu item that has an arrow pointing to the right. The cascading menu that results is a pop-up menu that can also have menu items with pullrights attached.

1.11.2 Menu Items

In addition to the menu types, there are different types of menu items: *choice*, *exclusive*, and *nonexclusive*. The different menu item types may be associated with each type of menu.

Each menu has a *default selection* associated with it. This item is displayed uniquely from other menu items and designates a default action to take if the user wants to select the menu without displaying it (see *pulldown menus* below). Typically, the 0th item in the menu is the default, but that may be changed either by the application or by the user.

Choice Items The *choice* item is the default menu item type used when a menu is created. The default selection in a menu has a ring around it. When a pop-up menu is displayed, it is positioned so that the mouse is pointing at the default item. Choice menu items may have pullright menus associated with them, in which case there is a pullright arrow at the right side of the item. If the selection of a menu item brings up a dialog box (command frame), then the label for the menu item typically ends in ellipses (. . .).

Exclusive Items When a choice item is selected, an action is taken and the menu forgets about it. Exclusive menu items retain the fact that they are selected even after the menu has popped down. If the user selects a new item, the new item is remembered. Because this is an exclusive menu, only one choice may be selected at a time. The *default* item is indicated by a double-lined box around the item.

When exclusive settings are used on menus, the current choice has a bold border when the pointer is not on a menu choice. When the user drags the pointer onto other settings, the bold border follows the pointer. Exclusive choice menus may not have items with pullright menus.

Nonexclusive Items Also called *toggle items*, menus that have toggle items support multiple choices from the menu to be selected at the same time. That is, the user may *toggle* whether a particular choice is selected. This action has no affect on the other menu items.

The MENUITEM package allows you to create separate menu items using separate calls to xv_create(). The attributes used are menu item-specific attributes—the same as those that are used for a menu's MENU_ITEM attribute.

1.12 The NOTICE Package

A notice is a pop-up window that notifies the user of a problem or asks a question that requires a response. Generally, notices report serious warnings or errors. OPEN LOOK notices do not have headers or footers and cannot be moved.

XView defines two types of notices, *standard notices* and *screen-locking* notices:

- *Standard notices* do not lock the screen and are placed centered in the "owner" frame. This type of notice may either block the application's thread of execution, or not block.

- *Screen-locking notices* lock the screen and block the thread of execution for all applications (the screen is locked with X grabs). These notices appear with a shadow that emanates from the location where an action in an application initiates the notice. This may be a panel button, such as "Quit", or some other XView object.

To use the NOTICE package, include the header file *<xview/notice.h>*. It provides the necessary types and definitions for using the package. A notice object's type is Xv_Notice.

1.13 The PANEL Package

The PANEL package implements the OPEN LOOK *control area*. Panels are used in many different contexts—property sheets, notices, and menus all use panels in their implementation. The main function of a panel is to manage a variety of *panel items*. Because some panel items may not contain windows that handle their own events, the PANEL package is responsible for propagating events to the appropriate panel item.

Panels set up and manage their own event handling masks and routines for themselves and their panel items. The application does not set event masks or install an event callback routine unless it needs to track events above and beyond what the PANEL package does by default (typical applications will not need to do this). The PANEL package handles all the repainting and resizing events automatically. Panels are not used to display graphics, so there is no need to capture repaint events. Rather than deal with other events specifically, callback routines are not installed on panels, but set for each panel item. Because of the varying types of panel items, each item's callback function may be invoked by a different action from the user. While clicking on a panel button is all that is necessary to activate the button's callback routine, a text panel item might be configured to call its notification callback routine upon the user pressing the RETURN key.

Since panel items express interest in different events, it is the responsibility of the PANEL package to track all events within the panel's window and dispatch events to the proper panel item depending on its type. In some cases, if an event happens over a certain panel item and that item is not interested in that event, the event may be sent to another panel item. For example, what happens if a key is pressed over a panel button? Because the panel button has no interest in the event, the panel will send the event to a text panel item, if one exists elsewhere in the panel.

A panel's owner is a frame. All programs that use panels or panel items must include <xview/panel.h>.

1.13.1 Panel Items

The user interacts with items through various methods ranging from mouse button selection to keyboard input. This interaction typically results in a *callback* function being called for the panel item. The callback functions also vary on a per-item basis. Each item type is described in the following sections.

1.13.1.1 Button Items

A button item allows the user to invoke a command or bring up a menu. The button's label identifies the name of the command or menu. A button label that ends in three dots (...) indicates that a pop-up menu will be displayed when the button is selected.

There are several types of panel button items:

- Panel Buttons
- Menu Buttons
- Abbreviated Menu Buttons

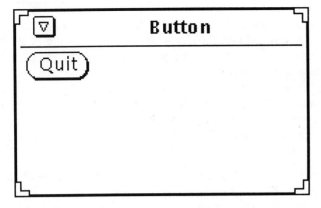

Figure 1-2. Panel item created with PANEL_BUTTON package

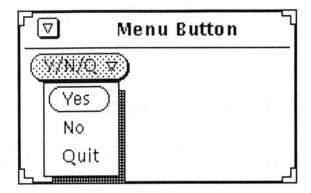

Figure 1-3. Panel button with an attached menu

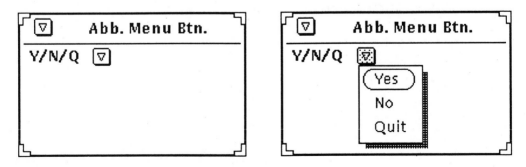

Figure 1-4. Panel item created with the PANEL_ABBREV_MENU_BUTTON package

1.13.1.2 Choice Items

Choice items provide a list of different choices to the user in which one or more choices may be selected. There are variations of choice items which implement different OPEN LOOK objects such as:

- Exclusive and Nonexclusive Choices (or Settings)

- Abbreviated Choice Items

- Checkboxes

The figures below show several, but not all of the different types of choice items.

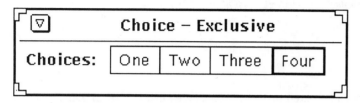

Figure 1-5. Panel item from the PANEL_CHOICE package

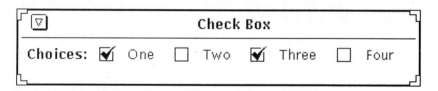

Figure 1-6. Panel item from the PANEL_CHECK_BOX package

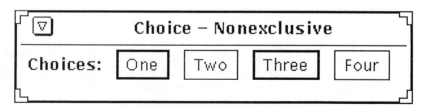

Figure 1-7. Panel item created with PANEL_TOGGLE macro

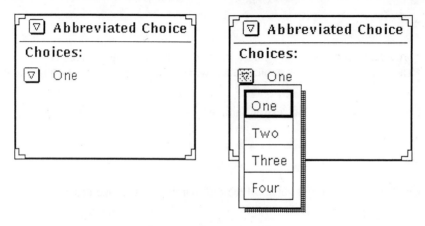

Figure 1-8. Panel item created with PANEL_CHOICE_STACK macro

1.13.1.3 Drop Target Items

A panel drop target item is a bordered image in a panel area that is used to transfer data to or from applications. Before you use a panel drop target item you need to be familiar with the SELECTION and DRAGDROP packages.

A panel drop target item is an object in the class `Panel_drop_target_item` which is equivalent to a `Panel_item`. A drop target item's owner is a `Panel`.

1.13.1.4 Panel Extension Items

Panel extension items support additional user defined panel items. Use of this type of panel item is an advanced topic that is covered in Chapter 25, *XView Internals* in the *XView Programming Manual*.

1.13.1.5 Gauges

Gauges are just like sliders, but they are "output only" items. That is, you set the value of the item and the display of the gauge changes just as it would for sliders. Also, there is no optional type-in field and there is no slider bar for the user to interactively change the value of the gauge. The gauge is intended to be used only as a feedback item.

To create a gauge, use the PANEL_GAUGE package.

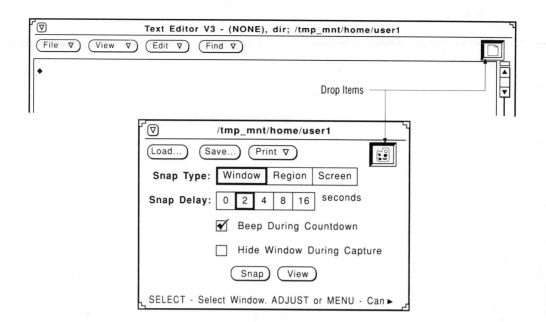

Figure 1-9. Panel drop target items

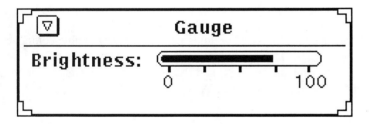

Figure 1-10. Panel item created with the PANEL_GAUGE package

1.13.1.6 List Items—Scrolling Lists

OPEN LOOK's specification for *scrolling lists* is implemented by the PANEL_LIST panel item. List items allow the user to make selections from a scrolling list of choices larger than can be displayed on the panel at one time. The selections can be exclusive or nonexclusive, like the choice items outlined in the previous section. The list is made up of strings or images and a scrollbar that functions like any scrollbar in XView, except that it cannot be split.

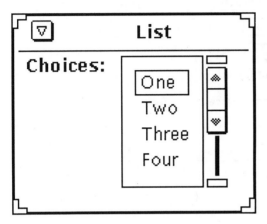

Figure 1-11. Panel list item created with the PANEL_LIST package

1.13.1.7 Message Items

Message items display a text or image message within a panel. The only visible component of a message item is the label itself. Message items are useful for annotations of all kinds, including titles, comments, descriptions, pictures, and dynamic status messages. The message is often used to identify elements on the panel. A message has no value.

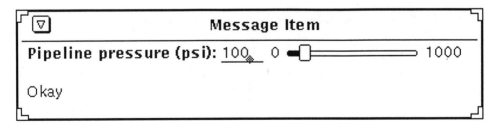

Figure 1-12. Panel item created with PANEL_MESSAGE package

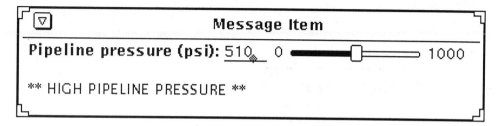

Figure 1-13. Another panel item created with PANEL_MESSAGE package

1.13.1.8 Multiline Text Items

Multiline text items are a special type of panel text item that allow a text field containing multiple lines.

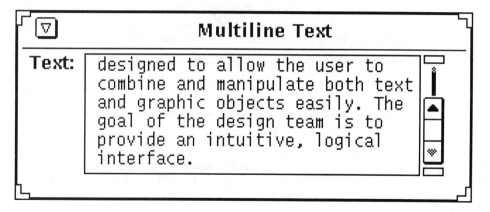

Figure 1-14. Panel item created with the PANEL_MULTILINE_TEXT package

1.13.1.9 Numeric Text Items

Panel numeric text items are virtually the same as panel text items except that the value displayed is of type int. Also, convenience features (such as increment and decrement buttons) ease the manipulation of the text string's numeric value, but there is little programmatic difference between the text item and the numeric text item. You can create a numeric text item using the PANEL_NUMERIC_TEXT package.

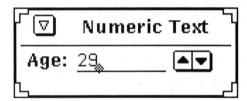

Figure 1-15. Panel item created with the PANEL_NUMERIC_TEXT package

1.13.1.10 Slider Items

Slider items allow the graphical representation and selection of a value within a range as shown in Figure 1-16. Sliders are appropriate for situations where it is desired to make fine adjustments over a continuous range of values. The user selects the slider bar and drags it to the value that he wishes. A slider has the following displayable components: the label, the current value, the slider bar, and the minimum and maximum allowable integral values (the range), end boxes, tick marks, tick mark minimum and maximum tick strings, as well as minimum and maximum value text strings.

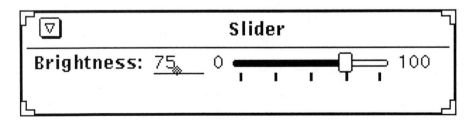

Figure 1-16. Panel item created with the PANEL_SLIDER package

1.13.1.11 Text Items

A panel text item contains as its value a NULL-terminated string. Typically, it contains only printable ASCII characters with no newlines. When a panel receives keyboard input (regardless of where the pointer is as long as it is within the boundaries of the panel), the keyboard event is passed to the item with the keyboard focus. A caret is used to indicate the insertion point where new text is added. You can type in more text than fits on the text field. If this happens, a right arrow pointing to the left will appear on the left on the field, indicating that some text to the left of the displayed text is no longer visible. Similarly, if text is inserted causing text on the right to move out of the visible portion of the text item, then an arrow pointing to the right will appear to the right of the text.

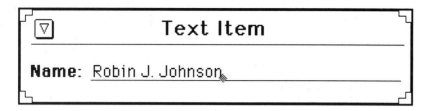

Figure 1-17. Panel item created with the PANEL_TEXT package

1.13.2 Scrollable Panels

Scrollable panels are not OPEN LOOK-compliant, but are provided for historical reasons. They are basically just like panels, except that typically not all panel items are in view. A vertical scrollbar attached to the panel allows the user to navigate to the panel items desired. Again, because this type of interface is not OPEN LOOK-compliant, you are discouraged from using this package.

Scrollable panels are created the same way panels are, but the package name to use is SCROLLABLE_PANEL. However, the scrollable panel package does not create the scrollbars, you must create them separately.

1.14 The SCREEN Object

An Xv_Screen is associated with virtually all XView objects. To use the Xv_Screen object, you must include the file *<xview/screen.h>*. The Xv_Screen object carries useful information such as the screen number of the root window, all the visuals, the colormap, the server and so on, that are associated with that screen.

The Xv_Screen object differs from the Screen data structure defined by Xlib and, in fact, has nothing to do with the X11 Screen data type (defined in *<X11/Xlib.h>*).

1.15 The SCROLLBAR Package

Scrollbars are used to change what you view in a subwindow. For instance, in a text subwindow, scrollbars are used to scroll through a document. In a canvas subwindow, scrollbars can be used to see another portion of the paint window (which can be larger than the canvas subwindow).

The definitions necessary to use scrollbars are found in the header file *<xview/scrollbar.h>*. The owner must be an object subclassed from the OPENWIN package or the FRAME package. The scrollbar inherits certain attributes from the parent while other attributes are initialized automatically. For example, if the owner of the scrollbar is a canvas, the scrollbar's color is inherited from the canvas, while the scrollbar's object length is set by the canvas explicitly; that is, you are not required to set it. This is usually desirable when creating objects that are used together.

1.16 The SELECTION Package

The X Window System provides several methods for applications to exchange information with one another. One of these methods is the use of the selections. A *selection* transfers arbitrary information between two clients. XView Version 3 provides a selection mechanism that is implemented using the SELECTION and SELECTION_ITEM packages. The selection package and its sub classes, including: the SELECTION_REQUESTOR package and the SELECTION_OWNER package, allow data to be move between applications or within an application. These packages replace the selection service used in previous versions of XView, which required special functions and structures. The old selection service is still supported; it is described Appendix A, *The Selection Service*, in the *XView Programming Manual*.

1.17 The SERVER Package

The SERVER package may be used to initialize the connection with the X server running on any workstation on the network. Once the connection has been made, the package allows you to query the server for information. xv_init(), the routine that initializes the XView Toolkit, opens a connection to the server and returns a handle to an Xv_Server object. While more than one server can be created, xv_init() only establishes a connection to *one* server. The server object returned by xv_init() is also the server pointed to by the external global variable, xv_default_server. Programs that do not save the Xv_Server object returned by xv_init() can reference this global variable instead.

Subsequent connections to other X11 servers must be made using separate calls to xv_create(). Note that using separate screens is not the same as establishing a connection to other servers—the same server can support multiple screens.

When making any reference to Xv_Server objects, applications should include *<xview/server.h>*. There is no owner for a server, the owner parameter is ignored and you may pass NULL.

1.18 The TEXTSW Package

This TEXTSW package allows a user or client to display and edit a sequence of ASCII characters. A text contains a vertical scrollbar but may not contain a horizontal scrollbar. The vertical scrollbar can be used to split views into several views. The font used by the text can be specified using the TEXTSW_FONT attribute, but only one font per text subwindow can be used, regardless of how many views there may be.

The contents of a text subwindow are stored in a file or in memory on the client side, not on the X server. Whether the *source* of the text is stored on disk or in memory is transparent to the user. When the user types characters in the text subwindow, the source might be changed immediately or synchronized later depending on how the text subwindow is configured. The TEXTSW package provides basic text editing features such as inserting arbitrary text into a file. It also provides complex operations such as searching for and replacing a string of text.

Applications need to include the file *<xview/textsw.h>* to use text subwindows.

1.19 The TTYSW Package

The TTY (or *terminal emulator*) subwindow emulates a standard terminal, the principal difference being that the row and column dimensions of a tty subwindow can vary from that of a standard terminal. In a tty subwindow, you can run arbitrary programs, including a complete interactive shell. Or you can emulate terminal interface applications that use the *curses*(3X) terminal screen optimization package without actually running a separate process. The TTY subwindow accepts the standard ANSI escape sequences for doing ASCII screen manipulation, so you can use *termcap* or *termio* screen-handling routines.

Programs using tty subwindows must include the file *<xview/tty.h>*. The default tty subwindow will fork a shell process and the user can use it interactively to enter commands. This program does not interact with the processing of the application in which the TTY subwindow resides; it is an entirely separate process.

1.20 The Notifier

The Notifier maintains the flow of control in an application. To understand the basic concepts of the Notifier, we must distinguish between two different styles of input handling, *mainline* input and *event-driven* input, and consider how they affect where the flow of control resides within a program.

1.20.1 Mainline Input Handling

The traditional type of input handling of most text-based applications is mainline-based and input-driven. The flow of control resides in the main routine and the program *blocks* when it expects input. That is to say, no other portion of the program may be executed while the program is waiting for input. For example, in a mainline-driven application, a C programmer will use `fgets()` or `getchar()` to wait for characters that the user types. Based on the user's input, the program chooses an action to take. Sometimes, that action requires more input, so the application calls `getchar()` again. The program does not return to the main routine until the processing for the current input is done.

The tight control represented by this form of input handling is the easiest to program since you have control at all times over what to expect from the user and you can control the direction that the application takes. There is only one source of input—the keyboard—and the user can only respond to one interface element at a time. A user's responses are predictable in the sense that you know that the user is going to type *something*, even if you do not know what it is.

1.20.2 Event-driven Input Handling

Windowing systems are designed such that many sources of input are available to the user at any given time. In addition to the keyboard, there are other input devices, such as the mouse. Each keystroke and mouse movement causes an *event* that the application might consider. Further, there are other sources of events such as the window system itself and other processes. Another aspect of event-driven input handling is that you are not guaranteed to have any predictable sequence of events from the user. That is, a user can position the mouse on an object that receives text as input. Before the user is done typing, the user can move the mouse to another window and select a panel button of some sort. The application cannot (and should not) expect the user to type in window *A* first, then move to window *B* and select the button. A well-written program should expect input from any window to happen at any time.

1.20.3 Functions of the Notifier

The Notifier can do any of the following:

- Handle *software interrupts*—specifically, UNIX signals such as SIGINT or SIGCONT.

- Notice state changes in processes that your process has spawned (e.g., a child process that has died).

- Read and write through file descriptors (e.g., files, pipes and sockets).

- Receive notification of the expiration of timers so that you can regularly flash a caret or display animation.

- Extend, modify or monitor XView Notifier clients (e.g., noticing when a frame is opened, closed or about to be destroyed.)

- Use a non-notification-based control structure while running under XView (e.g., porting programs to XView).

The Notifier also has provisions, to a limited degree, to allow programs to run in the Notifier environment without inverting their control structure.

1.20.4 How the Notifier Works

When you specify *callbacks* or *notify procedures*, the XView objects specified is said to be the *client* of the Notifier. Generally stated, the Notifier detects events in which its clients have expressed an interest and dispatches these events to the proper clients in a predictable order. In the X Window System, events are delivered to the application by the X server. In XView, it is the Notifier that receives the events from the server and dispatches them to its clients. After the client's notify procedure processes the event, control is returned to the Notifier.

1.20.4.1 Restrictions

The Notifier imposes some restrictions on its clients. Designers should be aware of these restrictions when developing software to work in the Notifier environment. These restrictions exist so that the application and the Notifier do not interfere with each other. More precisely, since the Notifier is multiplexing access to user process resources, the application needs to respect this effort so as not to violate the sharing mechanism.

For example, a client should not call `signal` (3). The Notifier is catching signals on behalf of its clients. If a client sets up its own signal handler, then the Notifier will never notice the signal. The program should call `notify_set_signal_func()` instead of `signal` (3).

2

XView Attributes

This section provides alphabetically arranged descriptions of all attributes, and the callback procedures that are supplied by the application programmer.

XView Attributes

This section lists all XView attributes in alphabetical order. Each attribute's description is in the format shown by the entry on this page. Only the fields appropriate to the particular attribute are shown.

INTRODUCTION

This field provides a brief description of the attribute.

Return Type: The return type describes the type that the attribute *should* return on a call to `xv_get()`. Note that this "return type" is normally coerced by the programmer. This field is only shown when the attribute is valid with `xv_get()`.

Argument: This shows the first programmer supplied value associated with the attribute. If an attribute has multiple values, then the type of each value is shown in multiple "Argument" fields.

Valid Values: Shows a list {in brackets} of values that are valid for the attribute.

Default: The default field shows the default value for the attribute.

Procs: Shows the attribute's valid procedures. In this field, `xv_create`, `xv_find`, `xv_get`, and `xv_set` exclude the `xv_` prefix.

Objects: The objects field shows the valid object or objects for the attribute. Attributes are divided into three classes: generic, common, and specific. (For more information, refer to the *XView Programming Manual*, Section 2.2.3, "Types of Attributes.")

Callback:

```
returntype
function_name_proc(arg1, arg2, arg3)
        type1    arg1;
        type2    *arg2;
        type3    *arg3;
```

The callback field shows the application programmer defined callback procedure associated with the attribute. If there are multiple callbacks associated with the attribute, each callback has its own "Callback" field. The function's return value is provided, along with a description of its arguments, if any.

Usage: If an example is provided it will be shown in this field.

See Also: Where there are numbers, they refer to chapters and sections in the *XView Programming Manual*, where the attribute is described (letters refer to appendices). A list of related attributes and/or other related information may also be shown.

ATTR_LIST

Specifies a NULL-terminated attribute-value list. It has no value type or default, but when used, it must be the first attribute in an attribute-value list. ATTR_STANDARD_SIZE, defined in *attr.h*, defines the maximum size of the attribute-value list.

Argument: Attr_avlist
Procs: create,set
Objects: All
Usage:

```
xv_create(object, pkg,
          ATTR_LIST, avlist,
          other_attrs, ..., 0);
```

See Also: 25.2.2, attr_create_list () in Section 3, *Procedures and Macros*

CANVAS_AUTO_CLEAR

Same as the OPENWIN_AUTO_CLEAR attribute.

CANVAS_AUTO_EXPAND

If TRUE, canvas width and height are never allowed to be less than the edges of the canvas window.

Argument: Boolean
Default: TRUE
Procs: create, get, set
Objects: Canvas
See Also: 5.4.1

CANVAS_AUTO_SHRINK

If TRUE, canvas width and height are never allowed to be greater than the edges of the canvas window.

Argument: Boolean
Default: TRUE
Procs: create, get, set
Objects: Canvas
See Also: 5.4.1

CANVAS_CMS_REPAINT

Specifies whether the canvas repaint procedure is called whenever a new colormap segment is set on the canvas, and/or the foreground and background colors of the canvas are changed.

Argument: Boolean
Default: FALSE
Procs: create, get, set
Objects: Canvas
See Also: 5.3

CANVAS_FIXED_IMAGE

Sets the BitGravity for the canvas paint windows to be NorthWestGravity when TRUE or ForgetGravity when FALSE.

Argument: Boolean
Default: TRUE
Procs: create, get, set
Objects: Canvas
See Also: 5.2, WIN_BIT_GRAVITY, CANVAS_RESIZE_PROC

CANVAS_HEIGHT

Specifies the height of the canvas paint window in pixels.

Argument: `int`
Default: `0`
Procs: `create,get,set`
Objects: `Canvas`
See Also: 5.4.2, `CANVAS_MIN_PAINT_HEIGHT, CANVAS_WIDTH, XV_RECT`

CANVAS_MIN_PAINT_HEIGHT

Specifies the minimum height of the canvas' paint window(s) in pixels. Any attempt to change the `CANVAS_HEIGHT` to be smaller than this value will have the effect of setting it to the value of `CANVAS_MIN_PAINT_HEIGHT`.

Argument: `int`
Default: `0`
Procs: `create,get,set`
Objects: `Canvas`
See Also: 5.4.1, `CANVAS_AUTO_EXPAND, CANVAS_AUTO_SHRINK, CANVAS_HEIGHT,`
              `CANVAS_WIDTH`

CANVAS_MIN_PAINT_WIDTH

Specifies the minimum width of the canvas' paint window(s) in pixels. Any attempt to change the `CANVAS_WIDTH` to be smaller than this value will have the effect of setting it to the value of `CANVAS_MIN_PAINT_WIDTH`.

Argument: `int`
Default: `0`
Procs: `create,get,set`
Objects: `Canvas`
See Also: 5.4.1, `CANVAS_AUTO_EXPAND, CANVAS_AUTO_SHRINK, CANVAS_HEIGHT,`
              `CANVAS_WIDTH`

CANVAS_NO_CLIPPING

This attribute is for SunView compatibility. For more information, refer to the manual, *Converting SunView Applications*.

CANVAS_NTH_PAINT_WINDOW

Returns the paint window associated with the *n*th view, and takes an argument of the value of *n*. 0 is the index of the first view. NULL is returned if the view does not exist.

Return Type: `Xv_Window`
Argument: `int`
Procs: `get`
Objects: `Canvas`
Usage:

```
Canvas   canvas;
Xv_Window paint_window;
paint_window = (Xv_Window)xv_get(canvas,
              CANVAS_NTH_PAINT_WINDOW, 1);
```

The example above will return the second paint window of the canvas.

See Also: 5.6.3

CANVAS_PAINT_CANVAS_WINDOW

Gets the canvas from a canvas paint window.

Return Type: `Canvas`
Procs: `get`
Objects: `Canvas_paint_window`
See Also: `CANVAS_VIEW_CANVAS_WINDOW`

CANVAS_PAINTWINDOW_ATTRS

Distributes specified attribute values across all paint windows in a given canvas. It takes an in-line attribute-value list of window attributes.

Argument: A-V list
Procs: `create, set`
Objects: `Canvas`
Usage:

```
xv_set (canvas,  CANVAS_PAINTWINDOW_ATTR,
                 WIN_EVENT_PROC, canvas_event,
                 WIN_FOREGROUND_COLOR, 0
                 NULL,
          NULL);
```

See Also: 20.3

CANVAS_REPAINT_PROC

Names a procedure called when canvas paint window has been damaged and must be repaired (repainted).

Argument `void (*canvas_repaint_proc) ()`
Default: `NULL`
Procs: `create, get, set`
Objects: `Canvas`
Callback: (Used when `CANVAS_X_PAINT_WINDOW` set to `FALSE`)

```
void
canvas_repaint_proc (canvas, paint_window, repaint_area)
     Canvas      canvas;
     Xv_Window   paint_window;
     Rectlist    *repaint_area;
```

Above, `canvas` is the canvas that was damaged,
`paint_window` is the window to repaint and,
`repaint_area` is a pointer to the list of `Rects` that is to be repainted.

Callback 2: (Used when `CANVAS_X_PAINT_WINDOW` set to `TRUE`)

When `CANVAS_X_PAINT_WINDOW` is `TRUE`, the `CANVAS_REPAINT_PROC` callback is called with the following parameters:

```
void
canvas_repaint_proc (canvas, paint_window, display, xid,
                     xrectlist)
          Canvas        canvas;
          Xv_Window     paint_window;
          Display       *display;
          Window        xid;
          Xv_xrectlist  *xrects;
```

canvas is the canvas that was damaged.
paint_window is the window to repaint.
display is the display handle to the X11 server connection.
xid is the X11 window identifier for the canvas paint window.
The Xv_xrectlist structure, defined in *<xview/xv_xrect.h>*, contains an array of
XRectangles and a count that specifies the repaint area for the canvas paint window.

See Also: 5.3 , CANVAS_RESIZE_PROC, CANVAS_X_PAINT_WINDOW, WIN_EVENT_PROC

CANVAS_RESIZE_PROC

Names a procedure called when canvas width or height changes. Note that if CANVAS_FIXED_
IMAGE is set to TRUE, which it is by default, the resize procedure will not be called when the canvas
is resized smaller.

Argument:	void (*canvas_resize_proc) ()
Default:	NULL
Procs:	create, get, set
Objects:	Canvas
Callback:	

```
void
canvas_resize_proc (canvas, width, height)
        Canvas    canvas;
        int       width;
        int       height;
```

canvas is the canvas being resized.
width and height are the new dimensions of the canvas.

See Also: 5.4.3 , CANVAS_FIXED_IMAGE, CANVAS_REPAINT_PROC, WIN_BIT_GRAVITY

CANVAS_RETAINED

Specifies whether the X server should attempt to retain backing store for the canvas paint windows.
Note that this does not guarantee that the window is retained as the server may not be able to comply.

Argument:	Boolean
Default:	TRUE
Procs:	create, get, set
Objects:	Canvas
See Also:	5.2

CANVAS_VIEW_CANVAS_WINDOW

Gets the canvas from a canvas view window.

Argument:	Canvas
Procs:	get
Objects:	Canvas_view
See Also:	CANVAS_PAINT_WINDOW_CANVAS, CANVAS_VIEW_PAINT_WINDOW

CANVAS_VIEW_PAINT_WINDOW

This attribute is used to get the canvas paint window associated with a given canvas view.

Return Type:	Canvas_paint_window
Procs:	get
Objects:	Canvas_view

XView Attributes

Usage:

```
                    Canvas_view view;
                    Xv_Window paint_window;

                    paint_window = (Xv_Window)xv_get(view,
                                       CANVAS_VIEW_PAINT_WINDOW);
```

See Also: 5.6.3 , `CANVAS_PAINT_WINDOW_CANVAS,  CANVAS_VIEW_PAINT_WINDOW`

CANVAS_VIEWABLE_RECT

Gets the visible part of the specified paint window in the paint window's coordinates. This attribute operates on a Canvas object and requires as an argument, a handle to one of the canvas' paint windows. The `Rect *` returned should not be freed, as it points to static storage.

Return Type: `Rect *`
Argument: `Canvas_paint_window`
Procs: `get`
Objects: `Canvas`
Usage:

```
                    Rect *rect;
                    Xv_Window canvas_pw = canvas_paint_window(canvas);
                    rect = (Rect *) xv_get(canvas,
                                       CANVAS_VIEWABLE_RECT,canvas_pw);
```

See Also: 5.3

CANVAS_WIDTH

Specifies the width of the canvas paint window in pixels.

Argument: `int`
Default: In general, the canvas inherits its parent's width.
Procs: `create, get, set`
Objects: `Canvas`
See Also: 5.4.2 , `CANVAS_MIN_PAINT_WIDTH`

CANVAS_X_PAINT_WINDOW

This attribute controls the parameters used in the `CANVAS_REPAINT_PROC`. Setting this attribute to `TRUE` will cause the `CANVAS_REPAINT_PROC` to be called back with the parameters `canvas`, `paint_window`, `display`, `xid`, and `xrectlist`; setting `CANVAS_X_PAINT_WINDOW` to `FALSE` will cause it to be called back with `canvas`, `paint_window`, and `repaint_area`.

Argument: `Boolean`
Default: `FALSE`
Procs: `create, get, set`
Objects: `Canvas`
See Also: 5.3 , `CANVAS_REPAINT_PROC`

CMS_BACKGROUND_PIXEL

Returns the background pixel (index 0) in a colormap segment.

Return Type: `unsigned long`
Default: `None`
Procs: `get`
Objects: `Cms`
See Also: 21.3.1

CMS_COLOR_COUNT

Used to specify the number of colors being set with CMS_COLORS or CMS_X_COLORS. This can be used in conjunction with CMS_INDEX to set a range of the colors in the cms.

Argument: `unsigned int`
Default: `CMS_SIZE` for a non-control cms, or `CMS_SIZE` - `CMS_CONTROL_COLORS` for a control cms.
Procs: `create, set`
Objects: Cms
Usage: To set the colors in the array colors to the range from 10 to 14 in a cms, you would do the following:

```
XColor colors[5];

xv_set(cms,
        CMS_X_COLORS, colors,
        CMS_INDEX, 10,
        CMS_COLOR_COUNT, 5,
        NULL);
```

See Also: 21.2

CMS_COLORS

Specifies the colors to be loaded into the colormap segment. Colors are specified as an array of `Xv_singlecolor`.

Argument: `Xv_singlecolor`
Default: None
Procs: `create, get, set`
Objects: Cms
See Also: 21.2.1

CMS_CONTROL_CMS

Indicates whether this colormap segment is a control colormap segment for use by control objects (like panel items and scrollbars).

Argument: `int`
Default: `FALSE`
Procs: `create, get, set`
Objects: Cms
See Also: 21.5

CMS_FOREGROUND_PIXEL

Returns the foreground pixel (index CMS_SIZE-1) in a colormap segment.

Return Type: `unsigned long`
Default: None
Procs: `get`
Objects: Cms
See Also: 21.3.1

XView Attributes

CMS_INDEX

Specifies the starting index to `CMS_COLOR_COUNT` entries into the colormap.

Argument: `unsigned long`
Default: 0 (If control cms, `CMS_CONTROL_COLORS`)
Procs: `create, set`
Objects: Cms
See Also: 21.2 , `CMS_COLOR_COUNT`

CMS_INDEX_TABLE

Used to translate the logical indices of the window's colormap segment into actual pixel values.

Return Type: `unsigned long *`
Default: N/A
Procs: `get`
Objects: Cms
See Also: 21.3

CMS_NAME

Specifies the name of the colormap segment.

Argument: `char *`
Default: Unique name generated internally
Procs: `create, get, set`
Objects: Cms
See Also: 21.6

CMS_NAMED_COLORS

Specifies the names of the colors to be loaded into the colormap segment. The `NULL`-terminated list of color names is parsed by `XParseColor()`.

Argument: List of `char *`
Default: None
Procs: `create, set`
Objects: Cms
See Also: 21.2.1

CMS_PIXEL

Translates a logical index into the actual colormap pixel value.

Argument: `unsigned long`
Default: None
Procs: `get`
Objects: Cms
Usage:

```
unsigned long pixel;
pixel=(unsigned long)xv_get(cms, CMS_PIXEL, 2);
```

See Also: 21.3

CMS_SCREEN

Returns the screen with which the colormap segment is associated.

Return Type: `Xv_Screen`
Default: Default screen
Procs: `get`
Objects: Cms

CMS_SIZE

Specifies the size of the colormap segment.

Argument: `int`
Default: `XV_DEFAULT_CMS_SIZE` or `CMS_CONTROL_COLORS`, for a control cms
Procs: `create, get`
Objects: Cms
See Also: 21.2

CMS_TYPE

Specifies the type of the colormap segment. If set to `XV_STATIC_CMS`, then only read-only colors can be allocated from the cms. If set to `XV_DYNAMIC_CMS`, then only read-write colors can be allocated from the cms. `XV_DYNAMIC_CMS` can only be used with a dynamic visual.

Argument: `Cms_type`
Default: `XV_STATIC_CMS`
Procs: `create`
Objects: Cms
See Also: 21.1.1

CMS_X_COLORS

Specifies the colors to be loaded into the colormap segment. Colors are specified as an array of `XColor`.

Argument: `XColor *`
Default: None
Procs: `create, set, get`
Objects: Cms
See Also: 21.2.1

CURSOR_BACKGROUND_COLOR

Specifies the background color of a cursor as an RGB triplet.

Argument: `Xv_singlecolor *`
Default: `white (255, 255, 255)`
Procs: `create, get, set`
Objects: `Xv_Cursor`
See Also: 13.4

CURSOR_DRAG_STATE

Indicates whether the cursor is over a "neutral" zone (`CURSOR_NEUTRAL`), a valid drop zone (`CURSOR_ACCEPT`), or an invalid drop zone (`CURSOR_REJECT`). The shape of the cursor varies depending on the state. Note that the current drag and drop protocol does not support a "reject" cursor.

Argument: `Cursor_drag_state`
Default: `CURSOR_NEUTRAL`
Proc: `create, get`
Objects: Cursor
See Also: 13.5, `CURSOR_DRAG_TYPE, CURSOR_STRING`

CURSOR_DRAG_TYPE

Indicates whether the cursor is "move" (`CURSOR_MOVE`) or "copy" (`CURSOR_DUPLICATE`). The duplicate version has a shadow. When combined with `CURSOR_STRING`, you get either a text move or text duplicate cursor.

Argument: `Cursor_drag_type`
Default: `CURSOR_MOVE`
Procs: `create, get`

Objects: `Cursor`
See Also: 13.5 , `CURSOR_DRAG_STATE`, `CURSOR_STRING`

CURSOR_FOREGROUND_COLOR
Specifies the foreground color of a cursor as an RGB triplet.

Argument: `Xv_singlecolor *`
Default: `black (0, 0, 0)`
Procs: `create, get, set`
Objects: `Xv_Cursor`
See Also: 13.4

CURSOR_IMAGE
Specifies the cursor's image.

Argument: `Server_image`
Default: None
Procs: `create, get, set`
Objects: `Xv_Cursor`
See Also: 13.1

CURSOR_MASK_CHAR
Specifies the index into the mask shape font. Predefined shapes are defined in *<xview/cursor.h>* .

Argument: `unsigned int`
Default: None
Procs: `create, get, set`
Objects: `Xv_Cursor`
Usage:

```
xv_set (cursor,
        CURSOR_MASK_CHAR, OLC_BASIC_MASK_PTR
        NULL);
```

See Also: 13.2 , `CURSOR_SRC_CHAR`

CURSOR_OP
The value for this attribute is the rasterop (defined in *<pixrect.h>*) which will be used to paint the cursor.

Argument: `int`
Default: `{ PIX_SRC | PIX_DST }`
Procs: `create, get, set`
Objects: `Xv_Cursor`

CURSOR_SRC_CHAR
Specifies the index into the shape font. Predefined shapes are in *<xview/cursor.h>*.

Argument: `unsigned int`
Default: -1
Procs: `create, get, set`
Objects: `Xv_Cursor`
Usage:

```
xv_set (cursor,
        CURSOR_SRC_CHAR, OLC_BASIC_PTR,
        CURSOR_MASK_CHAR, OLC_BASIC_MASK_PTR,
        NULL);
```

See Also: 13.2 , `CURSOR_MASK_CHAR`

CURSOR_STRING

Creates a text drag and drop cursor. The value of the attribute is the string which is to be displayed inside the "flying punch card." If the string exceeds 3 characters, then only the first 3 characters are displayed, and a "More arrow" is shown within the cursor. CURSOR_STRING is mutually exclusive of CURSOR_IMAGE, CURSOR_SRC_CHAR, and CURSOR_MASK_CHAR. The string is not copied. Once the drag and drop operation is complete, the text cursor objects used in the operation must be destroyed.

Argument:	char *
Default:	None
Procs:	create, get
Objects:	Cursor
See Also:	13.5, CURSOR_DRAG_STATE, CURSOR_DRAG_TYPE

CURSOR_XHOT

Specifies the x coordinate of the hotspot. Its value cannot be negative.

Argument:	int
Default:	0
Procs:	create, get, set
Objects:	Cursor
See Also:	13.3

CURSOR_YHOT

Specifies the y coordinate of the hotspot. Its value cannot be negative.

Argument:	int
Default:	0
Procs:	create, get, set
Objects:	Cursor
See Also:	13.3

DND_ACCEPT_CURSOR

During a drag and drop operation, this defines the mouse cursor that is used when the cursor is over an acceptable drop-site.

Argument:	Xv_cursor
Default:	Predefined OPEN LOOK drag and drop cursor
Procs:	create, get, set
Objects:	Dnd
See Also:	19.3.3

DND_ACCEPT_X_CURSOR

An alternative to DND_ACCEPT_CURSOR, this attribute accepts an XID of a cursor instead of an Xv_cursor.

Argument:	XID
Default:	Predefined OPEN LOOK drag and drop cursor
Procs:	create, get, set
Objects:	Dnd
See Also:	19.3.3

DND_CURSOR

Defines the mouse cursor that will be used during the drag portion of the drag and drop operation.

Argument: `Xv_cursor`
Default: Predefined OPEN LOOK drag and drop cursor
Procs: `create,get,set`
Objects: `Dnd`
See Also: 19.3.3 , `DND_ACCEPT_CURSOR`

DND_TIMEOUT_VALUE

Defines the amount of time to wait for an acknowledgment from the drop destination after the kicker message has been sent (`ACTION_DRAG_COPY` or `ACTION_DRAG_MOVE`). The kicker message is sent when the user releases the mouse button, forcing the drop.

Argument: `struct timeval *`
Default: Default selection package timeout
Procs: `create,get,set`
Objects: `Dnd`
See Also: 19.3.4

DND_TYPE

Defines whether this drag and drop operation will be a copy or a move. This is just a hint to the destination. If the type is a "move" operation and if the destination honors the hint, the destination will ask the source to convert the DELETE target.

Valid Values: `DND_COPY` or `DND_MOVE`
Default: `DND_MOVE`
Procs: `create,get,set`
See Also: 19.3

DND_X_CURSOR

An alternative to `DND_CURSOR`, but accepts an XID of a cursor instead of an `Xv_cursor`.

Argument: `XID`
Default: Predefined OPEN LOOK drag and drop cursor
Procs: `create,get,set`
Objects: `Dnd`
See Also: 19.3.3 , `DND_ACCEPT_X_CURSOR`

DROP_SITE_DEFAULT

Specifies that this drop-site wants forwarded drops from the window manager. Such drops include drops on icons and window manager decorations. Only one drop-site default should be specified per base frame (specifying more than one will have unpredictable results). This attribute is only a hint to the window manager.

Argument: `Boolean`
Default: `False`
Procs: `create,get,set`
Objects: `Drop_site_item`
See Also: 19.2

DROP_SITE_DELETE_REGION

Used to remove a region from the drop item. If the owner is destroyed with `xv_destroy()`, any drop-site regions attached to it will also be destroyed. When a NULL is passed as an argument, all regions in the drop-site will be removed.

Argument:	`Rect *`
Default:	N/A
Procs:	`create,set`
Objects:	`Drop_site_item`
See Also:	19.2.1

DROP_SITE_DELETE_REGION_PTR

Used to remove a list of regions from the drop item. Passing a NULL as an argument removes all regions in the drop-site.

Argument:	`Rect *` (a NULL-terminated array of `Rect` structs)
Default:	N/A
Procs:	`create,set`
Objects:	`Drop_site_item`
See Also:	19.2.1

DROP_SITE_EVENT_MASK

A mask used to specify if the regions within the site will receive synthetic previewing events. The previewing events will come with `event_action()` set to `ACTION_DRAG_PREVIEW` and `event_id()` set to one of `LOC_WINENTER`, `LOC_WINEXIT` or `LOC_DRAG`. These events will be delivered to the event procedure of the owner of the drop-site item. This mask is only a hint to the source. There is no guarantee the source will send these previewing events.

Argument:	`int`
Valid Values:	{`DND_ENTERLEAVE, DND_MOTION`} Defined in *<xview/dragdrop.h>*
Default:	`NULL`
Procs:	`create,get,set`
Objects:	`Drop_site_item`
See Also:	19.2.2

DROP_SITE_ID

An uninterpreted ID used to distinguish one drop-site from the next. Ideal when more than one site has been set on an object.

Argument:	`long`
Default:	A value generated from `xv_unique_key()`
Procs:	`create,get,set`
Objects:	`Drop_site_item`
See Also:	19.2.2

DROP_SITE_REGION

This attribute is used to associate a region to a drop-site item. The region is a `Rect *`. `DROP_SITE_REGION` will add to any existing regions within the drop-site item. The rect pointed to by `Rect *` will be copied. The coordinates in the rect should be relative to the drop-site item's owner's window. An `xv_get()` of a region of type `Rect *` will return an allocated `Rect` structure. This should be freed using `xv_free()` once the application has finished using it.

Argument:	`Rect *`
Default:	`NULL`
Procs:	`create,get,set`
Objects:	`Drop_site_item`
See Also:	19.2.1, `DROP_SITE_DELETE_REGION`

DROP_SITE_REGION_PTR

This attribute is similar to `DROP_SITE_REGION` except that it accepts a `NULL`-terminated array of regions. It will add to any existing regions that exist within the drop item. A `NULL` rect is defined to be one with width or height equal to 0. An `xv_get()` of a region list will return a `NULL`-terminated list of Rects. This data should be freed once the application has finished using it.

Argument:	`Rect *` (A `NULL`-terminated array of `Rect` structs)
Default:	`NULL`
Procs:	`create,get,set`
Objects:	`Drop_site_item`
See Also:	19.2.1 , `DROP_SITE_DELETE_REGION`

FONT_CHAR_HEIGHT

Returns the height (an `int`) of a specified character (a `char`) of the font. This is actually the height of the bounding rectangle, good for any character of the font.

Return Type:	`int`
Argument:	`char`
Procs:	`get`
Objects:	`Xv_Font`
Usage:	

```
Xv_font    font;
int        height;
height = (int)xv_get(font, FONT_CHAR_HEIGHT, 'm');
```

See Also: 16.2

FONT_CHAR_WIDTH

Returns the width (`int`) of a specified character (`char`) of the font.

Return Type:	`int`
Argument:	`char`
Procs:	`get`
Objects:	`Xv_Font`
See Also:	16.2

FONT_DEFAULT_CHAR_HEIGHT

Returns the default character height of the font. Does not take a value.

Return Type:	`int`
Procs:	`get`
Objects:	`Xv_Font`
Usage:	

```
Xv_font    font;
int        height;
height = (int)xv_get(font, FONT_DEFAULT_CHAR_HEIGHT);
```

See Also: 16.2

FONT_DEFAULT_CHAR_WIDTH

Returns the default character width of the font. Does not take a value.

Return Type:	`int`
Procs:	`get`
Objects:	`Xv_Font`
See Also:	16.2

FONT_FAMILY

Specifies the name of a font family.

Argument: `char *`
Default: None
Procs: `create, find, get`
Objects: `Xv_Font`
See Also: 16.1.1

FONT_INFO

Returns a pointer to the X structure `XFontStruct` containing X-related information for the font.

Return Type: `XFontStruct *`
Default: N/A
Procs: `get`
Objects: `Xv_Font`
Usage:

```
#include <X11/Xlib.h>
Xv_font        font;
XFontStruct   *font_info;
font_info =   (XFontStruct *)xv_get(font, FONT_INFO);
```

See Also: 16.2

FONT_NAME

Specifies the name of the font desired. This takes precedence over all other `Font` attributes. The list of valid names that can be used can be displayed using the `xlsfonts` command.

Argument: `char *`
Procs: `create, find`
Objects: `Xv_Font`
Usage:

```
Xv_font    font;

font = xv_create (frame, FONT,
    FONT_NAME,
    "-adobe-courier-bold-r-normal—14-140-75-75-m-90-iso8859-1"
    NULL) ;
height = (int)xv_get(font, FONT_DEFAULT_CHAR_HEIGHT);
```

See Also: 16.1.4

FONT_PIXFONT

This attribute is for SunView compatibility. For more information, refer to the manual, *Converting SunView Applications*. Returns the pixfont representation of the font.

FONT_RESCALE_OF

Given an existing font and a rescale factor, the returned font will be a similar font in the specified scale.

Argument1: `Xv_Font`
Argument2: `Window_rescale_state` (see *<xview/window.h>*)
Procs: `create, find`
Objects: `Xv_Font`
Usage:

```
Xv_font    font1,  font2;
```

```
                    /*
                     * Find a font similar to font1 but in the large
                     * scale
                     */
                    font2 = (Xv_FONT) xv_find (frame, FONT,
                                FONT_RESCALE_OF, font1, WIN_SCALE_LARGE,
                                NULL) ;
```

See Also: 16.1.3 , FONT_SIZES_FOR_SCALE, FONT_SCALE

FONT_SCALE

Specifies the scale desired for a font. The scale settings map to certain pixel sizes (defaults are 10, 12, 14, and 19). If FONT_SIZE is used, it will take precedence over FONT_SCALE.

Argument: Window_rescale_state (see <xview/window.h>)
Default: WIN_SCALE_MEDIUM
Procs: create, find, get
Objects: Xv_Font
See Also: 16.1.3 , FONT_RESCALE_OF, FONT_SIZES_FOR_SCALE

FONT_SIZE

Specifies the size of a font in pixels. Note that the valid values for size depend on what font sizes are available on the X server.

Argument: int
Default: 12
Procs: create, find, get
Objects: Xv_Font
Usage:

```
                Xv_font     font;

                /*
                 * This creates a lucida font with normal style
                 * with its size = 14
                 */
                font = (Xv_FONT) xv_find (frame, FONT
                            FONT_FAMILY_LUCIDA,
                            FONT_STYLE, FONT_STYLE_NORMAL
                            FONT_SIZE, 14,
                            NULL) ;
```

See Also: 16.1.2

FONT_SIZES_FOR_SCALE

Specifies a set of four integral sizes (measured in *points*) to which a font can be scaled.

Argument 1: int, for fonts scaled in small size
Argument 2: int, for fonts scaled in medium size
Argument 3: int, for fonts scaled in large size
Argument 4: int, for fonts scaled in extra_large size
Default: 10, 12, 14, 19
Procs: create, find
Objects: Xv_Font

Usage:

```
Xv_font                  font;

/*
 * This creates a lucida font with normal style
 * with its size = 19
 */
font = (Xv_FONT) xv_find (frame, FONT,
            FONT_FAMILY_LUCIDA,
            FONT_STYLE, FONT_STYLE_NORMAL,
            FONT_SIZES_FOR_SCALE, 12, 14, 19, 26,
            FONT_SCALE, WIN_SCALE_LARGE,
            NULL) ;
```

See Also: 16.1.3 , FONT_RESCALE_OF, FONT_SCALE

FONT_STRING_DIMS

Given a string and the address of a `Font_string_dims` structure (see *<xview/font.h>*), `xv_get()` fills it in with the width and height dimensions of the string. The pointer to the structure is returned by `xv_get`.

Return Type: `Font_string_dims *`
Argument1:   `char *`
Argument2:   `Font_string_dims *`
Procs: `get`
Objects: `Xv_Font`
Usage:

```
Xv_font                  font;
Font_string_dims         dims;

(void)xv_get (font, FONT_STRING_DIMS, "Hello World", dims);

/*
 * At this point 'dims' will contain the width and height
 * (in pixels) of the entire string "Hello World" as
 * rendered in the font 'font'.
 */
```

See Also: 16.2

FONT_STYLE

Specifies a font style.

Argument: `char *`
Default: `FONT_STYLE_NORMAL`
Procs: `create, find, get`
Objects: `Xv_Font`
See Also: 16.1.1

FRAME_ACCELERATOR

Specifies a window-level accelerator. The character in the first argument is used to call the procedure in the second argument with the data in the third argument. On `xv_get`, the frame package searches through the linked list of accelerators, and returns a pointer to the `Frame_accelerator` structure whose code or keysym matches the specified code and keysym. Applications do not normally use `xv_get` with this attribute.

On `create`, `set`:

Argument 1:   `char`
Argument 2:   `void (*) ()`
Argument 3:   `Xv_opaque`

On `get`:

Argument 1:   `char`
Argument 2:   `KeySym`
Procs: `create, get, set`
Objects: `Frame`
Callback:

```
void
accelerator_notify_proc (value, event)
    Xv_opaque    value;      /* from Argument 3 */
    Event        *event;
```

See Also: 6.14

FRAME_BACKGROUND_COLOR

This attribute is obsolete. To change a frame's background color, create a cms and set it on the frame.

FRAME_BUSY

Sets label to gray and changes cursor to hour-glass.

Argument: `Boolean`
Default: `FALSE`
Procs: `create, get, set`
Objects: `Frame`
See Also: 4.5

FRAME_CLOSED

Controls the frame's mapped state (either open or iconic).

Argument: `Boolean`
Default: `FALSE`
Procs: `create, get, set`
Objects: `Frame`
See Also: 14.2 , `XV_SHOW`

FRAME_CLOSED_RECT

Sets the *size* of the frame's icon.

Argument: `Rect *`
Default: `64 x 64`
Procs: `create, get, set`
Objects: `Frame`
See Also: 4.2.3

FRAME_CMD_DEFAULT_PIN_STATE

This attribute controls the initial state of the pin when the frame goes from unmapped (withdrawn) to mapped state. It is valid for both mapped and unmapped frames. However, if the frame is currently mapped, the effects of the change will be visible only on the next transition from unmapped to mapped state.

Argument: `int`
Valid Values: {`FRAME_CMD_PIN_IN`, `FRAME_CMD_PIN_OUT`} defined in *<xview/frame.h>* .
Procs: `create,get,set`
Objects: `Frame_cmd`
See Also: 4.3.2 , `FRAME_CMD_PIN_STATE`

FRAME_CMD_PANEL

Gets the default panel in the command frame.

Return Type: `Panel`
Procs: `get`
Objects: `Frame`
See Also: 11.12

FRAME_CMD_PIN_STATE

This attribute returns the current state of the pin. It is valid for both mapped and unmapped frames. Though, for unmapped frames it will always return `FRAME_CMD_PIN_OUT`.

Argument: `int`
Valid Values: {`FRAME_CMD_PIN_IN`, `FRAME_CMD_PIN_OUT`}defined in *<xview/frame.h>*
Procs: `get,set`
Objects: `Frame_cmd`
See Also: 4.3.2 `FRAME_CMD_DEFAULT_PIN_STATE`

FRAME_CMD_PUSHPIN_IN

This attribute is obsolete. It is supported only for compatibility reasons. Applications should use `FRAME_CMD_DEFAULT_PIN_STATE` and `FRAME_CMD_PIN_STATE` instead. Indicates whether the pushpin is in or out.

Argument: `Boolean`
Default: `FALSE`
Procs: `create,get,set`
Objects: `Frame`
See Also: `FRAME_CMD_PIN_STATE`

FRAME_DEFAULT_DONE_PROC

The default procedure is to set the subframe to `WIN_SHOW`, `FALSE`.

Default: `FRAME_DEFAULT_DONE_PROC`
Procs: `create,get,set`
Objects: `Frame`
See Also: 4.3.3 , `FRAME_DONE_PROC`

FRAME_DONE_PROC

Names a procedure to be called when the command frame is dismissed by the user (by taking the pushpin out).

Argument: `void` (**frame_done_proc*) ()
Default: `FRAME_DEFAULT_DONE_PROC`
Procs: `create,get,set`
Objects: `Frame`

Callback:

```
        void
        frame_done_proc (frame)
              Frame   frame;
```

See Also: 4.3.3

FRAME_FOCUS_DIRECTION
The direction in which the Location Cursor is pointing.

Argument: `Frame_focus_direction(enum)`
Valid Values: `{FRAME_FOCUS_RIGHT, FRAME_FOCUS_UP}`
Procs: `create,set,get`
Objects: `Frame`
See Also: 6.13.4

FRAME_FOCUS_WIN
Returns the handle of the Location Cursor (focus) window.

Return Type: `Xv_window`
Procs: `get`
Objects: `Frame`
See Also: 6.13.4

FRAME_FOREGROUND_COLOR
This attribute is obsolete. To change a frame's foreground color, create a cms and set it on the frame.

FRAME_ICON
Identifies the base frame's icon.

Argument: `Xv_opaque`
Default: A default empty icon.
Procs: `create,get,set`
Objects: `Frame`
See Also: 4.2.3

FRAME_INHERIT_COLORS
This attribute is obsolete. To implement this functionality, use `WIN_INHERIT_COLORS` on the frame.

FRAME_LABEL
Specifies the label used in the window manager's titlebar for the frame. XView copies the string on set.

Argument: `char *`
Default: `NULL`
Procs: `create,get,set`
Objects: `Frame`
See Also: 4.2.2 , `FRAME_SHOW_LABEL`

FRAME_LEFT_FOOTER
Specifies the left-justified footer. XView copies the string on set.

Argument: `char *`
Default: `NULL`
Procs: `create,get,set`
Objects: `Frame`
See Also: `FRAME_SHOW_FOOTER, FRAME_RIGHT_FOOTER`

FRAME_MAX_SIZE

This attribute is similar to FRAME_MIN_SIZE, but allows the application programmer to specify a maximum size the frame can be resized to by a user. All other aspects of this attribute are exactly the same as FRAME_MIN_SIZE.

Return Type: void
Argument 1:   int (maximum width of frame)
Argument 2:   int (maximum height of frame)
Default: The default value is 0. In other words there is no application specified minimum or maximum size. Keep in mind that the window manager may impose one though.
Procs: create, get, set
Objects: Frame
See Also: 4.3.5

FRAME_MIN_SIZE

This attribute allows the application programmer to specify a minimum size a frame can be resized to by a user. The FRAME_MIN_SIZE attribute takes two integer parameters, specifying the minimum width and height of the frame. This information is passed onto the window manager as part of the WM_NORMAL_HINTS property. Note that the minimum size is only a hint to the window manager. Some window managers may choose to ignore certain application specified hints. Setting both the minimum width and height to 0 effectively removes any application controlled minimum restriction on size.

Return Type: void
Argument 1:   int (minimum width of frame)
Argument 2:   int (minimum height of frame)
Default: The default value is 0. In other words there is no application specified minimum or maximum size. Keep in mind that the window manager may impose one .
Procs: create, get, set
Objects: Frame
Usage: To get the previous set values of FRAME_MIN_SIZE use xv_get() and pass in two parameters:

                    int width, height;

                    (void)xv_get(frame, FRAME_MIN_SIZE, &width, &height);

                Note that some window managers may choose to ignore changes to the WM_NORMAL_HINTS property on frames that are already mapped. Thus, depending on the window manager, it may be necessary to unmap and then remap the frame before the FRAME_MIN_SIZE values take effect.
See Also: 4.3.5

FRAME_NEXT_PANE

Set the input focus to the next pane that can accept input focus.

Argument: None
Valid Values: {FRAME_FOCUS_RIGHT, FRAME_FOCUS_UP}
Procs: set
Objects: Frame

FRAME_NO_CONFIRM

Controls whether a notice is displayed when a frame is destroyed.

Argument:	Boolean
Default:	TRUE
Procs:	create, get, set
Objects:	Frame
See Also:	4.2.4

FRAME_NTH_SUBFRAME

Gets the frame's nth (from 1) subframe. Returns NULL if requested Subframe does not exist.

Return Type:	Frame
Argument:	int
Procs:	get
Objects:	Frame
Usage:	

```
Frame  frame;
frame = xv_get (base_frame, FRAME_NTH_SUBFRAME, 1);
```

See Also:	4.8 , FRAME_NTH_SUBWINDOW

FRAME_NTH_SUBWINDOW

Gets the frame's nth (from 0) subwindow. Returns NULL if requested Subwindow does not exist.

Return Type:	Xv_Window
Argument:	int
Procs:	get
Objects:	Frame
See Also:	4.8 , FRAME_NTH_SUBFRAME

FRAME_PREVIOUS_ELEMENT

When set on a canvas, the focus is set to the view's horizontal scrollbar, vertical scrollbar, or the last element in the canvas.

Argument:	None
Procs:	set
Objects:	Frame

FRAME_PREVIOUS_PANE

Set the input focus to the previous pane that can accept input focus.

Argument:	None
Procs:	set
Objects:	Frame

FRAME_RIGHT_FOOTER

Specifies the right-justified footer. XView copies the string on set.

Argument:	char *
Default:	NULL
Procs:	create, get, set
Objects:	Frame
See Also:	FRAME_SHOW_FOOTER , FRAME_LEFT_FOOTER

FRAME_SHOW_FOOTER

Indicates whether the footer is visible.

Argument:	`Boolean`
Default:	`FALSE`
Procs:	`create`, `get`, `set`
Objects:	`Frame`
See Also:	4.2.2 , `FRAME_LEFT_FOOTER`, `FRAME_RIGHT_FOOTER`

FRAME_SHOW_HEADER

Indicates whether the header is visible. This is only a hint to the window manager. Some window managers may not honor this hint, some window managers may only honor this hint when the frame leaves the withdrawn state. Thus, to see the effect of setting this attribute to `FALSE`, the frame may need to be unmapped, and then mapped again.

Argument:	`Boolean`
Default:	`TRUE`
Procs:	`create`, `get`, `set`
Objects:	`Frame`
See Also:	4.2.2

FRAME_SHOW_LABEL

Indicates whether the frame's label is displayed. This is equivalent to `FRAME_SHOW_HEADER`.

Argument:	`Boolean`
Default:	`TRUE`
Procs:	`create`, `get`, `set`
Objects:	`Frame`

FRAME_SHOW_RESIZE_CORNER

Determines whether a frame has resize corners. This is only a hint to the window manager. Some window managers may not honor this hint, some window managers may only honor this hint when the frame leaves the withdrawn state. Thus, to see the effect of setting this attribute to `FALSE`, the frame may need to be unmapped, and then mapped again. This attribute has no effect on window managers that are not OPEN LOOK compliant.

Argument:	`Boolean`
Default:	`TRUE`
Procs:	`create`, `get`, `set`
Objects:	`Frame`
See Also:	4.3.4

FRAME_WM_COMMAND_ARGC

Returns the number of command-line option strings stored on the frame.

Return Type:	`int`
Default:	0
Procs:	`get`
Objects:	`Frame`
See Also:	4.11 , `FRAME_WM_COMMAND_ARGC_ARGV`, `FRAME_WM_COMMAND_ARGV`, `FRAME_WM_COMMAND_STRINGS`, `WIN_CMD_LINE`, *Xlib Programming Manual, Interclient Communication* Chapter

FRAME_WM_COMMAND_ARGC_ARGV

Lets an application set the command-line options that can be used to (re)start it. The options passed, in addition to XView options, are stored on a property called WM_COMMAND on the frame window. The options passed are stored by XView and will be added to the XView options on the WM_COMMAND property on the frame window, upon receiving a WM_SAVE_YOURSELF request from the session/window manager. The program *xprop* can be used to display a window's properties. Only one base frame window of the application needs to have this property set. This property is read possibly by a session manager to restart clients. Setting this attribute's arguments to NULL and -1 prevents any command-line option information from being saved on the frame. If there are two or more base frames in the application, the second and subsequent base frames should set their FRAME_WM_COMMAND_ARGC_ARGV attributes' arguments to NULL and -1 if they want to avoid multiple invocations of the same application by the session manager. The first argument is the number of strings passed in the second argument. The second argument is a pointer to an array containing the command-line option strings. The strings passed are copied and cached on the frame.

Argument1:	int
Argument2:	(char **)
Default:	0 for Argument1 NULL for Argument2
Procs:	create, set
Objects:	Frame
Usage:	

```
        Frame    base_frame, second_frame;
        char     *argv[10];
        int      argc = 0;

        argv[argc++] = "-I"
        argv[argc++] = "ls"
        argv[argc++] = "-bold_font"
        argv[argc++] = "courier-bold-14"

        /*
         * This ensures that the above options are stored
         * on the base frame
         */
        xv_set(base_frame, FRAME_WM_COMMAND_ARGC_ARGV,
                               argc, argv, NULL);

        /*
         * This ensures that no command-line information will
         * be stored on this frame.
         */
        xv_set(second_frame,
                FRAME_WM_COMMAND_ARGC_ARGV, NULL, -1, NULL);
```

See Also: 4.11, 20.9.5 , FRAME_WM_COMMAND_ARGV, FRAME_WM_COMMAND_ARGC, FRAME_WM_COMMAND_STRINGS, WIN_CMD_LINE, *Xlib Programming Manual, Interclient Communication* Chapter

FRAME_WM_COMMAND_ARGV

Returns the array containing the command-line option strings stored on the frame. The strings in the array must not be modified by client programs. If the value returned is -1, this means that no command-line information is stored on the frame.

Return Type: (char **) or -1
Default: NULL
Procs: get
Objects: Frame
See Also: 4.11 , FRAME_WM_COMMAND_ARGC_ARGV, FRAME_WM_COMMAND_ARGC,
               FRAME_WM_COMMAND_STRINGS, WIN_CMD_LINE,
               Xlib Programming Manual, Interclient Communication Chapter

FRAME_WM_COMMAND_STRINGS

Lets an application set the command-line options that can be used to (re)start it. The options passed, in addition to XView options are stored on a property called WM_COMMAND on the frame window. The options passed are stored by XView and will be added to the XView options on the WM_COMMAND property on the frame window, upon receiving a WM_SAVE_YOURSELF request from the session/window manager. (The program xprop can be used to display a window's properties). Only one base frame window of the application needs to have this property set. This property is read, possibly by a session manager to restart clients. Setting this attribute to -1 prevents any command-line option information from being saved on the frame. If there are two or more base frames in the application, the second and subsequent base frames should set their FRAME_WM_COMMAND_ARGC_ARGV attributes to -1 if they want to avoid multiple invocations of the same application by the session manager. The strings passed are copied and cached on the frame.

Argument: NULL-terminated list of (char *) or, -1 followed by NULL
Default: None
Procs: create, set
Objects: Frame
Usage:

```
        Frame    base_frame, second_frame;

        /*  Ensure that the given options are stored on
         *  on the base frame
         */
        xv_set (base_frame, FRAME_WM_COMMAND_STRINGS,
                "-I",
                "ls",
                "-bold_font",
                "courier-bold-14",
                NULL,
            NULL);

        /* This ensures that no command-line information will
         * be stored on this frame.
         */
        xv_set (second_frame, FRAME_WM_COMMAND_STRINGS,
                            -1, NULL, NULL);
```

See Also: 4.11 , FRAME_WM_COMMAND_ARGC_ARGV, FRAME_WM_COMMAND_ARGC,
               FRAME_WM_COMMAND_ARGV, WIN_CMD_LINE,
               Xlib Programming Manual, Interclient Communication Chapter

FRAME_X_ACCELERATOR

Specifies a window-level accelerator. The character in the first argument is used to call the procedure in the second argument with the data in the third argument. On `xv_get`, the Frame package searches through the linked list of accelerators, and returns a pointer to the `Frame_accelerator` structure whose code or keysym matches the specified code and keysym. Applications do not normally use `xv_get` with this attribute.

On `create`, `set`:

Argument 1: `char`
Argument 2: X11 KeySym
Argument 3: `Xv_opaque`

On get:

Argument 1: `char`
Argument 2: KeySym
Procs: `create,get,set`
Objects: `Frame`
Callback:

```
void
accelerator_notify_proc (value, event)
Xv_opaque    value;     /* from Argument 3 */
Event        *event;
```

See Also: 6.14

FULLSCREEN_ALLOW_EVENTS

When in a fullscreen grab and the pointer and/or the keyboard is "frozen," specifies how the events that are queued up in the server due to X grabs, are processed.

Argument: `int` (where the value is any of the `AllowEvents` modes in *<X11/X.h>*)
Procs: `create,set`
Objects: `Fullscreen`
See Also: `XAllowEvents ()`, *Xlib Reference Manual*.

FULLSCREEN_ALLOW_SYNC_EVENT

When in a synchronous grab mode, where the keyboard and/or pointer is frozen by a client; specifies that normal event processing continue until the next mouse button or keyboard event.

Argument: No value
Procs: `create,set`
Objects: `Fullscreen`

FULLSCREEN_CURSOR_WINDOW

Restricts the cursor to a specified window. `xv_get` identifies the window.

Argument: `Xv_window`
Default: None
Procs: `create,get`
Objects: `Fullscreen`

FULLSCREEN_GRAB_KEYBOARD

Specifies whether keyboard should be grabbed.

Argument:	Boolean
Default:	TRUE
Procs:	create, get, set
Objects:	Fullscreen

FULLSCREEN_GRAB_POINTER

Specifies whether pointer should be grabbed.

Argument:	Boolean
Default:	TRUE
Procs:	create, get, set
Objects:	Fullscreen

FULLSCREEN_GRAB_SERVER

Specifies whether server should be grabbed.

Argument:	Boolean
Default:	TRUE
Procs:	create, get, set
Objects:	Fullscreen

FULLSCREEN_INPUT_WINDOW

Specifies the window from which input is read; xv_get identifies that window. The server, keyboard, and pointer are grabbed for this window.

Argument:	Xv_window
Default:	Owner window
Procs:	create, get
Objects:	Fullscreen

FULLSCREEN_KEYBOARD_GRAB_KBD_MODE

Determines the grab mode for the keyboard when grabbing the keyboard.

Argument:	Fullscreen_grab_mode
Default:	FULLSCREEN_ASYNCHRONOUS
Procs:	create, get, set
Objects:	Fullscreen

FULLSCREEN_KEYBOARD_GRAB_PTR_MODE

Determines the grab mode for the pointer when grabbing the keyboard.

Argument:	Fullscreen_grab_mode
Default:	FULLSCREEN_ASYNCHRONOUS
Procs:	create, get, set
Objects:	Fullscreen

FULLSCREEN_OWNER_EVENTS

When a window grabs the server/keyboard/pointer, the value of this attribute determines the distribution of events to the the application's windows.

All events occurring outside all the application's windows, are reported to the grab window (see FULLSCREEN_INPUT_WINDOW).

For events occurring within the application's windows: If FULLSCREEN_OWNER_EVENTS is TRUE, the events are reported to the window indicated by the pointer. If FULLSCREEN_OWNER_EVENTS is FALSE, the events are reported to the grab window.

Argument:	Boolean
Default:	FALSE
Procs:	create, get, set
Objects:	Fullscreen

FULLSCREEN_PAINT_WINDOW

Specifies or gets the paint window that will be or is already in fullscreen.

Argument:	Xv_opaque
Default:	Owner window
Procs:	create, get
Objects:	Fullscreen

FULLSCREEN_POINTER_GRAB_KBD_MODE

Determines the grab mode for the keyboard when grabbing the pointer.

Argument:	Fullscreen_grab_mode
Default:	FULLSCREEN_ASYNCHRONOUS
Procs:	create, get, set
Objects:	Fullscreen

FULLSCREEN_POINTER_GRAB_PTR_MODE

Determines the grab mode for the pointer when grabbing the pointer.

Argument:	Fullscreen_grab_mode
Default:	FULLSCREEN_ASYNCHRONOUS
Procs:	create, get, set
Objects:	Fullscreen

FULLSCREEN_RECT

Returns a pointer to the rectangle containing the paint window that is currently fullscreen.

Argument:	Rect *
Default:	Owner window's bounding box
Procs:	get
Objects:	Fullscreen

FULLSCREEN_SYNC

Specifies whether to grab in synchronous (TRUE) or asynchronous (FALSE) mode.

Argument:	Boolean
Default:	FALSE
Procs:	create, get, set
Objects:	Fullscreen

HELP_STRING_FILENAME

The name of a file containing a list of string pairs. The file is searched for in the directories listed in the environment variable HELPPATH. Each line in the file contains two words: the first word is the help string for which help is available, and the second word is of the form "file:target", which XView uses to find the Spot Help text and More Help data. The first word must be less than 128 characters, and the second less than 64 characters. HELP_STRING_FILENAME is to be set on the paint window, or any of its owners, where the strings are to be painted.

Argument:	Char *
Default:	No string-help available
Procs:	create, get, set
Objects:	Icon
See Also:	23.2.3

ICON_FONT

Specifies the icon's font.

Argument:	Xv_font
Default:	lucida medium
Procs:	create, get, set
Objects:	Icon

ICON_HEIGHT

Icon's height in pixels.

Argument:	int
Default:	64
Procs:	create, get, set
Objects:	Icon

ICON_IMAGE

Sets or gets the remote image for icon's image.

Argument:	Server_image
Default:	NULL
Procs:	create, get, set
Objects:	Icon
See Also:	14.2

ICON_IMAGE_RECT

Sets or gets the bounding box (rect) for the icon's image.

Argument:	Rect *
Default:	Origin (0,0), width 64, height 64
Procs:	create, get, set
Objects:	Icon
See Also:	14.2

ICON_LABEL

Specifies the icon's label.

Argument:	char *
Default:	NULL
Procs:	create, get, set
Objects:	Icon
See Also:	14.2.1

ICON_LABEL_RECT

Sets or gets the bounding box for the icon's label. Relative to the icon, 0, 0 is the upper-left corner of the icon.

Argument: `Rect *`
Default: Bottom left-hand corner of the icon
Procs: `create,get,set`
Objects: `Icon`
See Also: 14.2.1

ICON_MASK_IMAGE

The icon's GC's clipmask is set to this bitmap. If this is set, `ICON_TRANSPARENT` is set to `TRUE` as a side effect.

Argument: `Pixmap or Server_image`
Default: `FALSE`
Procs: `create,get,set`
Objects: `Icon`
See Also: 14.2

ICON_TRANSPARENT

Sets the background color of the icon to be the same as the workspace's background color.

Argument: `int`
Default: `FALSE`
Procs: `create,get,set`
Objects: `Icon`
See Also: 14.2

ICON_TRANSPARENT_LABEL

Draws the given string into an icon using the foreground only. It does not affect any other pixels in the bounding box for each character. Creating, setting, and getting `ICON_TRANSPARENT_LABEL` is equivalent to creating, setting, and getting `ICON_LABEL` except that the string is drawn in the foreground color only.

Argument: `char *`
Default: `NULL`
Procs: `create,get,set`
Objects: `Icon`
See Also: 14.2.2

ICON_WIDTH

Icon's width in pixels.

Argument: `int`
Default: 64
Procs: `create,get,set`
Objects: `Icon`

MENU_ACTION_IMAGE

This attribute is for SunView compatibility. For more information, refer to the manual, *Converting SunView Applications*.

MENU_ACTION_ITEM

This attribute is for SunView compatibility. For more information, refer to the manual, *Converting SunView Applications*.

MENU_APPEND_ITEM

Appends an item to the end of menu.

Argument:	Menu_item
Default:	N/A
Procs:	set
Objects:	Menu
See Also:	11.6.3

MENU_CLASS

Gets an enumerated type that identifies the menu class, as set by the package. This may be one of MENU_CHOICE, MENU_COMMAND, or MENU_TOGGLE.

Argument:	Menu_class
Default:	Defined by package
Procs:	get
Objects:	Menu

MENU_CLIENT_DATA

Specifies an arbitrary value to be attached to a menu or a menu item.

Argument:	caddr_t
Default:	None
Procs:	create, get, set
Objects:	Menu, Menu_item
See Also:	11.17.3

MENU_COLOR

Specifies the color index to use for the foreground color for a menu or a menu item.

Argument:	int
Default:	size-1 (where size is the number of colors in the colormap segment associated with the window), for a menu. Same as the color index specified in the menu item's menu or for the window, for a menu item.
Procs:	create, get, set
Objects:	Menu, Menu_item

MENU_COL_MAJOR

If TRUE, string items in the menu will be sorted in column-major order (like ls (1)) instead of row-major order. This attribute does not apply unless the menu uses multiple columns.

Argument:	Boolean
Default:	TRUE
Procs:	create, get, set
Objects:	Menu

MENU_DEFAULT

Default menu item as a position. The first menu item has position one. Note that a menu title is also a menu item.

Argument:	int
Default:	1, without a menu title; 2, with a menu title
Procs:	create, get, set
Objects:	Menu

MENU_DEFAULT_ITEM

Default menu item as opaque handle.

Argument:	`Menu_handle`
Default:	Handle of first non-title item
Procs:	`create,get,set`
Objects:	`Menu`
See Also:	11.15

MENU_DESCEND_FIRST

If this attribute is specified in `xv_find`, then the search will be done "depth first." If it is not specified, the search will be "deferred"; that is, it will be done horizontally through the menu structure.

Argument:	No value
Default:	Deferred
Procs:	`find`
Objects:	`Menu`
See Also:	11.14

MENU_DONE_PROC

Specifies a callback procedure that is called when the menu group is dismissed.

Argument	`void (*`*menu_done_proc*`) ()`
Default:	`menu_return_value()`, for a menu object; `NULL`, for a menu item object
Procs:	`create, get, set`
Objects:	`Menu`
Callback:	

```
void
menu_done_proc (menu, result)
     menu      menu;
     Xv_opaque result;
```

`menu` is the base (top) level menu, as specified in `menu_show()`.

`result` is the return value from the menu notify procedure.

If the menu notify procedure is user-specified, then *result* is invalid, since user-specified menu notify procedures do not return a value. If the menu notify procedure is `menu_return_value()`; then `result` is the value of the selected menu item. If the menu notify procedure is `menu_return_item()`, the `result` is the handle of the selected menu item. You can get notification that any menu in a menu group is done by attaching `MENU_DONE_PROC` to each menu. However, you will get better results with `menu_item` notify procedures.

See Also:	11.4

MENU_FEEDBACK

This attribute is for SunView compatibility. For more informations, refer to the manual, *Converting SunView Applications*.

MENU_FIRST_EVENT

Gets the event which was initially passed into `menu_show`. The event's contents *can* be modified.

Return Type:	`Event *`
Procs:	`get`
Objects:	`Menu`
See Also:	11.4

MENU_GEN_PIN_WINDOW

Creates a command window as the pin window based on the menu's contents. The frame (argument 1) is the parent frame; the name (argument 2) is the pin window's name. All menu items *must* have notify procedures; MENU_NOTIFY_PROC for the menu itself is ignored.

Argument 1:	Frame
Argument 2:	char *
Default:	No pin window
Procs:	create, set
Objects:	Menu
See Also:	11.12

MENU_GEN_PROC

Names a client-provided procedure that is called to generate a menu or menu item.

Argument:	void (*menu_gen_proc) ()
Default:	None
Procs:	create, get, set
Objects:	Menu , Menu_item
Callback:	

```
Menu
menu_gen_proc (m, op)
        Menu            m;
        Menu_generate   op;
```

This menu generating procedure is called whenever a menu item that has the MENU_GEN_PROC attribute set and the menu needs to be displayed or traversed. It should return a handle to a menu that has either been dynamically created or statically stored. The *op* argument tells the state of the menu when the function is called. The argument *op* has one of the values: MENU_DISPLAY, MENU_DISPLAY_DONE, MENU_NOTIFY, or MENU_NOTIFY_DONE as defined by **Menu_generate** in *openmenu.h*.

See Also:	11.9

MENU_GEN_PROC_IMAGE

This attribute is for SunView compatibility. For more information, refer to the manual, *Converting SunView Applications*.

MENU_GEN_PROC_ITEM

This attribute is for SunView compatibility. For more information, refer to the manual, *Converting SunView Applications*.

MENU_GEN_PULLRIGHT

Defines the generate procedure for the menu item's submenu.

Argument: `void (*menu_gen_proc) ()`
Default: `NULL`
Procs: `create, get, set`
Objects: `Menu_item`
Callback:

```
        Menu
    menu_gen_proc (m, op)
            Menu          m;
            Menu_generate op;
```

This menu generating procedure is called whenever a menu item has `MENU_GEN_PROC` set and the menu needs to be displayed or traversed. It should return a handle to a menu that has either been dynamically created or statically stored.

See Also: 11.9

MENU_GEN_PULLRIGHT_IMAGE

This attribute is for SunView compatibility. For more information, refer to the manual, *Converting SunView Applications*.

MENU_GEN_PULLRIGHT_ITEM

This attribute is for SunView compatibility. For more information, refer to the manual, *Converting SunView Applications*.

MENU_IMAGE

Specifies the menu item's server image.

Argument: `Server_image`
Default: `NULL`
Procs: `create, get, set`
Objects: `Menu_item`
See Also: 11.6.1

MENU_IMAGE_ITEM

This attribute is for SunView compatibility. For more information, refer to the manual, *Converting SunView Applications*.

MENU_IMAGES

Creates menu items with the specified server images. The new menu items are appended to the menu.

Argument: list of `Server_image`
Default: None
Procs: `create, set`
Objects: `Menu`
See Also: 11.8

MENU_INACTIVE

If `TRUE`, the menu item is grayed out and not selectable.

Argument: `Boolean`
Default: `FALSE`
Procs: `create, get, set`
Objects: `Menu_item`
See Also: 11.13

MENU_INSERT

Inserts a new menu item after *n*th item in the menu.

Argument 1:   `int`
Argument 2:   `Menu_item`
Default: N/A
Procs: `create, get, set`
Objects: `Menu`

MENU_INSERT_ITEM

Inserts the menu item given as the next value after the menu item given as the first value.

Argument 1:   `Menu_item`
Argument 2:   `Menu_item`
Procs: `create, set`
Objects: `Menu`

MENU_ITEM

Allows you to create menu items *in-line* with the call to the `xv_create()` used to create your menu. Takes a *menu item*-specific attribute-value list that would otherwise be used in a separate call to `xv_create()` to create menu items with the MENUITEM package.

Argument: A-V list
Procs: `create, set`
Objects: `Menu`
Usage:

```
xv_create(NULL, MENU,
          MENU_ITEM,
              MENU_STRING, "foo",
              MENU_NOTIFY_PROC, foo_notify_proc,
              NULL,
          MENU_ITEM,
              MENU_STRING, "bar",
              MENU_NOTIFY_PROC, bar_notify_proc,
              NULL,
          NULL);
```

See Also: 11.6.1

MENU_LAST_EVENT

Gets the last event read by the menu. The event's contents can be modified.

Return Type: `Event *`
Procs: `get`
Objects: `Menu`
See Also: 11.4

MENU_NCOLS

Specifies the number of columns in a menu.

Argument: `int`
Default: 1
Procs: `create, get, set`
Objects: `Menu`
See Also: 11.11

XView Attributes

MENU_NITEMS

Returns the number of items in a menu.

Return Type: `int`
Procs: `get`
Objects: `Menu`
See Also: 11.9

MENU_NOTIFY_PROC

Names a procedure to be called when the user selects a menu item.

Argument: `void (*`*menu_notify_proc*`) ()`
Default: `NULL`
Procs: `create, get, set`
Objects: `Menu, Menu_item`
Callback:

```
void
menu_notify_proc (menu, menu_item)
        Menu        menu;
        Menu_item   menu_item;
```

The notify procedure is attached to menus and menu items using `MENU_NOTIFY_PROC`. This function is called whenever the user selects a menu item. The `menu` identifies which menu the `menu_item` belongs to.

See Also: 11.13

MENU_NOTIFY_STATUS

If the menu is attached to a menu button that is part of an unpinned pop-up window, then the window is dismissed if `MENU_NOTIFY_STATUS` is `XV_OK`. If `MENU_NOTIFY_STATUS` is set to `XV_ERROR`, then the window is not dismissed. You probably will only need to `xv_get ()` or `xv_set ()` this attribute from within a notify procedure. When a notify procedure exits for an unpinned command frame, XView internally uses the value of this attribute to determine whether or not the command frame is dismissed. XView sets the value of this attribute to `XV_OK` before calling the notify procedure.

Argument: `int`
Default: `XV_OK`
Valid Values: {`XV_OK, XV_ERROR`}
Procs: `get, set`
Objects: `Menu`
See Also: 11.16

MENU_NROWS

Sets or gets the number of rows in a menu.

Argument: `int`
Default: The number of menu items in the menu
Procs: `create, get, set`
Objects: `Menu`
See Also: 11.11

MENU_NTH_ITEM

Gets the *n*th menu item (*n* starts at 1).

Return Type: `Menu_item`
Argument: `int`
Procs: `get`
Objects: `Menu`
See Also: 11.9

MENU_PARENT

On a Menu object, this attribute is only valid from within a notify or generate procedure. With a sub-menu the return value is the Menu Item from which the submenu was pulled-right. For a top-level menu the `xv_get()` returns `NULL`.

On a Menu_item object, the return value is the handle of the enclosing Menu.

Return Type: `Menu` or `Menu_item`
Procs: `get`
Objects: `Menu, Menu_item`
See Also: 11.9.1

MENU_PIN

Determines whether the menu will have pushpin.

Argument: `Boolean`
Default: `FALSE`
Procs: `create, get, set`
Objects: `Menu`
See Also: 11.12

MENU_PIN_PROC

Names a procedure called if a user chooses the pin menu item. The default procedure displays a window whose layout is similar to the menu it replaces.

Argument: `void (*menu_pin_proc)()`
Default: `menu_default_pin_proc()`
Procs: `create, get, set`
Objects: `Menu`
Callback:

```
void
menu_pin_proc (menu, x, y)
        Menu    menu;
        int     x, y;
```

This client-supplied procedure is called whenever the user attempts to pin-up a menu. Attached to menus using the attribute, `MENU_PIN_PROC`. `x` and `y` are the fullscreen co-ordinates of the upper-left corner of the pin window.

See Also: 11.12

MENU_PIN_WINDOW

The handle of the command frame representing the pin window for the menu when pinned-up. Use `MENU_GEN_PIN_WINDOW` to have XView manage this frame automatically. When using `MENU_GEN_PIN_WINDOW`, the value returned by `xv_get()` for `MENU_PIN_WINDOW` will be `NULL` until a menu is initially pinned.

Argument:	`Frame_cmd`
Default:	None
Procs:	`create, get, set`
Objects:	`Menu`
See Also:	11.12

MENU_PULLRIGHT

Item's pullright menu.

Argument:	`Menu`
Default:	`NULL`
Procs:	`create, get, set`
Objects:	`Menu_item`
See Also:	11.8

MENU_PULLRIGHT_IMAGE

This attribute is for SunView compatibility. For more information, refer to the manual, *Converting SunView Applications*.

MENU_PULLRIGHT_ITEM

This attribute is for SunView compatibility. For more information, refer to the manual, *Converting SunView Applications*.

MENU_RELEASE

Specifies that the menu item gets destroyed when its parent menu is destroyed. This is the default for menu items created in-line.

Argument:	No value
Default:	Destroy item, if in-line; do *not* destroy item if `Append` or `Replace`.
Procs:	`create, set`
Objects:	`Menu_item`
See Also:	11.17

MENU_RELEASE_IMAGE

Specifies that the string or `Server_image` associated with the item is freed when the item is destroyed.

Argument:	No value
Default:	Do not release text string or server image.
Procs:	`create, set`
Objects:	`Menu_item`
See Also:	11.8

MENU_REMOVE

Removes the *n*th item from the menu (*n* starts at 1).

Argument:	`int`
Procs:	`set`
Objects:	`Menu`
See Also:	11.9

MENU_REMOVE_ITEM

Removes the specified menu item.

Argument: `Menu_item`
Procs: `set`
Objects: `Menu`

MENU_REPLACE

Replaces the *n*th menu item (argument 1) with the menu item specified in argument 2 (*n* starts at 1).

Argument 1: `int`
Argument 2: `Menu_item`
Procs: `create, set`
Objects: `Menu`

MENU_REPLACE_ITEM

Replaces the menu item given as first value with the one given as the second value in the menu (the old item is *not* replaced in any other menus in which it may appear).

Argument 1: `Menu_item`
Argument 2: `Menu_item`
Procs: `create, set`
Objects: `Menu`

MENU_SELECTED

This attribute is valid for both a menu and a menu item. On a menu, it returns the selected menu item number. On a menu item, it returns `TRUE` if the item is selected, otherwise it returns `FALSE`.

Argument: `int` or `Boolean`
Default: `FALSE`
Procs: `get`
Objects: `Menu, Menu_item`

MENU_SELECTED_ITEM

Returns the selected menu item.

Argument: `Menu_item`
Default: None
Procs: `get`
Objects: `Menu`
See Also: 11.15

MENU_STRING

Sets or gets the menu item's string. The string is *not* copied when this attribute is set.

Argument: `char *`
Default: `NULL`
Procs: `create, get, set`
Objects: `Menu_item`
See Also: 11.6.1

MENU_STRING_ITEM

This attribute is for SunView compatibility. For more information, refer to the manual, *Converting SunView Applications*.

MENU_STRINGS

Creates menu items with the specified strings. The new menu items are appended to the menu. The strings are *not* copied when this attribute is set.

Argument: list of char *
Procs: create, set
Objects: Menu
See Also: 11.5

MENU_TITLE

Specifies that the item is the menu's title. Returns TRUE or FALSE on get.

Return Type: Boolean
Argument: No value
Default: FALSE
Procs: create, get, set
Objects: Menu_item

MENU_TITLE_ITEM

Creates a string title item. Must be used with menus that do not originate from pullright items or pull-down menu buttons. The string is *not* copied when this attribute is set.

Argument: char *
Procs: create, set
Objects: Menu
See Also: 11.5

MENU_TYPE

Returns MENU_MENU or MENU_ITEM. Informs you whether the object is a menu or a menu item.

Argument: Menu_attribute (an enum)
Default: MENU_MENU
Procs: get
Objects: Menu, Menu_item

MENU_VALID_RESULT

If TRUE, then a zero return value represents a legitimate value. This attribute is used only when the menu notify procedure that is invoked is the public procedure menu_return_value().

Argument: Boolean
Default: FALSE
Procs: create, get, set
Objects: Menu

MENU_VALUE

Sets or gets the item's value. This attribute is used only when the menu notify procedure that is invoked is the public procedure menu_return_value().

Argument: Xv_opaque
Default: NULL
Procs: create, get, set
Objects: Menu_item

NOTICE_BLOCK_THREAD

Specifies the type of notice desired. If TRUE, the notice, when mapped (via XV_SHOW) will block the thread of execution.

Argument:	Boolean
Default:	TRUE
Procs:	create,set
Objects:	Xv_Notice
See Also:	12.2

NOTICE_BUSY_FRAMES

Specifies the frames or windows to appear busy during notice pop-up. This applies only when NOTICE_LOCK_SCREEN is FALSE.

Argument:	NULL-terminated list, Frame
Default:	NULL
Procs:	create,set
Objects:	Xv_Notice
See Also:	12.2.1

NOTICE_BUTTON

Specifies a string to be displayed in a button and a value to use if the button is selected.

Return Type:	int (notice_prompt () returns the value of the button selected)
Argument 1:	char *
Argument 2:	int
Default:	None
Procs:	create,set,notice_prompt ()
Objects:	Xv_Notice
See Also:	B.1.1, 12.1.1

NOTICE_BUTTON_NO

Specifies a string associated with the NO button. The value returned if this button is selected is NOTICE_NO.

Return Type:	int (notice_prompt () returns the value of the button selected)
Argument:	char *
Default:	None
Procs:	create,set,notice_prompt ()
Objects:	Xv_Notice
See Also:	B.1.1, 12.1.1

NOTICE_BUTTON_YES

Specifies a string to associate with the YES (confirm) button. The value returned when this button is selected is NOTICE_YES.

Return Type:	int (notice_prompt () returns the value of the button selected)
Argument:	char *
Default:	None
Procs:	create,set,notice_prompt ()
Objects:	Xv_Notice
See Also:	B.1.1, 12.1.1

NOTICE_EVENT_PROC

Specifies the function to be called when a notice button is clicked on. This applies only when NOTICE_LOCK_SCREEN is FALSE.

Argument:	void (*my_notice_proc) ()
Default:	NULL
Procs:	create, set
Objects:	Xv_Notice
Callback:	

```
void
my_notice_proc(notice, value, event)
        Xv_Notice   *notice;
        int         value;
        Event       *event;
```

See Also:	12.2.1

NOTICE_FOCUS_XY

Specifies the x, y position from which the notice shadow emanates. The x, y position is relative to the *owner* window. This applies to a notice object only when NOTICE_LOCK_SCREEN is TRUE.

Argument 1:	int
Argument 2:	int
Default:	Current mouse position
Procs:	create, set, notice_prompt()
Objects:	Xv_Notice
See Also:	B.1, 12.2.2

NOTICE_FONT

Specifies the font to be used in the notice.

Argument:	Xv_Font
Default:	The font of the owner frame
Procs:	create, get, notice_prompt()
Objects:	Xv_Notice

NOTICE_LOCK_SCREEN

Specifies the type of notice desired. If TRUE, the notice locks up the screen when mapped.

Argument:	Boolean
Default:	FALSE
Procs:	create, get, set
Objects:	Xv_Notice
See Also:	12.2

NOTICE_MESSAGE_STRING

Specifies the text to print in a notice. The argument is a single NULL-terminated string, which may contain "\n" as a line break.

Argument:	(char *)
Default:	NULL
Procs:	create, set, notice_prompt()
Objects:	Xv_Notice
See Also:	12.1

NOTICE_MESSAGE_STRINGS

Specifies the text to print in a notice. Argument is a NULL–terminated list of strings, which may contain "\n" as a line break.

Argument:	`list of char *`
Default:	NULL
Procs:	`create,set,notice_prompt()`
Objects:	`Xv_Notice`
See Also:	12.1

NOTICE_MESSAGE_STRINGS_ARRAY_PTR

Specifies the text to print in a notice. The argument is a variable pointing to a NULL-terminated array of strings, which may contain "\n" as a line break.

Argument:	`char**`
Default:	NULL
Procs:	`create,set,notice_prompt()`
Objects:	`Xv_Notice`
See Also:	24.4.2, 12.1

NOTICE_NO_BEEPING

Allows a client to specify that no beeping should take place, regardless of the default resource database setting. The default for this option is FALSE; that is, beep the number of times specified in the database.

Argument:	`int`
Default:	TRUE
Procs:	`create,get,set,notice_prompt()`
Objects:	`Xv_Notice`
See Also:	B.1.2, 12.2.2

NOTICE_STATUS

Specifies the address of the return code of the notice when it pops-down. If not specified, the notice return code is stored in the notice object and can be obtained by doing `(int)xv_get(notice NOTICE_STATUS)`. In `xv_set()` we pass in an `(int *)`, and the `xv_get()` returns an `(int)`.

Return Type:	`(int)`
Argument:	`(int *)`
Default:	See description
Procs:	`create,get,set`
Objects:	`Xv_Notice`
See Also:	12.1.1

NOTICE_TRIGGER

Specifies an XView event ID or type, other than clicking on mouse buttons, that will cause the notice to pop down. The notice pops down and the thread of execution continues. This applies to a notice object only when NOTICE_LOCK_SCREEN is TRUE. When this event occurs, the value returned is NOTICE_TRIGGERED. The event parameter to `notice_prompt` contains specifics about the event that triggered it.

Argument:	`int` (for example, MS_LEFT)
Default:	N/A
Procs:	`create,set,notice_prompt()`
Objects:	`Xv_Notice`
See Also:	12.2.2, `NOTICE_TRIGGER_EVENT`

NOTICE_TRIGGER_EVENT

Specifies the address of the XView Event structure that caused the notice to pop down, the thread of execution continues. This is used with the NOTICE_TRIGGER attribute and applies only when NOTICE_LOCK_SCREEN is TRUE.

Argument: (Event *)
Default: N/A
Procs: create, set
Objects: Xv_Notice
See Also: 12.2.2, NOTICE_TRIGGER

OPENWIN_ADJUST_FOR_HORIZONTAL_SCROLLBAR

Reserves space in openwin-class objects (e.g., canvas) for a horizontal scrollbar. On xv_set, adjusts (extends) the height of a subwindow that does *not* have a horizontal scrollbar to align properly with one that does.

Argument: Boolean
Default: TRUE
Procs: create, get, set
Objects: Openwin

OPENWIN_ADJUST_FOR_VERTICAL_SCROLLBAR

Reserves space in openwin-class objects (e.g., canvas) for a vertical scrollbar. On xv_set, adjusts (extends) the width of a subwindow that does *not* have a vertical scrollbar to align properly with one that does.

Argument: Boolean
Default: TRUE
Procs: create, get, set
Objects: Openwin

OPENWIN_AUTO_CLEAR

If TRUE, exposed areas of windows are cleared (i.e., painted the background color) before the repaint procedure is called.

Argument: Boolean
Default: TRUE unless subwindow's canvas is retained
Procs: create, get, set
Objects: Openwin
See Also: 5.3

OPENWIN_HORIZONTAL_SCROLLBAR

Returns the handle of the horizontal scrollbar associated with the specified view.

Return Type: Scrollbar
Argument: Xv_Window
Procs: get
Objects: Openwin
Usage:

```
Scrollbar   sb;
Xv_Window   view;
Openwin     openwin;

sb = (Scrollbar)xv_get(openwin,
        OPENWIN_HORIZONTAL_SCROLLBAR, view);
```

OPENWIN_NO_MARGIN

If TRUE, the view window's two pixel bottom and right margins are turned off.

Argument: Boolean
Default: FALSE
Procs: create, get, set
Objects: Openwin

OPENWIN_NTH_VIEW

Gets the handle of a specified openwin view window. Openwin view windows are numbered from 0.

Return Type: Xv_window
Argument: int
Procs: get
Objects: Openwin
See Also: 5.6.3

OPENWIN_NVIEWS

Gets the number of views contained in the open window.

Return Type: int
Default: 1
Procs: get
Objects: Openwin

OPENWIN_SHOW_BORDERS

Displays openwin borders. This must remain on for openwin objects to have scrollbars attached to them.

Argument: Boolean
Default: TRUE (FALSE for scrollable panels)
Procs: create, get
Objects: Openwin

OPENWIN_SPLIT

Takes as its value a list of attribute-value pairs beginning with OPENWIN_SPLIT_.

Argument: A-V list
Procs: create, set
Objects: Openwin
Callback:

> void
> *openwin_split_destroy_proc* (openwin)
>   Openwin   openwin;

OPENWIN_SPLIT_ used to install this procedure. This function is called when the user *joins* two views.

See Also: 5.6.2

OPENWIN_SPLIT_DESTROY_PROC

Names a procedure to call when a split openwin is joined. This attribute can only be set in an OPENWIN_SPLIT attribute-value list.

Argument	void (*openwin_split_destroy_proc) ()
Default:	NULL
Procs:	create, get, set
Objects:	Openwin
See Also:	5.6.3 , OPENWIN_SPLIT

OPENWIN_SPLIT_DIRECTION

Sets the direction of the split either horizontally or vertically. This attribute can only be set in an OPENWIN_SPLIT attribute-value list.

Argument:	Openwin_split_direction
Default:	OPENWIN_SPLIT_HORIZONTAL
Procs:	create, set
Objects:	Openwin
See Also:	OPENWIN_SPLIT

OPENWIN_SPLIT_INIT_PROC

Names a procedure to call when a split window is created. This attribute can only be set in an OPENWIN_SPLIT attribute-value list.

Argument	void (*openwin_split_init_proc) ()
Default:	NULL
Procs:	create, get, set
Objects:	Openwin
See Also:	5.6.3 , OPENWIN_SPLIT

OPENWIN_SPLIT_POSITION

Sets the position (in pixels) of the view. This attribute can only be set in an OPENWIN_SPLIT attribute-value list.

Argument:	int
Default:	None
Procs:	create,set
Objects:	Openwin
See Also:	OPENWIN_SPLIT

OPENWIN_SPLIT_VIEW

Specifies which view to split. Its value is the handle of the view you want to split. This attribute can only be set in an OPENWIN_SPLIT attribute-value list.

Argument:	Xv_window
Procs:	set
Objects:	Openwin
See Also:	OPENWIN_SPLIT

OPENWIN_SPLIT_VIEW_START

Specifies which part of the data (measured in scrollbar-units) is displayed at the start of the view (*top* for vertical; *left* for horizontal). This attribute can only be set in an OPENWIN_SPLIT attribute-value list.

Argument:	int
Default:	Continue from previous view
Procs:	create,get,set
Objects:	Openwin
See Also:	OPENWIN_SPLIT

OPENWIN_VERTICAL_SCROLLBAR

Returns the handle of the vertical scrollbar associated with the specified view.

Argument:	Scrollbar
Procs:	get
Objects:	Openwin
See Also:	OPENWIN_HORIZONTAL_SCROLLBAR

OPENWIN_VIEW_ATTRS

Distributes modifications across all *views* in a given openwin. Note that this does not affect canvas paint windows.

Argument:	A-V list
Procs:	create, set
Objects:	Openwin
See Also:	CANVAS_PAINTWINDOW_ATTRS

PANEL_ACCEPT_KEYSTROKE

Specifies whether the panel background or panel item should consume keyboard events. When an item wants keystrokes, set PANEL_ACCEPT_KEYSTROKE to TRUE on the panel item in the item's init routine. Setting PANEL_ACCEPT_KEYSTROKE to TRUE on the panel background is not recommended, since this is not supported by OPEN LOOK. This mode is maintained for SunView1 compatibility. **Warning**: this attribute should *only* be used from within a panel item extension.

Argument:	Boolean
Default:	FALSE for panel background. Default for panel items depends on the state of Open-Windows.KeyboardCommands. If its SunView1 or Basic, then only PANEL_TEXT, PANEL_NUMERIC_TEXT, and PANEL_MULTILINE_TEXT accept keyboard input focus. If its Full, then all panel items accept keyboard input focus.
Procs:	create, get, set
Objects:	Panel, Panel_item
See Also:	7.19.7

PANEL_BACKGROUND_PROC

Names an event-handling procedure called when an event falls on the background of the panel.

Argument: `void (*panel_background_proc) ()`
Default: `panel_default_handle_event`
Procs: `create, get, set`
Objects: `Panel`
Callback:

```
void
panel_background_proc (panel, event)
        Panel      panel
        Event      *event
```

Event-handling procedure called when an event falls on the background of the panel (e.g., not on any panel items).

See Also: 7.19.7

PANEL_BLINK_CARET

This attribute is for SunView compatibility. For more information, refer to the manual, *Converting SunView Applications.*

PANEL_BUSY

Sets a button's or a drop target item's busy state. While a button or drop target is busy, it will not accept further input (e.g., SELECT-down). By default, a button or Drop Target Item will be in the busy state while in its notify procedure and be cleared upon exiting. The busy state can be maintained after exiting the notify procedure by setting PANEL_BUSY to TRUE from within the notify procedure. Setting PANEL_BUSY back to FALSE, at a later time, clears the button's busy state. This attribute can also be used for similar functionality in panel item extensions.

Argument: `Boolean`
Default: Set to FALSE prior to entering button's or drop target's notify procedure
Procs: `get, set`
Objects: `Panel_button_item, Panel_item, Panel_drop_target_item`
See Also: 7.9.1

PANEL_CARET_ITEM

Specifies the panel item that currently has the input focus.

Argument: `Panel_item`
Default: First item that can accept keyboard input
Procs: `create, get, set`
Objects: `Panel`
See Also: 7.15.1

PANEL_CHILD_CARET_ITEM

Specifies what embedded (child) panel item to set the keyboard focus to when the application sets PANEL_CARET_ITEM to the parent panel item. PANEL_CHILD_CARET_ITEM should be NULL, if there are no embedded (child) panel items, or if the parent panel item itself can take the keyboard focus.

Argument: `Panel_item`
Default: NULL
Procs: `create, get, set`
Objects: `Panel_item` with an embedded (child) panel item.

PANEL_CHOICE_COLOR

Specifies the foreground color index (argument 2) for the specified choice (argument 1).

Argument 1:   `int` (choice index)
Argument 2:   `int` (color_index)
Default: Panel foreground color
Procs: `create,get,set`
Objects: `Panel_choice_item`
Usage:

```
xv_set(pchoice, PANEL_CHOICE_COLOR, 1, RED, NULL);
```

See Also: 7.10.6, 21.5

PANEL_CHOICE_FONT

This attribute is for SunView compatibility. For more information, refer to the manual, *Converting SunView Applications.*

PANEL_CHOICE_FONTS

This attribute is for SunView compatibility. For more information, refer to the manual, *Converting SunView Applications.*

PANEL_CHOICE_IMAGE

Specifies the image (argument 2) for the specified choice (argument 1).

Argument 1:   `int`
Argument 2:   `server_image`
Default: None
Procs: `create,get,set`
Objects: `Panel_choice_item`
See Also: 7.10.2

PANEL_CHOICE_IMAGES

Specifies the image for each of several choices.

Argument: `NULL`-terminated list of `Server_images`
Default: `NULL`
Procs: `create,set`
Objects: `Panel_choice_item`
See Also: 7.10

PANEL_CHOICE_NCOLS

Specifies the number of columns to use in the layout of panel choices.

Argument: `int`
Default: 1 for vertical layout (`PANEL_LAYOUT`)
Procs: `create,get,set`
Objects: `Panel_choice_item`
See Also: 7.10.1

PANEL_CHOICE_NROWS

Specifies the number of rows to use in the layout of panel choices.

Argument: `int`
Default: 1 for horizontal layout (`PANEL_LAYOUT`)
Procs: `create,get,set`
Objects: `Panel_choice_item`
See Also: 7.10.1

PANEL_CHOICE_RECT

The rectangle that encloses the specified choice. The first argument is the index of the choice (0= first choice). This attribute is not valid for `PANEL_CHOICE_STACK` objects.

Argument: `int`
Return Type: `Rect *`
Procs: `get`
Objects: `Panel_choice_item`
See Also: 7.10.7

PANEL_CHOICE_STRING

Specifies the string (argument 2) for the specified choice (argument 1). The string is copied when this attribute is set.

Argument 1:   `int`
Argument 2:   `char *`
Default: `NULL`
Procs: `create, get, set`
Objects: `Panel_choice_item`
See Also: 7.10

PANEL_CHOICE_STRINGS

Specifies the string for each choice. You must specify at least one choice. The least you can specify is a single `NULL`-terminated string. The strings are copied when this attribute is set.

Argument: `NULL`-terminated list of `char *`
Default: `NULL`
Procs: `create, set`
Objects: `Panel_choice_item`
See Also: 7.10, 25.2.1

PANEL_CHOICE_X

This attribute is for SunView compatibility. For more information, refer to the manual, *Converting SunView Applications*.

PANEL_CHOICE_XS

This attribute is for SunView compatibility. For more information, refer to the manual, *Converting SunView Applications*.

PANEL_CHOICE_Y

This attribute is for SunView compatibility. For more information, refer to the manual, *Converting SunView Applications*.

PANEL_CHOICE_YS

This attribute is for SunView compatibility. For more information, refer to the manual, *Converting SunView Applications*.

PANEL_CHOOSE_NONE

Allows scrolling lists or choice items to have no currently selected item. Not applicable if `PANEL_CHOOSE_ONE` is `FALSE`.

Argument: `Boolean`
Default: `TRUE`
Procs: `create, get, set`
Objects: `item, Panel_list_item`
See Also: 7.10.2

PANEL_CHOOSE_ONE

If TRUE, creates an exclusive scrolling list or choice. If FALSE, creates a non-exclusive scrolling list or choice. PANEL_CHOOSE_ONE is used as part of the PANEL_TOGGLE macro. When creating a toggle, it is recommended that you use the macro instead of the attribute.

Argument: Boolean
Default: TRUE
Procs: create, get
Objects: Panel_choice_item, Panel_list_item
See Also: 7.11.3

PANEL_CLIENT_DATA

Specifies an arbitrary value to be attached to a panel or to individual panel items.

Argument: caddr_t
Default: None
Procs: create, get, set
Objects: Panel, Panel_item
See Also: 7.19.1

PANEL_CURRENT_ITEM

Returns the handle of the currently active panel item. An item is considered current when there is a mouse button down event pending on that item (for example, after a SELECT-down over a text scrolling button, but before the corresponding SELECT-up). NULL implies no panel item is currently active.

Argument: Panel_item
Procs: get
Objects: Panel

PANEL_DEFAULT_ITEM

Sets the default panel item in the panel or gets the handle of the default panel item. Only buttons are valid as default items. Application programmers use this attribute to indicate the default button in a popup frame. Then, using the DefaultAction key, usually RETURN, causes the default button to be activated.

Argument: Panel_item
Default: NULL
Procs: create, get, set
Objects: Panel

PANEL_DEFAULT_VALUE

Identifies the default choice in PANEL_CHOICE_STACK items.

Argument: int or unsigned
Default: First choice
Procs: create, get, set
Objects: Panel_choice_item

PANEL_DIRECTION

Identifies the horizontal or vertical orientation of a slider or gauge.

Argument: Panel_setting
Valid Values: {PANEL_HORIZONTAL, PANEL_VERTICAL}
Default: PANEL_HORIZONTAL
Procs: create, get, set
Objects: Panel_slider_item, Panel_gauge_item
See Also: 7.13

PANEL_DISPLAY_LEVEL

Specifies the number of choices to display. Values are one of `PANEL_ALL`, `PANEL_CURRENT`, or `PANEL_NONE`. `PANEL_DISPLAY_LEVEL` is used as part of the `PANEL_CHOICE_STACK` macro; it is recommended that you use the macro instead of the attribute.

Argument: `Panel_setting`
Valid Values: {`PANEL_ALL`, `PANEL_CURRENT`, `PANEL_NONE`}
Default: `PANEL_ALL`
Procs: `create,get`
Objects: `Panel_choice_item`
See Also: 7.10.1

PANEL_DISPLAY_ROWS

Number of rows to display in the multiline text field.

Argument: `int`
Default: 5
Procs: `create,get,set`
Objects: `Panel_multiline_text_item`
See Also: 7.17

PANEL_DROP_BUSY_GLYPH

Busy drop target glyph, as defined by drag and drop specification.

Argument: `Server_image`
Default: Use normal drop target glyph
Procs: `create,get,set`
Objects: `Panel_drop_target_item`
See Also: 7.18.1

PANEL_DROP_DND

Drag and drop object (`DRAGDROP`) associated with panel drop target item. The `DRAGDROP` object is used to initiate a drag and drop operation. If no `PANEL_DROP_DND` exists, then the panel Drop Target Item does not support drags, and is termed an "empty" drop target (`PANEL_DROP_FULL = FALSE`).

Argument: `Drag_drop`
Default: `NULL`
Procs: `create,get,set`
Objects: `Panel_drop_target_item`
See Also: 7.18.1

PANEL_DROP_FULL

If `TRUE`, then the drop target item has draggable data set on the `PANEL_DROP_DND` object's selection items. The normal glyph is displayed. Setting `PANEL_DROP_FULL` to `TRUE` when no `PANEL_DROP_DND` is defined is not valid; `PANEL_DROP_FULL` will remain `FALSE`. If `FALSE`, then no draggable data is available (i.e., the drop target is empty). No glyph is displayed.

Argument: `Boolean`
Default: `FALSE`
Procs: `create,get,set`
Objects: `Panel_drop_target_item`
See Also: 7.18.1

PANEL_DROP_GLYPH

Normal drop target glyph, as defined by drag and drop package.

Argument:	`Server_image`
Default:	None
Procs:	`create,get,set`
Objects:	`Panel_drop_target_item`
See Also:	7.18.1

PANEL_DROP_HEIGHT

Dimensions of drag target box, in pixels, excluding border and margin.

Argument:	`int`
Default:	16
Procs:	`create,get,set`
Objects:	`Panel_drop_target_item`

PANEL_DROP_SEL_REQ

Selection requestor object (SELECTION_REQUESTOR) associated with the panel drop target item. The `Selection_requestor` object is used to receive a drop.

Argument:	`Selection_requestor`
Procs:	`get`
Objects:	`Panel_drop_target_item`
See Also:	7.18.1

PANEL_DROP_SITE_DEFAULT

Specifies whether or not the panel drop target's drop site is the default drop site. Only one panel drop target in a frame may be the default drop target. See DROP_SITE_DEFAULT attribute for more information.

Argument:	`Boolean`
Default:	`FALSE`
Procs:	`create,get,set`
Objects:	`Panel_drop_target_item`

PANEL_DROP_WIDTH

Dimensions of drag target box, in pixels, excluding border and margin.

Argument:	`int`
Default:	12
Procs:	`create,get,set`
Objects:	`Panel_drop_target_item`

XView Attributes

PANEL_EVENT_PROC

Event handler for panel items.

Argument: `void (*panel_event_proc) ()`
Default: Panel_item specific.
Procs: `create,get,set`
Objects: `Panel_item`
Callback:

```
        void
        panel_event_proc (item, event)
                Panel_item    item
                Event       *event
```

Client-specified event-handling procedure for handling events on panel items. This procedure is installed using `PANEL_EVENT_PROC`.

See Also: 7.19.8

PANEL_EXTRA_PAINT_HEIGHT

Defines the increment by which the panel grows in the **y** direction. It is used when `window_fit_height ()` is called.

Argument: `int`
Default: 1 pixel
Procs: `create,get,set`
Objects: `Panel`
See Also: 7.5

PANEL_EXTRA_PAINT_WIDTH

Defines the increment by which the panel grows in the **x** direction. It is used when `window_fit_width ()` is called.

Argument: `int`
Default: 1 pixel
Procs: `create,get,set`
Objects: `Panel`
See Also: 7.5

PANEL_FEEDBACK

Specifies feedback to give when an item is selected. If `PANEL_DISPLAY_LEVEL` is `PANEL_CURRENT`, the default value is `PANEL_NONE`; otherwise, it is `PANEL_MARKED`. `PANEL_FEED_BACK` is used as part of the `PANEL_CHECK_BOX` macro. It is recommended that you use the macro instead of the attribute.

Argument: `Panel_setting`
Default: See description
Procs: `create,get,set`
Objects: `Panel_choice_item`

PANEL_FIRST_ITEM

Gets the handle of the first item on a panel. The `PANEL_EACH_ITEM` macro (Section 3, *Summary of Procedures and Macros*) can be used to iterate over each item in a panel, starting with this first item.

Argument: `Panel_item`
Procs: `get`
Objects: `Panel`
See Also: 7.7

PANEL_FIRST_PAINT_WINDOW

Returns a pointer to the first `Panel_paint_window` struct, which defines the paint window and view window associated with the first view in the scrollable panel.

Argument:	`Panel_paint_window *`
Procs:	`get`
Objects:	`Scrollable_panel`

PANEL_FOCUS_PW

The paint window which currently has or last had the input focus. The `has_input_focus` `Panel_status` flag indicates whether or not the scrollable panel currently has the input focus. Initially, the focus paint window is set to the first paint window created in the scrollable panel.

Warning: This attribute should *only* be used from within a panel item extension.

Argument:	`Xv_Window`
Procs:	`get`
Objects:	`Scrollable_panel`

PANEL_GAUGE_WIDTH

Specifies the length of the panel gauge "thermometer" bar, in pixels, regardless of its horizontal or vertical orientation.

Argument:	`int`
Default:	`100`
Procs:	`create, get, set`
Objects:	`Panel_gauge_item`
See Also:	7.14

PANEL_GINFO

The OLGX Graphics Information structure for the specified panel or panel item. This attribute is only of interest to those panel item extensions that are calling OLGX functions or using OLGX macros.

Warning: This attribute should *only* be used from within a panel item extension.

Argument:	`Graphics_info *`
Procs:	`get`
Objects:	`Panel, Panel_item`

PANEL_INACTIVE

If TRUE, panel item cannot be selected. Inactive items are displayed with gray-out pattern.

Argument:	`Boolean`
Default:	`FALSE`
Procs:	`create, get, set`
Objects:	`Panel_item`
See Also:	7.9.1

PANEL_ITEM_CLASS

Gets the panel item *type* of the panel item specified.

Argument:	`Panel_item_type`
Procs:	`get`
Objects:	`Panel_item`

PANEL_ITEM_COLOR

Specifies the colormap index to use for the item. A value of –1 implies the foreground color for the panel window.

Argument: `int`
Default: `-1`
Procs: `create,get,set`
Objects: `Panel_item`
See Also: 21.5.1

PANEL_ITEM_CREATED

The `Panel_item` has finished processing the `XV_END_CREATE` phase of the generic panel item package (i.e. `xv_panel_item_pkg`). All `Panel_items` are subclassed from `xv_panel_item_pkg`.
Warning: This attribute should *only* be used from within a panel item extension.

Argument: `Boolean`
Procs: `get`
Objects: `Panel_item`

PANEL_ITEM_DEAF

The item does not want any events. This is used for items that contain one or more windows that are located within the item's rectangle. These windows are interposed on in order to process their events and maintain the panel's internal variables. An example of this is `PANEL_MULTILINE_TEXT`.
Warning: This attribute should *only* be used from within a panel item extension.

Argument: `Boolean`
Procs: `get,set`
Objects: `Panel_item`

PANEL_ITEM_LABEL_RECT

The rectangle describing the label portion of an item.
Warning: This attribute should *only* be used from within a panel item extension.

Argument: `Rect *`
Procs: `get,set`
Objects: `Panel_item`

PANEL_ITEM_MENU

Specifies the menu associated with the panel item.

Argument: `Menu`
Default: `NULL`
Procs: `create,get,set`
Objects: `Panel_item`

PANEL_ITEM_NTH_WINDOW

Returns the nth embedded window that receives events in the specified panel item. The first embedded window has index 0. This attribute functions exactly like OPENWIN_NTH_VIEW. This attribute is an "advanced" attribute; the general application programmer will not need to use this attribute.

Return Type: Xv_Window
Argument: int
Procs: get
Objects: Panel_item
Usage:

```
textsw_view = xv_get(mltxt_item,
                PANEL_ITEM_NTH_WINDOW, 0, NULL);
```

See Also: OPENWIN_NTH_VIEW

PANEL_ITEM_NWINDOWS

Returns the number of embedded windows in the specified panel item that receives events. Zero indicates that there are no embedded windows. This attribute functions exactly like OPENWIN_NVIEWS. This attribute is an "advanced" attribute; the general application programmer will not need to use this attribute.

Return Type: int
Procs: get
Objects: Panel_item
See Also: OPENWIN_NVIEWS

PANEL_ITEM_RECT

Gets the rectangle surrounding the panel item.

Argument: Rect *
Procs: get
Objects: Panel_item

PANEL_ITEM_VALUE_RECT

The rectangle describing the value portion of an item.
Warning: This attribute should *only* be used from within a panel item extension.

Argument: Rect *
Procs: get, set
Objects: Panel_item

PANEL_ITEM_WANTS_ADJUST

The panel item wants ACTION_ADJUST events.
Warning: This attribute should *only* be used from within a panel item extension.

Argument: Boolean
Procs: get, set
Objects: Panel_item

PANEL_ITEM_WANTS_ISO

This flag indicates that the panel item wants all ISO characters. Unmodified ASCII characters are not to be interpreted as mouseless keyboard commands. Currently, `PANEL_TEXT` and `PANEL_MULTILINE_TEXT` items have this flag set.

Warning: This attribute should *only* be used from within a panel item extension.

Argument:	`Boolean`
Default:	`FALSE`
Procs:	`get,set`
Objects:	`Panel_item`

PANEL_ITEM_X

Specifies the x position (in pixels) where the last panel item was created. If no item was created, then it specifies the x position where the first item will be created.

Argument:	`int`
Procs:	`get`
Objects:	`Panel`
See Also:	7.4.2

PANEL_ITEM_X_GAP

When set on a panel, the horizontal space, in pixels, between the last panel item created and the next panel item; when set on a panel item it is the horizontal space, in pixels, between the last panel item created and this panel item. This attribute allows applications to more easily use relative item positioning instead of absolute positioning. Relative item positioning is the recommended method of positioning panel items, since the size of items may change between invocations (e.g., different scales) or versions of the toolkit.

Argument:	`int`
Default:	10, for Panel; the panel's `PANEL_ITEM_X_GAP`, for panel item
Procs:	`create,get,set`, for panel; `create,get`, for panel item
Objects:	`Panel,Panel_item`
See Also:	7.3.1

PANEL_ITEM_X_POSITION

The default x coordinate of the panel item.

Warning: This attribute should *only* be used from within a panel item extension.

Argument:	`int`
Procs:	`get,set`
Objects:	`Panel`

PANEL_ITEM_Y

Specifies the y position (in pixels) where the last panel item was created. If no item was created, then it specifies the y position where the first item will be created.

Argument:	`int`
Default:	None
Procs:	`get`
Objects:	`Panel`
See Also:	7.4.2

PANEL_ITEM_Y_GAP

When set on a panel, this is the vertical space, in pixels, between the last panel item created and the next panel item when set on a panel item, PANEL_ITEM_Y_GAP is the vertical space, in pixels, between the last panel item created and this panel item. This attribute allows applications to more easily use relative item positioning instead of absolute positioning. Relative item positioning is the recommended method of positioning panel items, since the size of items may change between invocations (e.g., different scales) or versions of the toolkit.

Argument: int
Default: 13 for panel, the panel's PANEL_ITEM_Y_GAP for panel item
Procs: create, get, set for panel; create, get for panel item
Objects: Panel, Panel_item
See Also: 7.3.1

PANEL_ITEM_Y_POSITION

The default y coordinate of the panel item.
Warning: This attribute should *only* be used from within a panel item extension.

Argument: int
Procs: get, set
Objects: Panel

PANEL_JUMP_DELTA

Specifies the number of client units to adjust the value when a JumpLeft or JumpRight keyboard command is issued for a horizontal slider. Also specifies the number of client units to adjust the value when a JumpUp or JumpDown keyboard command is issued for a vertical slider or numeric text item. Used in conjunction with the OPEN LOOK Mouseless Model.

Argument: int
Default: 10
Procs: create, get, set
Objects: Panel_slider_item, Panel_numeric_text_item

PANEL_LABEL_BOLD

If TRUE, PANEL_MESSAGE_ITEM's label is rendered in bold.

Argument: Boolean
Default: FALSE
Procs: create, get, set
Objects: Panel_message_item
See Also: 7.12

PANEL_LABEL_FONT

Defines the font to use in the label portion of a panel item.
Warning: Use of this attribute may cause your application to violate the OPEN LOOK Graphical User Interface Functional Specification.

Argument: Xv_Font
Default: Panel font
Procs: create, get, set
Objects: Panel_item

PANEL_LABEL_IMAGE

Specifies the image for an item's label.

Argument:	`Server_image`
Default:	`NULL`
Procs:	`create, get, set`
Objects:	`Panel_item`
See Also:	15.4.1

PANEL_LABEL_STRING

Specifies the string for the item's label. The string is copied when this attribute is set.

Argument:	`char *`
Default:	`NULL`
Procs:	`create, get, set`
Objects:	`Panel_item`
See Also:	7.9

PANEL_LABEL_WIDTH

Specifies the width of the panel item label in pixels. For buttons, `PANEL_LABEL_WIDTH` does not include endcaps and menu marks (if any are present). `PANEL_LABEL_WIDTH` has no effect on a panel button until the panel button's `PANEL_LABEL_STRING` or `PANEL_LABEL_IMAGE` is set.

Argument:	`int`
Default:	Width of text string or server image
Procs:	`create, get, set`
Objects:	`Panel_item`
See Also:	7.9.3

PANEL_LABEL_X

Specifies the x coordinate of the *label* portion of panel items that have *values* associated with them (e.g., text items). Intended to be used when `PANEL_VALUE_X` is specified.

Argument:	`int` (in pixels)
Default:	`PANEL_ITEM_X` from parent panel
Procs:	`create, get, set`
Objects:	`Panel_item`
See Also:	`PANEL_VALUE_X`

PANEL_LABEL_Y

Specifies the y coordinate of the *label* portion of panel items that have *values* associated with them (e.g., text items). Intended to be used only if `PANEL_VALUE_Y` is specified.

Argument:	`int` (in pixels)
Default:	`PANEL_ITEM_Y` from parent panel
Procs:	`create, get, set`
Objects:	`Panel_item`
See Also:	`PANEL_VALUE_Y`

PANEL_LAYOUT

In a `PANEL` create call, this attribute controls the layout of panel items. When used in a create panel item call, this attribute controls the direction in which the item's components are laid out.

Argument:	`Panel_setting`
Default:	`PANEL_HORIZONTAL`
Procs:	`create, get, set`
Objects:	`Panel, Panel_item`
See Also:	7.3.1

PANEL_LINE_BREAK_ACTION

At the end of each line, wrap to the next line at either the character (`PANEL_WRAP_AT_CHAR`) or word (`PANEL_WRAP_AT_WORD`) level.

Argument: `Panel_setting`
Valid values: {`PANEL_WRAP_AT_CHAR`, `PANEL_WRAP_AT_WORD`}
Default: value of "text.lineBreak" default, or `PANEL_WRAP_AT_WORD`
Procs: `create,get,set`
Objects: `Panel_multiline_text_item`
See Also: 7.17

PANEL_LIST_CLIENT_DATA

Sets or gets up to 32 bits of user-entered data (argument 2) from a row number (argument 1) on the list.

Argument 1:   `int`
Argument 2:   `Xv_opaque`
Default: `NULL`
Procs: `create,get,set`
Objects: `Panel_list_item`
See Also: 7.11.4

PANEL_LIST_CLIENT_DATAS

Works much like its companion attribute, `PANEL_LIST_CLIENT_DATA`, except that it takes a `NULL`-terminated value list of client data as its value. Position in the value list determines the row to which the data will be associated.

Argument: `NULL`-terminated `list` of `Xv_opaque`
Default: `NULL`
Procs: `create,set`
Objects: `Panel_list_item`
See Also: 7.11.4

PANEL_LIST_DELETE

Deletes a row from the scrolling list. The list is adjusted automatically after the deletion.

Argument: `int` (row number)
Default: None
Procs: `create,set`
Objects: `Panel_list_item`
See Also: 7.11.2

PANEL_LIST_DELETE_ROWS

Deletes the specified number of rows, starting at the specified row. The first argument is the row number, and the second argument is the number of rows to delete.

Argument 1:   `int`
Argument 2:   `int`
Procs: `create,set`
Objects: `Panel_list_item`
See Also: 7.11.2

PANEL_LIST_DELETE_SELECTED_ROWS

Deletes all selected rows. Not valid in edit mode.

Argument:	No value
Procs:	`set`
Objects:	`Panel_list_item`
See Also:	7.11.2

PANEL_LIST_DISPLAY_ROWS

Sets the number of rows in a list that will be displayed.

Argument:	`int`
Default:	5
Procs:	`create,get,set`
Objects:	`Panel_list_item`
See Also:	7.11.1

PANEL_LIST_FIRST_SELECTED

Returns the row number of the first selected row. If no row is selected, it returns -1.

Return Type:	`int`
Argument:	No argument
Procs:	`get`
Objects:	`Panel_list_item`
See Also:	7.11.3

PANEL_LIST_FONT

Set the specified row (argument 1) to the specified font (argument 2).

Argument 1:	`int` (row number)
Argument 2:	`Xv_Font`
Default:	Use panel font
Procs:	`create,get,set`
Objects:	`Panel_list_item`
See Also:	7.11.1

PANEL_LIST_FONTS

Set the first n rows to the specified fonts.

Argument:	`NULL`-terminated list of `Xv_Font`
Default:	Use panel font
Procs:	`create,set`
Objects:	`Panel_list_item`
See Also:	7.11.1

PANEL_LIST_GLYPH

Takes a row number (argument 1) and `Server_image` (argument 2) to let you assign a glyph or icon to a row. The height of the glyph may not exceed the height of the scrolling list row. Also see `PANEL_LIST_ROW_HEIGHT`.

Return Type:	`Server_image`
Argument 1:	`int`
Argument 2:	`Server_image`
Default:	`NULL`
Procs:	`create,get,set`
Objects:	`Panel_list_item`
See Also:	7.11.1

PANEL_LIST_GLYPHS

Works the same as its companion attribute, `PANEL_LIST_GLYPH`, except that it takes a `NULL`-terminated value list as its value. The height of the glyph may not exceed the height of the scrolling list row. Also see `PANEL_LIST_ROW_HEIGHT`.

Argument:	`NULL`-terminated list of `Server_image`
Default:	`NULL`
Procs:	`create, set`
Objects:	`Panel_list_item`
See Also:	7.11.1

PANEL_LIST_INSERT

Inserts a list item at a specified row number. This attribute allocates space, attaches a row number to the list, and inserts an empty string. Clients must set `PANEL_LIST_GLYPH` and/or `PANEL_LIST_STRING` at this row number to set the glyph item and/or string.

Argument:	`int`
Procs:	`create, set`
Objects:	`Panel_list_item`
See Also:	7.11.2

PANEL_LIST_INSERT_DUPLICATE

Allow (`TRUE`) or disallow (`FALSE`) duplicate strings to be inserted into the scrolling list.

Argument:	`Boolean`
Default:	`TRUE`
Procs:	`create, get, set`
Objects:	`Panel_list_item`
See Also:	7.11.2

PANEL_LIST_INSERT_GLYPHS

Insert the specified glyphs into the scrolling list before the specified row. The first argument is a row number, and the second argument is a pointer to a `NULL`-terminated array of server images.

Argument 1:	`int`
Argument 2:	`NULL`-terminated list of `Server_image`
Procs:	`create, set`
Objects:	`Panel_list_item`
See Also:	7.11.2

PANEL_LIST_INSERT_STRINGS

Insert the specified strings into the scrolling list before the specified row. The first argument is a row number, and the second argument is a pointer to a `NULL`-terminated array of strings. The strings are copied when this attribute is set.

Argument 1:	`int`
Argument 2:	`NULL`-terminated list of `char *`
Procs:	`create, set`
Objects:	`Panel_list_item`
See Also:	7.11.2

PANEL_LIST_MODE

Sets or gets the mode of the scrolling list. Setting the mode to `PANEL_LIST_READ`, when in edit mode is equivalent to selecting the "End Editing" menu item. Setting the mode to `PANEL_LIST_EDIT` when in read mode is equivalent to selecting the "Edit List" menu item.

Argument:	`Panel_list_mode`
Valid Values:	{`PANEL_LIST_READ`, `PANEL_LIST_EDIT`}
Default:	`PANEL_LIST_READ`
Procs:	`get, set`
Objects:	`Panel_list_item`
See Also:	7.11.5

PANEL_LIST_NEXT_SELECTED

Returns the row number of the first selected row following the row specified. If no row after the row specified is selected, returns -1.

Argument:	`int`
Procs:	`get`
Objects:	`Panel_list_item`
See Also:	7.11.3

PANEL_LIST_NROWS

Gets the total number of rows in the scrolling list.

Return Type:	`int`
Procs:	`get`
Objects:	`Panel_list_item`

PANEL_LIST_ROW_HEIGHT

Specifies the height of each row in the scrolling list.

Argument:	`int`
Default:	Height of panel's font
Procs:	`create, get`
Objects:	`Panel_list_item`
See Also:	7.11.1

PANEL_LIST_SCROLLBAR

Returns the scrollbar attached to a `PANEL_LIST` panel item.

Return Type:	`Scrollbar`
Procs:	`get`
Objects:	`Panel_list_item`

PANEL_LIST_SELECT

Takes two values: a row number (argument 1) and a Boolean (argument 2) that lets you select (TRUE) or deselect (FALSE) the specified row. If the scrolling list is not hidden (XV_SHOW is TRUE) then the specified row will be made visible, which may entail scrolling the scrolling list. To disable this scrolling, set XV_SHOW to FALSE before setting PANEL_LIST_SELECT and then reset XV_SHOW to TRUE afterwards.

Argument 1:	`int`
Argument 2:	`Boolean`
Default:	`FALSE`
Procs:	`set, create`
Objects:	`Panel_list_item`
See Also:	7.11.3

PANEL_LIST_SELECTED

Returns whether the specified row number is selected (TRUE) or not (FALSE).

Argument: `int`
Return Type: `Boolean`
Procs: `get`
Objects: `Panel_list_item`

PANEL_LIST_SORT

Sort the list in forward (PANEL_FORWARD) or reverse (PANEL_REVERSE) alphabetical order.

Argument: `Panel_setting`
Valid values: `PANEL_FORWARD` or `PANEL_REVERSE`
Procs: `set`
Objects: `Panel_list_item`

PANEL_LIST_STRING

Specifies the string (argument 2) of a specified row (argument 1). `xv_get` returns the pointer to the character string assigned to the row. The string is copied when this attribute is set.

Return Type: `char *`
Argument 1: `int` (row number)
Argument 2: `char *`
Default: Empty string
Procs: `create, get, set`
Objects: `Panel_list_item`
See Also: 7.11.1

PANEL_LIST_STRINGS

Works the same as its companion attribute, PANEL_LIST_STRING, except that it takes a NULL-terminated list of strings as its value. The strings are copied when this attribute is set.

Argument: `NULL`-terminated list of `char *`
Default: Empty string
Procs: `create, set`
Objects: `Panel_list_item`
See Also: 7.11.1

PANEL_LIST_TITLE

The title of the scrolling list.

`PANEL_LIST_TITLE` does not copy the string. If the string is cleared or freed, the Scrolling List's title will be removed.

Argument: `char *`
Default: No title
Procs: `create, get, set`
Objects: `Panel_list_item`
See Also: 7.11.1

PANEL_LIST_WIDTH

Specifies the width of the scrolling list: -1 extends the scrolling list to the right edge of the panel. A value of 0 sets the width slightly wider than the widest row, and other values specify the width of the scrolling list in pixels. To get the width of a `PANEL_LIST` item's rectangle, use `XV_WIDTH`. To get the width of the label rectangle, use `PANEL_LABEL_WIDTH`.

Argument: `int`
Default: 0
Procs: `create,get,set`
Objects: `Panel_list_item`
See Also: 7.11.1

PANEL_MASK_CHAR

Specifies the character used to mask type-in characters. Use the space character for no character echo (caret does not advance). Use the `NULL` character to disable masking.

Argument: `char`
Default: `NULL`
Procs: `create,set,get`
Objects: `Panel_text_item,Panel_numeric_text_item`
See Also: 7.15

PANEL_MAX_TICK_STRING

String which appears underneath the maximum tick mark on horizontal sliders or gauges, or to the right of the maximum tick mark on vertical sliders or gauges. If `PANEL_TICKS` is 0, `PANEL_MAX_TICK_STRING` is ignored. The width of the slider or gauge may be adjusted to insure that there is enough space to accommodate both the minimum and maximum tick strings. The string is copied when this attribute is set.

Argument: `char *`
Default: No maximum tick string
Procs: `create,get,set`
Objects: `Panel_slider_item, Panel_gauge_item`
See Also: 7.13

PANEL_MAX_VALUE

Specifies the maximum value of the slider, gauge, or numeric text item.

Argument: `int`
Default: `100`
Procs: `create,get,set`
Objects: `Panel_numeric_text_item,Panel_gauge_item,Panel_slider_item`
See Also: 7.13

PANEL_MAX_VALUE_STRING

Maximum value string for the slider. On horizontal sliders, the maximum value string appears to the right of the maximum end box. On vertical sliders, the maximum value string appears above the maximum end box. The string is copied when this attribute is set.

Argument: `char *`
Default: No maximum value string
Procs: `create,get,set`
Objects: `Panel_slider_item`
See Also: 7.13

PANEL_MIN_TICK_STRING

String which appears underneath the minimum tick mark on horizontal sliders or gauges, or to the right of the minimum tick mark on vertical sliders or gauges. If `PANEL_TICKS` is 0 `PANEL_MIN_TICK_STRING` is ignored. The width of the slider or gauge may be adjusted to insure that there is enough space to accommodate both the minimum and maximum tick strings. The string is copied when this attribute is set.

Argument: `char *`
Default: No minimum tick string
Procs: `create, get, set`
Objects: `Panel_slider_item, Panel_gauge_item`
See Also: 7.13

PANEL_MIN_VALUE

Specifies the minimum value of the slider, gauge, or numeric text item.

Argument: `int`
Default: 0
Procs: `create, get, set`
Objects: `Panel_slider_item, Panel_numeric_text_item, Panel_gauge_item`
See Also: 7.13

PANEL_MIN_VALUE_STRING

Minimum value string for the slider. On horizontal sliders, the minimum value string appears to the left of the minimum end box. On vertical sliders, the minimum value string appears below the minimum end box. The string is copied when this attribute is set.

Argument: `char *`
Default: No minimum value string
Procs: `create, get, set`
Objects: `Panel_slider_item`
See Also: 7.13

PANEL_NCHOICES

Returns the number of choices available in a choice or toggle item.

Return Type: `int`
Procs: `get`
Objects: `Panel_choice_item`
See Also: 7.10

PANEL_NEXT_COL

This attribute is used when the panel layout is `PANEL_VERTICAL`. It specifies that the item is to start a new column and specifies the amount of white space (in pixels) between the last column and the next (new) column. If you specify −1, the default gap (`PANEL_ITEM_X_GAP`) is used.

Argument: `Panel_item`
Default: None
Procs: `create`
Objects: `Panel_item`
See Also: 7.3.1

PANEL_NEXT_ITEM

Gets the handle of the next item on a panel.

Argument: `Panel_item`
Procs: `get`
Objects: `Panel_item`
Usage:

next_item = xv_get(this_item, PANEL_NEXT_ITEM);

See Also: · 7.7

PANEL_NEXT_ROW

This attribute is used when the panel layout is `PANEL_HORIZONTAL`. It specifies that the item is to start a new row and specifies the amount of white space (in pixels) between the last row and the next (new) row. If you specify –1, the default gap (`PANEL_ITEM_Y_GAP`) is used.

Argument: `Panel_item`
Default: None
Procs: `create`
Objects: `Panel_item`
See Also: 7.3.1

PANEL_NO_REDISPLAY_ITEM

This flag is useful if you intend to call `xv_super_set_avlist()` at the beginning of the set routine. Setting this attribute to `TRUE` prevents the parent panel from redisplaying while the attributes are being set. This attribute should be reset to `FALSE` after the call to `xv_super_set_avlist()`.
Warning: This attribute should *only* be used from within a panel item extension.

Argument: `Boolean`
Procs: `get,set`
Objects: `Panel`
See Also: 25.11.6

PANEL_NOTIFY_LEVEL

Specifies when to call the notify function. The valid values are `PANEL_ALL`, `PANEL_NONE`, `PANEL_SPECIFIED`, and `PANEL_NON_PRINTABLE`. For sliders, any setting other than `PANEL_ALL` results in notification only on `SELECT`-up.

Argument: `Panel_setting`
Valid Values: {`PANEL_ALL`, `PANEL_NONE` , `PANEL_SPECIFIED`, `PANEL_NON_PRINTABLE`}
Default: `PANEL_SPECIFIED`
Procs: `create,get,set`
Objects: `Panel_numeric_text_item`, `Panel_multiline_text_item`,
               `Panel_slider_item`, `Panel_text_item`
See Also: 7.13.2

PANEL_NOTIFY_PROC

Procedure to call when a panel item is activated.

Argument: Varies—see callbacks below
Default: `NULL`
Procs: `create,get,set`
Objects: `Panel_item`

Callback: (For Button Items)

```
void
notify_proc (item, event)
        Panel_item    item;
        Event         *event;
```

Client-specified callback routine invoked when the user *activates* the button (accepts preview).

Callback: (For Message Items)

```
void
notify_proc (item, event)
        Panel_item    item;
        Event         *event;
```

Client-specified callback routine invoked when the user *activates* the message (accepts preview).

Callback: (For Text Items, Numeric Text Items, and Multiline Text Items)

```
Panel_setting
notify_proc (item, event)
        Panel_item    item;
        Event         *event;
```

Client-specified callback routine invoked when the user *activates* the text (accepts preview). For text, numeric text, and multiline text items, the return value type is Panel_setting and is one of PANEL_INSERT, PANEL_NEXT, PANEL_NONE, or PANEL_PREVIOUS.

Callback: (For Exclusive Choice Items and Slider Items)

```
void
notify_proc (item, value, event)
        Panel_item    item;
        int           value;
        Event         *event;
```

Client-specified callback routine invoked when the user *activates* the exclusive choice or slider (accepts preview).

Callback: (For Non-exclusive Choice Items, toggles)

```
void
notify_proc (item, value, event)
        Panel_item     item;
        unsigned int   value;
        Event          *event;
```

Client-specified callback routine invoked when the user *activates* the non-exclusive choice (accepts preview). The value parameter is of type unsigned int because it represents a *mask* of choices that are selected. For example, if the first and third items are selected, then the first and third bits in the value parameter are on—this value happens to be five.

Callback: (For List Items)

```
int
notify_proc(item, string, client data, op, event, row)
        Panel_item        item;
        Panel_list_op     op;
        char              *string;
        Xv_opaque         client_data;
        Event             *event;
        int               row;
```

Client-specified callback routine invoked when the user *activates* the list item (accepts preview).

`string` is the string associated with the `row`.

`client_data` is the client data associated with the `row`.

`op` indicates a select, validate, or delete operation. Of these, only `PANEL_LIST_OP_VALIDATE` requires a return value.

`row` indicates the row in the scrolling list. Returns `XV_OK` to validate a change or `XV_ERROR` to invalidate a change.

Callback: (For Drop Target Item)

```
int
notify_proc(item, event)
        Panel_item     item;
        Event          *event;
```

A return value of `XV_OK` indicates that XView should call `dnd_done()`. A return value of `XV_ERROR` indicates that XView should not call `dnd_done()`.

See Also: 7.10.5

PANEL_NOTIFY_STATUS

If the panel item is part of an unpinned command frame, then the window is dismissed if `PANEL_NOTIFY_STATUS` is `XV_OK`. If `PANEL_NOTIFY_STATUS` is set to `XV_ERROR`, then the window is not dismissed. You only `xv_get()` or `xv_set()` this attribute from within a notify procedure. When a notify procedure exits, for an unpinned command frame, XView internally uses the value of this attribute to determine whether or not the command frame is dismissed. XView sets the value of this attribute to `XV_OK` before calling the notify procedure.

Argument: `int`
Valid Values: {`XV_OK`, `XV_ERROR`}
Default: `XV_OK`
Procs: `get`, `set`
Objects: `Panel_item`
See Also: 7.9.1

PANEL_NOTIFY_STRING

String of characters that triggers notification when one of the characters is typed in a text item. Applies only when `PANEL_NOTIFY_LEVEL` is `PANEL_SPECIFIED`. The string is copied when this attribute is set.

Argument: `char *`
Default: \n \r \t (i.e., newline, carriage return, and tab)
Procs: `create`, `get`, `set`
Objects: `Panel_numeric_text_item`, `Panel_text_item`,
             `Panel_multiline_text_item`
See Also: 7.15.3

PANEL_OPS_VECTOR

The panel operations vector, which is the method by which the panel package dispatches events to panel items. For more information, see Section 25.11, "The Wizzy Package" in the *XView Programming Manual*.

Argument:	`Panel_ops *`
Procs:	`get,set`
Objects:	`Panel_item`

PANEL_PAINT

Controls the panel item's painting behavior in **xv_set** calls. The specified value applies only to the **xv_set** call. As the **xv_set** call exits, it restores PANEL_PAINT to its previous value. Possible values are PANEL_CLEAR, PANEL_NO_CLEAR, or PANEL_NONE. PANEL_PAINT operates on Panel and Panel_item objects. The default for Panel item objects is the value of PANEL_PAINT for the Panel to which the Panel item is attached. This attribute is used strictly for performance enhancements and, normally, is not required.

Argument:	`Panel_setting`
Default:	PANEL_CLEAR for panel objects, the panel's PANEL_PAINT for panel item objects
Procs:	`create,set`
Objects:	`Panel,Panel_item`
See Also:	7.19.3

PANEL_PRIMARY_FOCUS_ITEM

The current or last panel item that is or was a primary (First-Class) focus client.
Warning: This attribute should *only* be used from within a panel item extension.

Argument:	`Panel_item`
Procs:	`get,set`
Objects:	`Panel`
Usage:	

```
if (xv_get(panel_public, PANEL_PRIMARY_FOCUS_ITEM) =^= item_public)
    xv_set(panel_public, PANEL_PRIMARY_FOCUS_ITEM, NULL, NULL);
```

This example should be executed when an item's remove procedure is called, if the item is a primary focus client.

PANEL_READ_ONLY

If TRUE, editing is disabled; if FALSE, editing is enabled. Note that **xv_set** does not apply to scrolling lists.

Argument:	`Boolean`
Default:	FALSE
Procs:	`create,get,set`
Objects:	`Panel_list_item, Panel_multiline_text_item,` `Panel_numeric_text_item, Panel_text_item,` `Panel_slider_item`

PANEL_REPAINT_PROC

Specifies the name of the client-supplied panel background repaint procedure.

Argument: `void (*panel_repaint_proc) ()`
Default: `NULL`
Procs: `create, get, set`
Objects: `Panel`
Callback:

```
void
panel_repaint_proc (panel, pw, repaint_area)
     Panel        panel;
     Xv_Window    pw;        /* paint window */
     Rectlist     *repaint_area;
```

See Also: 7.19.2

PANEL_SHOW_RANGE

If TRUE, shows the minimum and maximum slider or gauge values.

Argument: `Boolean`
Default: `TRUE`
Procs: `create, get, set`
Objects: `Panel_slider_item, Panel_gauge_item`
See Also: 7.13

PANEL_SHOW_VALUE

If TRUE, shows current slider value.

Argument: `Boolean`
Default: `TRUE`
Procs: `create, get, set`
Objects: `Panel_slider_item`
See Also: 7.13

PANEL_SLIDER_END_BOXES

Shows or hides the slider end boxes.

Argument: `Boolean`
Default: `FALSE`
Procs: `create, get, set`
Objects: `Panel_slider_item`
See Also: 7.13

PANEL_SLIDER_WIDTH

Specifies the length of the slider bar in pixels. The length is set whether the slider is horizontally or vertically oriented.

Argument: `int`
Default: `100`
Procs: `create, get, set`
Objects: `Panel_slider_item`
See Also: 7.13

PANEL_STATUS

Returns the state of the panel. See *<xview/panel.h>* for more information.

Warning: This attribute should *only* be used from within a panel item extension.

Argument: `Panel_status *`
Procs: `get`
Objects: `Panel`

PANEL_TEXT_SELECT_LINE

Selects and highlights the entire contents of the text field.

Argument: No value
Procs: `set`
Objects: `Panel_text_item`
Usage:

        `xv_set(ptext, PANEL_TEXT_SELECT_LINE, NULL);`

See Also: 7.15.2

PANEL_TICKS

Specifies the number of evenly-spaced tick marks to be displayed on slider or gauge panel items.

Argument: `int`
Default: 0
Procs: `create, get, set`
Objects: `Panel_slider_item, Panel_gauge_item`
See Also: 7.13

PANEL_TOGGLE_VALUE

Specifies the value (argument 2) of a particular toggle choice (argument 1).

Argument 1:   `int`
Argument 2:   `int`
Default: `NULL`
Procs: `create, get, set`
Objects: `Panel_choice_item`

PANEL_VALUE

Indicates the current value of a panel item. Its type varies depending on the type of panel item specified. See Chapter 7, *Panels* for details.

Argument: Varies with panel item type
Procs: `create, get, set`
Objects: `Panel_item`
See Also: 7.6

PANEL_VALUE_DISPLAY_LENGTH

Maximum number of characters to display in a text string. Note that the length of the value display may not be less than the combined width of the left and right "more text" buttons. In 12-point font, this is four characters. This attribute is intended for use with fixed-width fonts. For variable-width fonts, use the attribute PANEL_VALUE_DISPLAY_WIDTH. For a Multiline Text Item, this specified the length of each row (line) in the Multiline Text Field, expressed in characters.

Argument:	int
Default:	80 (for Slider, Text, and Numeric Text Items)
	40 (for a Multiline Text Item)
Procs:	create,get,set
Objects:	Panel_slider_item, Panel_numeric_text_item, Panel_text_item, Panel_multiline_text_item
See Also:	7.17, 7.15

PANEL_VALUE_DISPLAY_WIDTH

The width, in pixels, of a text field's value. For a Multiline Text Item, this is the width of each row (line) in the Multiline Text Field.

Argument:	int
Default:	80 default character widths (for Text and Numeric Text Items).
	Width corresponding to value of PANEL_VALUE_DISPLAY_LENGTH (for a Multiline Text Item)
Procs:	create,get,set
Objects:	Panel_text_item, Panel_numeric_text_item, Panel_multiline_text_item
See Also:	7.17, 7.15

PANEL_VALUE_FONT

Specifies the font to use in the value portion of the Panel Item.

Warning: Use of this attribute may cause your application to violate the OPEN LOOK Graphical User Interface Functional Specification.

Argument:	Xv_Font
Default:	Panel's font
Procs:	create,get,set
Objects:	Panel_numeric_text_item, Panel_slider_item, Panel_text_item

PANEL_VALUE_STORED_LENGTH

Maximum number of characters allowed in string value for a text item. For Multiline Text Items, if PANEL_VALUE_STORED_LENGTH is greater than PANEL_VALUE_DISPLAY_LENGTH times PANEL_DISPLAY_ROWS, then a scrollbar will be visible on the Multiline Text Field. (An outstanding bug in TEXTSW_MEMORY_MAXIMUM prevents PANEL_VALUE_STORED_LENGTH from being set to less than 1024; thus a Multiline Text Item will always have a scrollbar.)

Argument:	int
Default:	Same as TEXTSW_MEMORY_MAXIMUM default (for Multiline Text Item)
	80 (for a Text or Numeric Text Item)
Procs:	create,get,set
Objects:	Panel_numeric_text_item, Panel_text_item, Panel_multiline_text_item Panel
See Also:	7.17, 7.15

PANEL_VALUE_UNDERLINED

Show or hide the text field value's underlining.

Argument: Boolean
Default: TRUE
Procs: create, get, set
Objects: Panel_text_item, Panel_numeric_text_item

PANEL_VALUE_X

Specifies the x coordinate of the *value* portion of panel items that have separate *label* and *value* entities (e.g., text items).

Argument: int
Default: (See Chapter 7, *Panels*.)
Procs: create, get, set
Objects: Panel_item
See Also: 7.4.3 , PANEL_LABEL_X

PANEL_VALUE_Y

Specifies the y coordinate of the *value* portion of panel items that have separate *label* and *value* entities (e.g., Text Items).

Argument: int
Default: (See Chapter 7, *Panels*, in the *XView Programming Manual.*)
Procs: create, get, set
Objects: Panel_item
See Also: 7.4.3 , PANEL_LABEL_Y

SCREEN_NUMBER

Specifies the number of the screen associated with object.

Argument: int
Default: 0
Procs: get
Objects: Screen
See Also: 15.2

SCREEN_SERVER

Specifies the server associated with this screen. By default, its value is the server created by opening the display specified by the value of the DISPLAY environment variable.

Return Type: Xv_Server
Procs: get
Objects: Screen
See Also: 15.3.3

SCROLLBAR_DIRECTION

Sets orientation of the scrollbar as SCROLLBAR_VERTICAL or SCROLLBAR_HORIZONTAL.

Argument: Scrollbar_setting
Valid Values: {SCROLLBAR_VERTICAL, SCROLLBAR_HORIZONTAL}
Default: None
Procs: create, get
Objects: Scrollbar

SCROLLBAR_LAST_VIEW_START

Specifies the offset of the view into the object prior to the last scroll.

Argument: int
Default: 0
Procs: get
Objects: Scrollbar

SCROLLBAR_MENU

Specifies a pointer to the scrollbar's menu. Clients can add items to the *default* menu but cannot remove items from it.

Argument: Menu
Default: Scrollbar creates a default menu
Procs: get
Objects: Scrollbar

SCROLLBAR_NOTIFY_CLIENT

Used by the Notifier. Indicates the client that is notified when the scrollbar is scrolled. See Chapter 10, *Scrollbars*, in the *XView Programming Manual*.

Argument: Xv_opaque
Default: Subwindow scrollbar is attached to contents
Procs: create, get, set
Objects: Scrollbar
See Also: 10.4.1

SCROLLBAR_OBJECT_LENGTH

Specifies the length of the scrollable object in scrollbar units. Value must be greater than or equal to zero.

Argument: int
Default: 0
Procs: create, get, set
Objects: Scrollbar
See Also: 10.2

SCROLLBAR_PAGE_LENGTH

Specifies the length of a page in scrollbar units for page-scrolling purposes.

Argument: int
Default: 0
Procs: create, get, set
Objects: Scrollbar
See Also: 10.2

SCROLLBAR_PIXELS_PER_UNIT

Specifies the number of pixels constituting a scrollbar unit. For example, when scrolling a list of icons, each unit might be 64 pixels.

Argument: int
Default: 1
Procs: create, get, set
Objects: Scrollbar
See Also: ' 10.2

SCROLLBAR_SPLITTABLE

Indicates whether the object that contains the scrollbar is splittable.

Argument: `Boolean`
Default: `FALSE`
Procs: `create, get, set`
Objects: `Scrollbar`
See Also: 5.6.1

SCROLLBAR_VIEW_LENGTH

Specifies the length of the viewing window in scrollbar units.

Argument: `int`
Default: 0
Procs: `create, get, set`
Objects: `Scrollbar`
See Also: 10.2

SCROLLBAR_VIEW_START

Specifies the current offset into the scrollbar object in scrollbar units. The value must be greater than or equal to zero.

Argument: `int`
Default: 0
Procs: `create, get, set`
Objects: `Scrollbar`
See Also: 10.2

SEL_APPEND_TYPE_NAMES

Same as `SEL_TYPE_NAMES` except that the new list is appended to the previously set type list.

Argument: List of string (`STRING, NULL`)
Default: N/A
Procs: `create, set`
Objects: `Selection_requestor`
Usage:

```
Selection_requestor  sel;
sel = xv_create(panel, SELECTION_REQUESTOR,
                SEL_REPLY_PROC, SelectionReplyProc,
                NULL);
xv_set(sel, SEL_APPEND_TYPE_NAMES, "TARGETS", NULL,
       NULL);
```

See Also: 18.2.3 , `SEL_TYPE_NAMES`

SEL_APPEND_TYPES

Same as SEL_TYPES except that the new list is appended to the previously set type list.

Argument: List of Atoms (XA_STRING, NULL)
Default: N/A
Procs: create,set
Objects: Selection_requestor
Usage:

```
Selection_requestor  sel;
sel = xv_create(panel, SELECTION_REQUESTOR,
                SEL_REPLY_PROC, SelectionReplyProc,
                NULL);
xv_set(sel, SEL_APPEND_TYPES, XA_STRING, NULL, NULL);
```

See Also: 18.2.3, SEL_TYPES

SEL_CONVERT_PROC

Specifies the procedure that is to be called whenever a client requests the current value of the selection.

Argument: int (*convert_proc) ()
Default: sel_convert_proc
Procs: create,get,set
Objects: Selection_owner
Callback:

```
int
convert_proc( sel, replyType, replyBuff, length, format )
    Selection_owner sel;
    Atom            *replyType;
    Xv_opaque       *replyBuff;
    unsigned long   *length;
    int             *format;
```

sel specifies the selection owner.
replyType specifies the type of the selection that has been requested. It should be explicitly set to an atom which describes the converted type of the selection (for example, TEXT might have the type XA_STRING).
replyBuff is a pointer to a buffer address which contains the converted data.
length specifies a pointer to the number of elements in *replyBuff*. The size of an element is defined by *format*.
The convert procedure is called with *length* set to the maximum allowed buffer size.
format specifies a pointer to the data format. Valid values are 8, 12, or 32 for 8-bit, 16-bit, or 32-bit quantities, respectively.

See Also: 18.2.4

SEL_COPY

SEL_COPY indicates whether or not to make a copy of the SEL_DATA data. If set to FALSE it is up to the client to maintain the data.

Argument: Boolean
Default: TRUE
Procs: create,set,get
Objects: Selection_item
See Also: 18.3.1

SEL_DATA

Used to initiate a blocking selection request. The arguments to this attribute are, a pointer to a long which will be set to the number of elements in the returned buffer and a pointer to an integer which will be set to the data format. `xv_get()` returns a pointer to the selection data. Clients should free the returned buffer. If the requestor client has not registered a `reply_proc()` with the selection package and is requesting for MULTIPLE or INCR, the call will return with *length* set to SEL_ERROR and format set to zero. If the requestor client has registered a `reply_proc()` with the selection package and requesting for MULTIPLE or INCR, the package will call the client's `reply_proc()` with the converted data. `xv_get()` returns after the transaction has completed with *length* set to XV_OK and format set to the returned data format. If the request fails the `xv_get()` will return with *length* set to SEL_ERROR and format set to zero. For a `Selection_item` object, this attribute specifies a pointer to the selection data.

Argument: Xv_opaque
Default: N/A
Procs: get for Selection_requestor objects
              get and set for Selection_item objects
Objects: Selection_requestor, Selection_item
Usage:

```
data = (char *) xv_get(sel_requestor, SEL_DATA,
                                &length, &format);
```

See Also: 18.3.1, 18.2.3

SEL_DONE_PROC

Specifies the procedure that is called after the requestor has received the selection or NULL if the owner is not interested in being called back.

Argument: void (*done_proc)()
Default: NULL
Procs: create, get, set
Objects: Selection_owner
Callback:

```
void
done_proc( sel, replyBuff, target )
      Selection_owner   sel;
      Xv_opaque         replyBuff;
      Atom              target;
```

sel specifies the selection owner.
replyBuff specifies the address which contains the converted data.
target specifies the target type returned by the convert procedure.

See Also: 18.2.7

SEL_FIRST_ITEM

Returns a selection item.

Argument: Selection_item
Default: N/A
Procs: get
Objects: Selection_owner
See Also: 18.3.1, SEL_NEXT_ITEM

SEL_FORMAT

Specifies the data format.

Argument:	`Xv_opaque`
Default:	8
Procs:	`create,get,set`
Objects:	`Selection_item`
See Also:	18.3.1

SEL_LENGTH

Specifies the number of 8, 16, 32-bit elements contained in the reply.

Argument:	`unsigned long`
Default:	Type-dependent
Procs:	`create,get,set`
Objects:	`Selection_item`
See Also:	18.3.1

SEL_LOSE_PROC

Used to register a procedure that is called back whenever the selection owner loses the selection that it holds.

Argument:	`void (*`*lose_proc*`) ()`
Default:	`NULL`
Procs:	`create,get,set`
Objects:	`Selection_owner`
Callback:	

```
void
lose_proc( sel )
     Selection_owner sel;
```

sel specifies the selection owner.

See Also:	18.2.6

SEL_NEXT_ITEM

Returns a selection item.

Argument:	`Selection_item`
Default:	N/A
Procs:	`get`
Objects:	`Selection_owner`
See Also:	18.3.1 , `SEL_FIRST_ITEM`

SEL_OWN

Setting `SEL_OWN` causes the selection to be acquired (`TRUE`) or lost (`FALSE`). Owning a selection without an external conversion procedure or any selection items will generate a `NULL`-data reply to any incoming requests.

Argument:	`Boolean`
Default:	`FALSE`
Procs:	`create,get,set`
Objects:	`Selection_owner`
See Also:	18.2.4

SEL_PROP_DATA

Specifies the data associated with a property. Should be used in conjunction with `SEL_TYPE_INDEX`.

Argument:	`Xv_opaque`
Default:	`NULL`
Procs:	`create,set`
Objects:	`Selection_requestor`
See Also:	18.6 , `SEL_TYPE_INDEX`

SEL_PROP_FORMAT

Specifies the format of the data associated with a property. Should be used in conjunction with `SEL_TYPE_INDEX`.

Argument:	`int`
Default:	N/A
Procs:	`create,set`
Objects:	`Selection_requestor`
See Also:	18.6 , `SEL_TYPE_INDEX`

SEL_PROP_INFO

Returns the property data. This attribute should be used from a conversion procedure. It returns the data that has been set on the selection notifier's property by the requestor client.

Argument:	`Sel_prop_info *`
Default:	N/A
Procs:	`get`
Objects:	`Selection_owner`
See Also:	18.6.1 , `SEL_TYPE_INDEX`

SEL_PROP_LENGTH

Specifies the length of the data associated with a property. Should be used in conjunction with `SEL_TYPE_INDEX`.

Argument:	`unsigned long`
Default:	N/A
Procs:	`create,set`
Objects:	`Selection_requestor`
See Also:	18.6 , `SEL_TYPE_INDEX`

SEL_PROP_TYPE

Specifies the type of the data associated with a property.

Argument:	`Atom`
Default:	N/A
Procs:	`create,set`
Objects:	`Selection_requestor`
See Also:	18.6 , `SEL_PROP_INFO, SEL_TYPE_INDEX`

SEL_PROP_TYPE_NAME

Specifies the type of the data associated with a property. It takes a string argument which is interned into an atom. Should be used in conjunction with `SEL_TYPE_INDEX`.

Argument:	`Atom`
Default:	N/A
Procs:	`create,set`
Objects:	`Selection_requestor`
See Also:	18.6 , `SEL_PROP_INFO, SEL_TYPE_INDEX`

SEL_RANK

Used to set the rank of the selection. Pre-defined atoms are XA_PRIMARY and XA_SECONDARY. The client should set the rank to the atom representing the selection.

Argument:	Atom
Default:	XA_PRIMARY
Procs:	create,get,set
Objects:	Selection
See Also:	18.2.2 and *Xlib Programming Manual, Interclient Communication* Chapter

SEL_RANK_NAME

Used to set the rank of the selection. The package will intern the selection atom using this atom name (a string).

Argument:	*char
Default:	XA_PRIMARY
Procs:	create,get,set
Objects:	Selection
See Also:	18.2.2

SEL_REPLY_PROC

A procedure that is called when a response to a request comes in.

Argument:	void (*reply_proc) ()
Default:	NULL
Procs:	create,get,set
Objects:	Selection_requestor
Callback:	

```
void
reply_proc( sel_req, target, type, replyValue, length, format )
    Selection_requestor  sel_req;
    Atom                 target;
    Atom                 type;
    Xv_opaque            replyValue;
    unsigned long        length;
    int                  format;
```

If the selection conversion fails, this routine is called with *replyValue* set to an error code and *length* set to SEL_ERROR.

sel_req specifies the selection requestor.

target specifies the target type set by the convert procedure.

type specifies the specifies the type returned by the convert procedure.

replyValue specifies the data content returned.

length specifies the length of the data returned by the convert procedure.

format specifies the format of the data returned by the convert procedure.

If the selection content is larger than the server's maximum request size or if the selection owner has decided to transfer the selection data in increments, the selection package will send the data to the requestor in chunks.

See Also:	18.2.5

SEL_TIME

Specifies the time of the acquisition or the request attempt.

Argument:	`struct timeval *`
Default:	Last event time
Procs:	`create, get, set`
Objects:	`Selection`
See Also:	18.2.3

SEL_TIMEOUT_VALUE

Selection timeout value. This value indicates the number of seconds that a requestor or a selection owner waits for a response during the selection transfer.

Argument:	`unsigned int`
Default:	From the value of the resource `Selection.Timeout`
Procs:	`create, get, set`
Objects:	`Selection`
See Also:	18.2.3, 18.2.2

SEL_TYPE

Specifies an atom type that the client is requesting. For a selection item, specifies the type that the package will convert to.

Argument:	`Atom`
Default:	`XA_STRING`
Procs:	`create, get, set`
Objects:	`Selection_item, Selection_requestor`
See Also:	18.2.3 , `SEL_TYPES`, `SEL_TYPE_NAME`, and *Xlib Programming Manual, Interclient Communication* Chapter

SEL_TYPE_INDEX

Specifies an index to the `SEL_TYPES` or `SEL_TYPE` list. This attribute is also used to specify an index to the `SEL_TYPE_NAME` and `SEL_TYPE_NAMES` lists. This attribute is used in conjunction with `SEL_PROP_DATA`, `SEL_PROP_LENGTH`, `SEL_PROP_FORMAT`, **SEL_PROP_TYPE**, and `SEL_PROP_TYPE_NAME` to associate data with a property used by the requestor.

Argument:	`int`
Default:	N/A
Procs:	`create, set`
Objects:	`Selection_requestor`
Usage:	(Multiple Request)

```
xv_set ( sel_req,
        SEL_TYPES, XA_STRING, INSERT_SELECTION, NULL,
        SEL_TYPE_INDEX, 1,
        SEL_PROP_DATA, dataPointer,
        SEL_PROP_LENGTH, 20,
        NULL );
```

Usage:	(Single Request)

```
xv_set ( sel_req, SEL_TYPE, XA_STRING,
                SEL_TYPE_INDEX, 0,
                SEL_PROP_DATA, dataPointer,
                SEL_PROP_LENGTH, 20,
        NULL );
```

See Also:	18.6

SEL_TYPE_NAME

Same as `SEL_TYPE` except that the argument is the name of the requested selection type instead of an atom. The package will intern the requested atom name. For a selection item, specifies the type name that the package will convert to.

Argument: `*char`
Default: `"STRING"`
Procs: `create,get,set`
Objects: `Selection_requestor Selection_item`
See Also: 18.2.3

SEL_TYPE_NAMES

Specifies a `NULL` -terminated list of atom type names that the client is requesting.

Argument: List of string
Default: `"STRING, NULL"`
Procs: `create,get,set`
Objects: `Selection_requestor`
See Also: 18.2.3

SEL_TYPES

Specifies a `NULL`-terminated list of atom types that the client is requesting. The effect will be as if a sequence of "SelectionRequest" events is delivered to the selection owner, one for each atom. This attribute will initiate a `MULTIPLE` request.

Argument: List of Atoms
Default: `XA_STRING,NULL`
Procs: `create,get,set`
Objects: `Selection_requestor`
See Also: 18.2.3

SELN_*

Appendix A presents all of the `SELN_` attributes.

SERVER_ATOM

`SERVER_ATOM` is equivalent to `XInternAtom()` (with the `only_if_exists` flag set to `FALSE`) except that it caches the results on the server object so that subsequent requests for the same atom will not require a round-trip to the X server.

Return Type: Atom
Procs: `get`
Usage:

```
Atom  atom;
atom = (Atom) xv_get(server_object,
                SERVER_ATOM, "TIMESTAMP");
```

See Also: 15.3.3 , `SERVER_ATOM_NAME`

SERVER_ATOM_NAME

SERVER_ATOM_NAME is equivalent to XGetAtomName() except that it caches the results on the server object so that subsequent requests will not require a roundtrip to the X server. The returned string is maintained by XView and should not be modified or freed. XView will free up all strings associated with atoms on that server when the server object is destroyed.

Return Type: char *
Procs: get
Usage:

```
char *atom_name;
atom_name  (char *)xv_get(server_object, atom);
```

See Also: 15.3.3 , SERVER_ATOM

SERVER_EXTENSION_PROC

Specifies the procedure used to handle server extension events.

Argument: void (*extension_proc)()
Default: NULL
Procs: create, get, set
Objects: Server
Callback:

```
void
extension_proc(display, xevent, window)
     Display   *display;
     Event     *xevent;
     Xv_window  window;
```

See Also: 6.10

SERVER_EXTERNAL_XEVENT_MASK

This attribute, together with SERVER_EXTERNAL_XEVENT_PROC, allows a client to receive notification for X events destined for X windows which are not local to a client. For each non-local X window, the client can specify a different set of X events for which it needs notification. Additionally, an XView object handle is provided as an argument which is returned as a parameter during callback. For xv_create and xv_set this attribute takes three arguments: an XID of a window, and an event mask (see <X11/X.h> for details), and an XView object handle. SERVER_EXTERNAL_XEVENT_MASK for xv_get takes two arguments: an XID of a window, and an XView object handle and returns a mask.

Argument 1:   unsigned long
Argument 2:   unsigned long
Argument 3:   Xv_opaque
Default: None
Procs: create, get, set
Objects: Server
Usage:

```
xv_set (server, SERVER_EXTERNAL_XEVENT_MASK,
               RootWindow(dpy, 0),
               ButtonPressMask | PropertyChangeMask,
               frame,
        SERVER_EXTERNAL_XEVENT_PROC,
               root_event_proc, frame,
        NULL);
```

See Also: 6.11 , SERVER_EXTERNAL_XEVENT_PROC

SERVER_EXTERNAL_XEVENT_PROC

This attribute, together with attribute SERVER_EXTERNAL_XEVENT_MASK allows a client to receive notification for X events destined for X windows which are not local to the client. A client can register a separate callback procedure for each XView object handle. For xv_create and xv_set this attribute takes two arguments. For xv_get it takes one argument: an XView object handle and returns a function name. A NULL first argument temporarily disables callbacks.

Argument 1:   void (*callback_proc) ()
Argument 2:   Xv_opaque
Default: None
Procs: create,get,set
Objects   Server
Usage:

```
xv_set (server,
        SERVER_EXTERNAL_XEVENT_MASK,
            RootWindow(dpy, 0),
            ButtonPressMask | PropertyChangeMask,
            frame,
        SERVER_EXTERNAL_XEVENT_PROC,
            root_event_proc, frame,
        NULL);
```

Callback:

```
void
callback_proc (server, display, xevent, handle)
    Xv_server   server;
    Display    *display;
    XEvent     *xevent;
    Xv_opaque   handle;
```

See Also: 6.11 , SERVER_EXTERNAL_XEVENT_MASK

SERVER_IMAGE_BITMAP_FILE

Specifies a file containing the X11 bitmap from which the server image is created.

Argument: char *
Default: None
Procs: create
Objects: Server
See Also: 15.4.1

SERVER_IMAGE_BITS

Specifies the SunView pixrect image bits for the server image. Use SERVER_IMAGE_X_BITS for standard X11 bitmaps.

Argument: short *
Default: Uninitialized
Procs: create,get,set
Objects: Server_image
See Also: 15.4.1

SERVER_IMAGE_CMS

Specifies the colormap segment to be used in converting the server image data (which are logical colormap indices) into pixel values in the pixmap used to draw the server image.

Argument:	cms
Default:	The default cms for the application
Procs:	create, get
Usage:	

```
Server_image image;

image = (Server_image)xv_create(NULL,
            SERVER_IMAGE,
            ...
            SERVER_IMAGE_CMS, cms,
            ...
            NULL);
```

See Also: 15.4.1

SERVER_IMAGE_COLORMAP

Specifies the name of the colormap segment to be used in converting the server image data (which are logical colormap indices) into pixel values in the pixmap used to draw the server image.

This is basically a backwards compatibility attribute, and where possible, SERVER_IMAGE_CMS should be used instead.

Argument:	char *
Default:	"xv_default_cms"
Procs:	get, create
Usage:	

```
Cms cms;
Server_image image;

cms = (Cms)xv_create(NULL, CMS,
    ...
    CMS_NAME, "palette",
    ...
    NULL);

image = (Server_image)xv_create(NULL, SERVER_IMAGE,
    ...
    SERVER_IMAGE_COLORMAP, "palette",
    ...
    NULL);
```

SERVER_IMAGE_DEPTH

Specifies the bit plane depth of the server image.

Argument:	int
Default:	1
Procs:	create, get, set
Objects:	Server_image
See Also:	15.4.1

SERVER_IMAGE_PIXMAP

Allows an existing pixmap to be associated with a server image. An `xv_get` using this attribute is equivalent to an `xv_get` of the `XV_XID` of the server image.

Argument: `Pixmap`
Default: None
Procs: `create,get,set`
Objects: `Server_image`
See Also: 15.4.1

SERVER_IMAGE_SAVE_PIXMAP

Allows the application to specify that the old pixmap must not be destroyed if a new pixmap is created as the result of changing any server image attributes or assigning a new pixmap directly. You should retain a handle to the old pixmap first.

Argument: `Boolean`
Default: `FALSE`
Procs: `create,get,set`
Objects: `Server_image`
See Also: 15.4.1

SERVER_IMAGE_X_BITS

Specifies the bits to use in a server image. Bits are stored in an array of `char`.

Argument: `char *`
Default: None
Procs: `create,set`
Objects: `Server_image`
See Also: 15.4.1

SERVER_NTH_SCREEN

Specifies the screen with given number. Returns `NULL` if screen does not exist.

Argument 1: `int`
Argument 2: `Screen`
Default: N/A
Procs: `create,get,set`
Objects: `Server`
See Also: 15.2.1

SERVER_SYNC

Flushes the request buffer and waits for all events and errors to be processed by the server. If the argument is `TRUE`, then `SERVER_SYNC` discards all events on the input queue.

Argument: `Boolean`
Default: N/A
Procs: `set`
Objects: `Server`

SERVER_SYNC_AND_PROCESS_EVENTS

Same as `SERVER_SYNC`, but this processes any events that arrive as a result of the `XSync()`.

Argument: No value
Default: None
Procs: `create,set`
Objects: `Server`
See Also: 15.3.3

TEXTSW_ACTION_*

Appendix C, *Textsw Action Attributes*, describes the `textsw` action attributes. These attributes are only valid for use with a `textsw` notify procedure.

TEXTSW_AGAIN_RECORDING

If FALSE, changes to the `textsw` are not repeated when the user invokes AGAIN. Disabling reduces memory overhead.

Argument: Boolean
Default: TRUE
Procs: create, get, set
Objects: Textsw

TEXTSW_AUTO_INDENT

If TRUE, automatically indents a new line to match the previous line.

Argument: Boolean
Default: FALSE
Procs: create, get, set
Objects: Textsw

TEXTSW_AUTO_SCROLL_BY

Specifies the number of lines to scroll when type-in moves insert point below the view.

Argument: int
Default: 1
Procs: create, get, set
Objects: Textsw

TEXTSW_BLINK_CARET

Determines whether the caret blinks (for better performance don't blink).

Argument: Boolean
Default: FALSE
Procs: create, get, set
Objects: Textsw

TEXTSW_BROWSING

If TRUE, prevents editing of displayed text. If another file is loaded in, browsing stays on.

Argument: Boolean
Default: FALSE
Procs: create, get, set
Objects: Textsw

TEXTSW_CHECKPOINT_FREQUENCY

Specifies the number of edits between checkpoints. Set to 0 to disable checkpointing.

Argument: int
Default: 0
Procs: create, get, set
Objects: Textsw

TEXTSW_CLIENT_DATA

Specifies the pointer to arbitrary client data.

Argument: Xv_opaque
Default: NULL
Procs: create, get, set
Objects: Textsw

TEXTSW_CONFIRM_OVERWRITE

Specifies confirmation of any request to write to an existing file.

Argument: Boolean
Default: TRUE
Procs: create, get, set
Objects: Textsw

TEXTSW_CONTENTS

Specifies the text for a subwindow. xv_get needs additional parameters (see Chapter 8, *Text Subwindows*, in the *XView Programming Manual*).

Argument: char *
Default: NULL
Procs: create, get, set
Objects: Textsw
See Also: 8.6.2

TEXTSW_CONTROL_CHARS_USE_FONT

If FALSE, control characters always display as an up arrow followed by a character instead of whatever glyph is in the current font.

Argument: Boolean
Default: FALSE
Procs: create, get, set
Objects: Textsw

TEXTSW_DESTROY_VIEW

The current view will be destroyed.
Argument: No value

TEXTSW_DISABLE_CD

Stops textsw from changing current working directory and grays out associated items in the menu.

Argument: Boolean
Default: FALSE
Procs: create, get, set
Objects: Textsw

TEXTSW_DISABLE_LOAD

Prevents files from being loaded into the textsw and grays out the associated items in the menu.

Argument: Boolean
Default: FALSE
Procs: create, get, set
Objects: Textsw

TEXTSW_EDIT_COUNT
Monotonically increments count of the number of edits made to the **textsw.**

Argument:	`int`
Procs:	`get`
Objects:	`Textsw`

TEXTSW_EXTRAS_CMD_MENU
Returns the "Extras" submenu of the TEXT PANE menu for the **textsw.**

Return Type:	`Menu`
Procs:	`get`
Objects:	`Textsw`

TEXTSW_FILE
For `xv_create` and `xv_set`, specifies the name of the file to load; for `xv_get`, returns the name of the file loaded or `NULL` if no file was loaded.

Argument:	`char *`
Default:	`NULL`
Procs:	`create, get, set`
Objects:	`Textsw`
See Also:	8.4.1

TEXTSW_FILE_CONTENTS
Initializes the text subwindow contents from a file, yet still edits the contents in memory as if specified using `TEXTSW_FILE`.

Argument:	`char *`
Default:	`NULL`
Procs:	`create, set`
Objects:	`Textsw`
See Also:	8.6.1

TEXTSW_FIRST
Specifies the zero-based index of first displayed character.

Argument:	`int`
Procs:	`create, get, set`
Objects:	`Textsw`
See Also:	8.4.1

TEXTSW_FIRST_LINE
Specifies the zero-based index of first displayed line.

Return Type:	`int`
Procs:	`get`
Objects:	`Textsw`
See Also:	8.7.2

TEXTSW_FONT
Specifies the font to use in a text subwindow.

Argument:	`Xv_Font`
Procs:	`create, get, set`
Objects:	`Textsw`
See Also:	8.1

TEXTSW_HISTORY_LIMIT
Specifies the number of user action sequences that can be undone.

Argument:	`int`
Default:	50
Procs:	`create, get, set`
Objects:	`Textsw`

TEXTSW_IGNORE_LIMIT
Specifies the number of edits `textsw` allows before vetoing `destroy`. Valid values are 0, which means the `destroy` will be vetoed if there have been any edits, and `TEXTSW_ INFINITY`, which means the `destroy` will never be vetoed. Vetoing a destroy means a confirm notice is displayed when the `textsw` is about to be destroyed. This veto confirm message is displayed only if the ignore limit is set to 0. A `textsw` is destroyed when the `textsw` or its enclosing frame is the object of an `xv_destroy()` call, which occurs when the application is quit from the Window Manager menu.

Argument:	`int`
Default:	0
Procs:	`create, get, set`
Objects:	`Textsw`

TEXTSW_INSERT_FROM_FILE
Inserts the contents of a file into a text subwindow at the current insertion point.

Argument:	`char *`
Default:	None
Procs:	`set, create`
Objects:	`Textsw`
See Also:	8.6.3

TEXTSW_INSERT_MAKES_VISIBLE
Controls whether insertion causes repositioning to make inserted text visible. Possible values are `TEXTSW_ALWAYS` or `TEXTSW_ IF_AUTO_SCROLL`.

Argument:	`Textsw_enum`
Default:	`TEXTSW_ALWAYS`
Procs:	`create, get, set`
Objects:	`Textsw`
See Also:	8.7.4

TEXTSW_INSERTION_POINT
Specifies the index of the current insertion point.

Argument:	`Textsw_index`
Default:	None
Procs:	`create, get, set`
Objects:	`Textsw`
See Also:	8.4.3

TEXTSW_LENGTH
Specifies the length of the `textsw`'s contents.

Argument:	`int`
Procs:	`get`
Objects:	`Textsw`
See Also:	8.3

TEXTSW_LINE_BREAK_ACTION

Determines how the `textsw` treats file lines that are too big to fit on one display line. `TEXTSW_CLIP` clips the line when it gets too long to fit; you don't see any additional characters typed on the line when the line exceeds the width of the textsw. `TEXTSW_WRAP_CHAR` "wraps" the line around so the part of the line that exceeds the width of the textsw is displayed on the next line(s). Textsw does not insert a CR. It just displays it as if a CR were there. If this happens in the middle of the word, the textsw will display the line as if a CR were inserted in the middle of the word. `TEXTSW_WRAP_WORD` "wraps" at the word level, thus, it will not break a word up to wrap around. It will figure out where the word starts and display as if a CR were inserted before the word.

Argument: `Textsw_enum`
Valid Values: {`TEXTSW_CLIP`, `TEXTSW_WRAP_AT_CHAR`, `TEXTSW_WRAP_AT_WORD`}
Default: `TEXTSW_WRAP_AT_WORD`
Procs: `create`, `get`, `set`
Objects: `Textsw`
See Also: 8.7.1

TEXTSW_LOWER_CONTEXT

Specifies the minimum number of lines to maintain between insertion point and bottom of view. A value of –1 turns auto scrolling off.

Argument: `int`
Default: 0
Procs: `create`, `get`, `set`
Objects: `Textsw`

TEXTSW_MEMORY_MAXIMUM

Specifies how much memory to use when not editing files (e.g., editing in memory). This attribute only takes effect at create time or after the window is reset with `textsw_reset`. The lower bound is 1K bytes, which is silently enforced.

Argument: `int`
Default: `20000`
Procs: `create`, `get`, `set`
Objects: `Textsw`
See Also: 8.4.8

TEXTSW_MODIFIED

Specifies whether the `textsw` has been modified.

Argument: `Boolean`
Procs: `get`
Objects: `Textsw`
See Also: 8.4.1

TEXTSW_MULTI_CLICK_SPACE

Specifies the maximum number of pixels between successive mouse clicks to still have the clicks considered a multi-click.

Argument: `int`
Default: 4
Procs: `create`, `get`, `set`
Objects: `Textsw`

XView Attributes

TEXTSW_MULTI_CLICK_TIMEOUT

Specifies the maximum number of milliseconds between successive mouse clicks to still have the clicks considered a multi-click.

Argument: `int`
Default: `390`
Procs: `create, get, set`
Objects: `Textsw`

TEXTSW_NOTIFY_PROC

Names a notify procedure.

Argument: `void (*notify_proc) ()`
Default: `NULL`
Procs: `create, set`
Objects: `Textsw`
Callback:

```
void
notify_proc (textsw, avlist)
        Textsw        textsw
        Attr_avlist   avlist
```

Notify procedure installed by application using `TEXTSW_NOTIFY_PROC`.
See Also: 8.12

TEXTSW_READ_ONLY

If `TRUE`, prevents editing of the displayed text. If another file is loaded in, read-only status is turned off again.

Argument: `Boolean`
Default: `FALSE`
Procs: `create, get, set`
Objects: `Textsw`

TEXTSW_STATUS

If set, specifies the address of a variable of type `Textsw_status`. A value that reflects what happened during the call to `xv_create` is then written into it.

Argument: `Textsw_status *`
Default: None
Procs: `create`
Objects: `Textsw`
See Also: 8.2

TEXTSW_STORE_CHANGES_FILE

Controls whether the *target* filename given to `textsw_store ()` to save the current contents to a file changes the name of the file being edited (`TEXTSW_FILE`).

Argument: `Boolean`
Default: `TRUE`
Procs: `create, set`
Objects: `Textsw`
See Also: 8.5.1

TEXTSW_SUBMENU_EDIT

Returns the submenu associated with the text pane menu `Edit` submenu.

Argument:	Menu
Procs:	get
Objects:	Textsw

TEXTSW_SUBMENU_FILE

Returns the submenu associated with the text pane menu `File` submenu.

Argument:	Menu
Procs:	get
Objects:	Textsw

TEXTSW_SUBMENU_FIND

Returns the submenu associated with the text pane menu `Find` submenu.

Argument:	Menu
Procs:	get
Objects:	Textsw

TEXTSW_SUBMENU_VIEW

Returns the submenu associated with the text pane menu `View` submenu.

Argument:	Menu
Procs:	get
Objects:	Textsw

TEXTSW_UPPER_CONTEXT

Specifies the minimum number of lines to maintain between the start of the selection and top of view. A value of –1 means defeat the normal actions.

Argument:	int
Default:	2
Procs:	create, get, set
Objects:	Textsw

TTY_ARGV

The command, specified as an argument vector, that the tty subwindow executes. Using the value `TTY_ARGV_DO_NOT_FORK` lets a user start a tty subwindow without forking off a shell.

Argument:	char**
Default:	None
Procs:	create, set
Objects:	Textsw
See Also:	9.1

TTY_CONSOLE

If `TRUE`, tty subwindow grabs console output.

Argument:	Boolean
Default:	FALSE
Procs:	set, create
Objects:	Tty

TTY_PAGE_MODE

If TRUE, output will stop after each page.

Argument: Boolean
Default: FALSE
Procs: create, get, set
Objects: Tty

TTY_PID

The process ID of the program being run in the tty subwindow.

Argument: int
Default: None
Procs: create, get, set
Objects: Tty
See Also: 9.3

TTY_QUIT_ON_CHILD_DEATH

If TRUE, window_done is called on the parent frame of the tty window when its child terminates.

Argument: Boolean
Default: FALSE
Procs: set, create
Objects: Tty
See Also: 9.3

TTY_TTY_FD

Gets the file descriptor of the pseudo-tty associated with the tty subwindow.

Argument: int
Procs: get
Objects: Tty
See Also: 9.4

WIN_ALARM

This attribute is for SunView compatibility. For more information, refer to the manual, *Converting SunView Applications*.

WIN_ALARM_DATA

This attribute is for SunView compatibility. For more information, refer to the manual, *Converting SunView Applications*.

WIN_BACKGROUND_COLOR

Specifies the background color of a window as an index into the colormap segment associated with the window.

Argument: int
Default: 0
Procs: create, get, set
Objects: Xv_Window
See Also: 4.7, 21.3.1, WIN_CMS, WIN_FOREGROUND_COLOR

WIN_BACKGROUND_PIXMAP

Specifies the background pixmap of a window.

Argument:	`Pixmap`
Default:	`NULL`
Procs:	`create, get, set`
Objects:	`Xv_Window`

WIN_BELOW

Causes the window to be positioned below the sibling window given as the value. Restricted to windows with the same immediate parent (i.e., subwindows). Does not affect the `xv_x` of the window.

Argument:	`Xv_Window`
Default:	N/A
Procs:	`set, create`
Objects:	`Xv_Window`

WIN_BIT_GRAVITY

Sets the Xlib-specific "bit gravity" on the underlying X window associated with the object. See *<X11/X.h>* for a list of legal values.

Argument:	`int`
Default:	`NorthWestGravity`
Procs:	`create, get`
Objects:	`Xv_Window`
See Also:	5.3 , `CANVAS_FIXED_IMAGE`, `CANVAS_RESIZE_PROC`

WIN_CLIENT_DATA

Specifies an arbitrary value to be attached to a window.

Argument:	`caddr_t`
Default:	None
Procs:	`create, get, set`
Objects:	`Xv_Window`
See Also:	7.19.1 , `XV_KEY_DATA`

WIN_CMD_LINE

Lets an application set the command-line options that can be used to (re)start it. The options passed, in addition to XView options are stored on a property called `WM_COMMAND` on the frame window. (The program *xprop* can be used to display a window's properties). Only one base frame window of the application needs to have this property set. This property is read possibly by a session manager to restart clients. Setting this attribute to -1 prevents any command-line option information from being saved on the frame. If there are two or more base frames in the application, the second and subsequent base frames should set their `WIN_CMD_LINE` attributes to -1 if they want to avoid multiple invocations of the same application by the session manager.

The string passed is copied and cached on the frame.

WARNING: Usage of this attribute will make the application non-ICCCM compliant. Use `FRAME_WM_COMMAND_ARGC_ARGV` instead. Intermixing the usage of `WIN_CMD_LINE` and `FRAME_WM_COMMAND_*` attributes has unpredictable results.

Argument: char *
Default: None
Procs: create,get,set
Objects: Xv_Window
See Also: FRAME_WM_COMMAND_ARGC_ARGV, FRAME_WM_COMMAND_ARGC,
             FRAME_WM_COMMAND_ARGV, FRAME_WM_COMMAND_STRINGS,
             Xlib Programming Manual, Interclient Communication Chapter

WIN_CMS

Window-based objects use colormap segments to get their colors. These objects get a default color-map segment when they are created, but you can assign a new one using this attribute.

Argument: Cms
Default: Depends on WIN_INHERIT_COLORS, typically inherits parent's cms
Procs: create,get,set
Objects: Xv_Window
See Also: 21.5, 21.2.2, 21.1, WIN_FOREGROUND_COLOR, WIN_BACKGROUND_COLOR

WIN_CMS_DATA

This attribute is obsolete, where possible, the Cms package should be used. It specifies the data for the colormap segment associated with the window. The data is written into the currently allocated colormap segment. If a new segment is desired, set it using WIN_CMS_NAME first.

Argument: Xv_cmsdata *
Default: None
Procs: create,get,set
Objects: Xv_Window

WIN_CMS_NAME

This attribute is obsolete, where possible, the Cms package should be used. Specifies the colormap segment to be associated with the window.

Argument: char *
Default: None
Procs: create,get,set
Objects: Xv_Window
See Also: 21.2.2

WIN_COLLAPSE_EXPOSURES

Collapses contiguous multiple Exposure (and GraphicsExpose) events destined for the same window that are grouped by the count field in the X Expose event.

Argument: Boolean
Default: TRUE
Procs: create,get,set
Objects: Xv_Window
See Also: 5.3

WIN_COLUMNS

Specifies the window's width (including left and right margins) in columns relative to the width of the window's font. WIN_COLUMNS is not a valid xv_create() attribute for a Textsw. Issue a separate xv_set() call after the xv_create() in order to set this attribute on a Textsw.

Argument: int
Default: Varies based on font, typically 80 columns
Procs: create,get,set
Objects: Xv_Window

WIN_CONSUME_EVENT

Specifies that the window will accept an event of type specified. The event is appended to the current input mask.

Argument:	Event code (defined in *<xview/win_input.h>*)
Default:	Varies from package to package
Procs:	`create, get, set`
Objects:	`Xv_Window`
See Also:	6.3.2, 5.7.1 , `WIN_CONSUME_X_EVENT_MASK,` `WIN_CONSUME_EVENTS,` `WIN_IGNORE_EVENT,` `WIN_IGNORE_EVENTS,` `WIN_X_EVENT_MASK`

WIN_CONSUME_EVENTS

Specifies a NULL-terminated list of event types that this window accepts. The event is appended to the current input mask.

Argument:	List of XView events
Default:	Varies from package to package
Procs:	`create, set`
Objects:	`Xv_Window`
See Also:	6.3.2, `WIN_CONSUME_X_EVENT_MASK,` `WIN_CONSUME_EVENT,` `WIN_IGNORE_EVENT,` `WIN_IGNORE_EVENTS,` `WIN_X_EVENT_MASK`

WIN_CONSUME_X_EVENT_MASK

The input mask is specified using X event masks found in *<X11/X.h>*. The event is appended to the current input mask.

Argument:	`unsigned long`
Default:	Varies from package to package
Procs:	`create, get, set`
Objects:	`Xv_Window`
See Also:	6.3.1 , `WIN_CONSUME_EVENT,` `WIN_CONSUME_X_EVENTS,` `WIN_IGNORE_EVENT,` `WIN_IGNORE_EVENTS,` `WIN_X_EVENT_MASK`

WIN_CURSOR

Specifies the window's cursor. You must supply the handle of an XView window as the parent parameter when getting WIN_CURSOR. Getting WIN_CURSOR on the root window returns NULL.

Argument:	`Xv_Cursor`
Default:	Default X server cursor
Procs:	`create, get, set`
Objects:	`Xv_Window`
Usage:	

```
default_cursor = (Xv_cursor)xv_get (
                        paint_win, WIN_CURSOR);


xv_set(paint_win, WIN_CURSOR, default_cursor, NULL);
```

XView Attributes

WIN_DEPTH

This attribute is obsolete. Use `XV_DEPTH` instead. Specifies the pixel depth of the window.

Argument:	`int`
Default:	Function of the screen
Procs:	`create, get`
Objects:	`Xv_Window`
See Also:	21.8, 2.4.2

WIN_DYNAMIC_VISUAL

This attribute is obsolete. Use the attribute `XV_VISUAL` to specify the visual used in the creation of the window or colormap segment.

Argument:	`Boolean`
Default:	`FALSE`
Procs:	`create`
Objects:	`Xv_Window`

WIN_EVENT_PROC

Specifies a callback procedure where window events are delivered.

Argument:	`void (*event_proc)()`
Default:	None
Procs:	`create, get, set`
Objects:	`Xv_Window`
Callback:	

```
void
event_proc (window, event, arg)
    Xv_Window    window;
    Event        *event;
    Notify_arg   arg;
```

See Also:	7.19.6 , Chapter 20, *The Notifier*, in the *XView Programming Manual*

WIN_FIT_HEIGHT

Causes the window to shrink or expand its height according to the window's contents leaving a margin specified by the value given. Typically used with panels to fit panel items.

Argument:	`int`
Default:	Depends on window size
Procs:	`create, get, set`
Objects:	`Xv_Window`
See Also:	`window_fit ()` macro in Section 3, *Procedures and Macros*, in the *XView Programming Manual*

WIN_FIT_WIDTH

Causes the window to shrink or expand its width according to the window's contents leaving a margin specified by the value given.

Argument:	`int`
Default:	Depends on window size
Procs:	`create, get, set`
Objects:	`Xv_Window`
See Also	`window_fit ()` macro in Section 3, *Procedures and Macros*

WIN_FOREGROUND_COLOR

Specifies the foreground color of a window as an index into the colormap segment associated with the window.

Argument: `int`
Default: `size` −1 (where `size` is the number of colors in the colormap segment associated with the window)
Procs: `create, get, set`
Objects: `Xv_Window`
See Also: 4.7, 21.3.1 , `WIN_CMS`, `WIN_BACKGROUND_COLOR`

WIN_FRAME

Returns the window's frame.

Return Type: `Frame`
Default: N/A
Procs: `get`
Objects: `Xv_Window`

WIN_FRONT

Indicates that the window should move to the front of the stacking order. Setting this attribute does *not* map the window. Use `XV_SHOW` to raise and map a window.

Argument: No value
Procs: `create, set`
Objects: `Xv_Window`

WIN_GRAB_ALL_INPUT

Specifies that the window will get all events regardless of location of the pointer. Performs a grab of the keyboard and the pointer.

Argument: `Boolean`
Default: `FALSE`
Procs: `set, create`
Objects: `Xv_Window`
See Also: 6.6.1 , `FULLSCREEN` attributes

WIN_HORIZONTAL_SCROLLBAR

This attribute is obsolete. Use `OPENWIN_HORIZONTAL_SCROLLBAR` instead. It is a handle to the horizontal scrollbar for that window.

Argument: `Scrollbar`
Default: `NULL`
Procs: `create, get, set`
Objects: `Xv_Window`

WIN_IGNORE_EVENT

Specifies that the window will not receive this event. (Certain events cannot be ignored.)

Argument: XView event code (see *<xview/win_input.h>*)
Default: None
Procs: `create, set`
Objects: `Xv_Window`
See Also: 6.3.2 , `WIN_CONSUME_EVENT`, `WIN_CONSUME_X_EVENT_MASK`, `WIN_CONSUME_EVENTS`, `WIN_IGNORE_EVENTS`

XView Attributes

WIN_IGNORE_EVENTS

Specifies a NULL-terminated list of events that this window will not receive. (Certain events cannot be ignored.)

Argument: List of event codes (see *<xview/win_input.h>*)
Default: None
Procs: `set,create`
Objects: `Xv_Window`
See Also: 6.3.2 , `WIN_CONSUME_EVENT, WIN_CONSUME_X_EVENT_MASK,`
            `WIN_CONSUME_EVENTS, WIN_IGNORE_EVENT`

WIN_IGNORE_X_EVENT_MASK

Prevents the specified event masks from being delivered to the event handler. The input mask is specified using X event masks found in *<X11/X.h>*.

Argument: `unsigned long`
Default: Varies from package to package
Procs: `create,get,set`
Objects: `Xv_Window`
See Also: 6.3.1 , `WIN_CONSUME_X_EVENT_MASK, WIN_EVENT_PROC, WIN_IGNORE_EVENT,`
            `WIN_IGNORE_EVENTS, WIN_X_EVENT_MASK`

WIN_INHERIT_COLORS

This attribute specifies whether the window should inherit the colors used by its parent. If TRUE, the window will inherit the WIN_CMS, XV_VISUAL, WIN_FOREGROUND_COLOR, and WIN_ BACKGROUND_COLOR attributes of its parent. If FALSE, it will use the defaults for all of these attributes.

Argument: `Boolean`
Default: `TRUE`
Procs: `create,get,set`
Objects: `Xv_Window`

WIN_INPUT_MASK

Specifies the window's input mask. This overwrites the current mask.

Argument: `Inputmask *`
Default: Varies from package to package
Procs: `create,get,set`
Objects: `Xv_Window`
See Also: 6.8

WIN_INPUT_ONLY

Specifies that a window is an input only window; although it has other window properties, it cannot be drawn into.

Argument: No value
Default: Input/Ouptut Window
Procs: `create`
Objects: `Xv_Window`

WIN_IS_CLIENT_PANE

When used with `xv_create()`, the attribute has no value; using the attribute sets it to TRUE. When used, the window is considered to be an OPEN LOOK GUI application-specific pane which can override resources, such as fonts. Currently, the only packages that support this are `text` and `tty/term`.

Argument: `Boolean`
Default: `FALSE`
Procs: `create,get`
Objects: `Xv_Window`

WIN_KBD_FOCUS

This attribute is for SunView compatibility. For more information, refer to the manual, *Converting SunView Applications*.

WIN_MAP

Indicates whether to map or unmap the window. Setting this attribute to true maps the window without changing the stacking order. This does not imply *raised* (to the top of the window tree). Use `XV_SHOW` to raise and map a window.

Argument: `Boolean`
Default: `FALSE`
Procs: `create,get,set`
Objects: `Xv_Window`
See Also: `WIN_FRONT, XV_SHOW`

WIN_MENU

This attribute is obsolete. The window manager now specifies the window's menu.

WIN_MESSAGE_DATA

Used to access the data portion of a window's client message.

Return Type: char
Procs: `get`
Objects: `Xv_Window`
See Also: 6.7.1 , `WIN_MESSAGE_FORMAT,WIN_MESSAGE_TYPE`

WIN_MESSAGE_FORMAT

Used to access the format portion of a window's client message.

Return Type: `unsigned char`
Procs: `get`
Objects: `Xv_Window`
See Also: 6.7.1 , `WIN_MESSAGE_DATA,WIN_MESSAGE_TYPE`

WIN_MESSAGE_TYPE

Used to access the type portion of a window's client message.

Return Type: Atom
Procs: `get`
Objects: `Xv_Window`
See Also: 6.7.1 , `WIN_MESSAGE_FORMAT,WIN_MESSAGE_DATA`

WIN_MOUSE_XY

Warps the mouse pointer to the specified position. Returns a static `Rect *` on `xv_get`.

Argument:	`int, int`
Default:	N/A
Procs:	`create, get, set`
Objects:	`Xv_Window`
See Also:	13.3

WIN_NO_CLIPPING

This attribute is for SunView compatibility. For more information, refer to the manual, *Converting SunView Applications*.

WIN_PARENT

Specifies the window's parent in the window tree. This attribute affectively reparents a window on set.

Argument:	`Xv_Window`
Default:	None
Procs:	`create, get, set`
Objects:	`Xv_Window`

WIN_PERCENT_HEIGHT

This attribute is for SunView compatibility. For more information, refer to the manual, *Converting SunView Applications*.

WIN_PERCENT_WIDTH

This attribute is for SunView compatibility. For more information, refer to the manual, *Converting SunView Applications*.

WIN_RECT

Specifies the bounding box of a window. Returns a static `Rect` on `xv_get`.

Argument:	`Rect *`
Default:	`NULL`
Procs:	`create, get, set`
Objects:	`Xv_Window`

WIN_RETAINED

Hint to the server to maintain backing store for this window. The server may not honor this request.

Argument:	`Boolean`
Default:	`FALSE`
Procs:	`create, get, set`
Objects:	`Xv_Window`
See Also:	5.5

WIN_RIGHT_OF

Causes a sibling window to be laid out just to the right of the window given as the value. Restricted to windows that share the same immediate parent. Does not set `XV_Y`.

Argument:	`Xv_Window`
Default:	Arbitrary
Procs:	`create, set`
Objects:	`Xv_Window`
See Also:	`WIN_BELOW`

WIN_ROW_GAP

This attribute is for SunView compatibility. For more information, refer to the manual, *Converting SunView Applications*.

WIN_ROW_HEIGHT

Specifies the height of a row in the window.

Argument:	`int`
Default:	Font's default height
Procs:	`create, get, set`
Objects:	`Xv_Window`

WIN_ROWS

Specifies the window's height (including top and bottom margins) in rows. `WIN_ROWS` is not a valid `xv_create()` attribute for a `Textsw`. Issue a separate `xv_set()` call after the `xv_create()` in order to set this attribute on a `Textsw`.

Argument:	`int`
Default:	`34`
Procs:	`create, get, set`
Objects:	`Xv_Window`

WIN_SAVE_UNDER

Provides a hint to the server about whether or not the screen area beneath a window should be saved while the window, such as a pop-up menu, is mapped. This is not the same as `WIN_RETAINED`.

Argument:	`Boolean`
Default:	`FALSE`
Procs:	`set`
Objects:	`Xv_Window`

WIN_SCREEN_RECT

Returns the bounding box of the screen containing the window. Data points to per-process static storage.

Argument:	`Rect *`
Default:	Screen dependent
Procs:	`get`
Objects:	`Xv_Window`

WIN_SET_FOCUS

Sets the input focus to this window, if possible. The X protocol restricts unmapped windows from holding the input focus. The window must select for `KBD_USE` and `KBD_DONE` events.

Argument:	No value
Default:	None
Procs:	`create,set`
Objects:	`Xv_Window`

WIN_SOFT_FNKEY_LABELS

Assigns labels for the soft function keys. The value for the `WIN_SOFT_FNKEY_LABELS` is a string of 12 labels separated by newline characters "\n".

Argument: `char *`
Procs: `get,set`
Usage:

```
canvas = (Canvas) xv_create (frame,CANVAS,
                CANVAS_X_PAINT_WINDOW,TRUE,
                NULL);


xv_set(canvas_paint_window(canvas),
        WIN_SOFT_FNKEY_LABELS,"Red\nGreen\nBlue\nMaroon\n
        Orchid\nViolet\nMagenta\nCoral\nTurquoise\n
        Yellow\nBrick\nBlack\n",
        WIN_EVENT_PROC, my_Event_proc,
        NULL);
```

In the above example, whenever the canvas gets the input focus, the soft function key labels will be updated to "Red Green Blue ...". To display the soft function key panel, select the Function Keys item from the Workspace Utilities menu.

See Also: 6.12.1

WIN_TOP_LEVEL

Returns whether the window is the child of another window or is a frame.

Return Type: `Boolean`
Default: N/A
Procs: `get`
Objects: `Xv_Window`

WIN_TOP_LEVEL_NO_DECOR

Controls whether this window is or is not controlled by the window manager. (This controls the `OverrideRedirect` flag.)

Argument: `Boolean`
Default: `FALSE`
Procs: `create,get,set`
Objects: `Xv_Window`
See Also: 4.10

WIN_TRANSPARENT

Specifies that the window's background pixmap should be be transparent (set to none). For more information, on the background pixmap refer to the section, "*The Window Background*" in Chapter Four of the *Xlib Programming Manual*.

Argument: No value
Default: Not transparent
Procs: `create`
Objects: `Xv_Window`

WIN_VERTICAL_SCROLLBAR

This attribute is obsolete. Use `OPENWIN_VERTICAL_SCROLLBAR` instead. Specifies that scrollbar orientation is vertical.

Argument:	`Scrollbar`
Default:	None
Procs:	`create, get, set`
Objects:	`Xv_Window`

WIN_WINDOW_GRAVITY

Defines how the window should be repositioned if its parent is resized. See *<X11/X.h>* for legal values.

Argument:	`int`
Default:	`NorthWestGravity`
Procs:	`create, get, set`
Objects:	`Xv_Window`
See Also:	5.3, `WIN_BIT_GRAVITY`

WIN_X_COLOR_INDICES

Translates the logical indices of the window's colormap segment (from 0 to `size-1`) into the actual indices into the colormap used by the window.

Argument:	`unsigned long *`
Procs:	`get`
Objects:	`Xv_Window`
See Also:	21.3

WIN_X_EVENT_MASK

Expects an X event mask. Acts in the same manner as `WIN_CONSUME_X_EVENT_MASK`; but instead of appending to the current input mask, replaces it with a new mask.

Argument:	`unsigned long`
Default:	Varies from package to package
Procs:	`create, get, set`
See Also:	`WIN_CONSUME_EVENTS, WIN_CONSUME_X_EVENT_MASK`

XV_AUTO_CREATE

Specifies whether to create an object not found by `xv_find()`.

Argument:	`Boolean`
Default:	`TRUE`
Procs:	`find`
Objects:	`Cms, Font, Menu_item`
See Also:	25.9.2

XV_BOTTOM_MARGIN

Specifies the margin at the bottom of an object.

Argument:	`int`
Default:	Varies with object
Procs:	`create, get, set`

XV_DEPTH

Specifies the pixel depth of the object.

Argument: int
Default: Function of the screen
Procs: create, get
Objects: Xv_Window

XV_DISPLAY

Returns the X Display data structure. The structure returned is maintained by the toolkit and should not be freed.

Argument: Display *
Default: Display structure for specified object
Procs: get
Objects: All Drawable objects and its subcalsses
See Also: 15.1

XV_ERROR_PROC

The application's *XView* error handler is called as a result of xv_error() being called.

Argument: int (*error_proc) ()
Default: None
Procs: xv_init
Objects: N/A
Callback:

```
            int
            error_proc (object, avlist)
                   Xv_object    object;
                   Attr_avlist avlist;
```

See Also: 24.2 , XV_X_ERROR_PROC

XV_FOCUS_ELEMENT

Set focus on the first (0) or last (-1) element in the pane.

Argument: int
Valid Values: {0, -1}
Procs: set
Objects: Xv_Window

XV_FONT

Specifies an object's font.

Argument: Xv_Font
Default: lucida medium
Procs: create, get, set
Object: Generally, all

XV_HEIGHT

Specifies the height of an object in pixels.

Argument: int
Default: N/A
Procs: create, get, set
Objects: All
See Also: 15.4

XV_HELP_DATA

Specifies the help string used by the help package to display on-line help. The text string has the form file:keyword. The help package looks for the key keyword in the file *$HELPDIR/file.info*. In the special case for a Textsw, set XV_HELP_DATA on the Textsw's view which you can get with the following call:

```
xv_get(textsw, OPENWIN_NTH_VIEW, NULL);
```

Argument: char *
Default: No help available notice
Procs: create, get, set
Objects: All
See Also: 23.1

XV_INIT_ARGC_PTR_ARGV

Interprets command-line args. Strips generic toolkit command-line arguments out of argv, and decrements argc accordingly.

Argument 1: int *
Argument 2: char **
Default: None
Procs: xv_init
Objects: N/A
Usage:

```
main(argc, argv
    int    argc;
    char   **argv;
{
    server = xv_init (XV_INIT_ARGC_PTR_ARGV,
                            &argc, argv, NULL);
}
```

See Also: 3.2.1 , XV_INIT_ARGS

XV_INIT_ARGS

Interprets command-line arguments. Does not strip generic toolkit command-line arguments out of argv.

Argument 1: int
Argument 2: char **
Default: None
Procs: xv_init
Objects: N/A
Usage:

```
main(argc, argv
    int    argc;
    char   **argv;
{
    server = xv_init (XV_INIT_ARGS, argc, argv, NULL);
}
```

See Also: 3.2.1 , XV_INIT_ARGC_PTR_ARGV

XV_INSTANCE_NAME

The attribute XV_INSTANCE_NAME is used to associate an instance name with an XView object. The instance name is used to construct the resource name used by the resource manager to perform look-ups. The resource name is constructed by concatenating the instance names of all objects in the current object's lineage, starting with the name of the application or whatever was passed in with the -name command-line option, ending with the XView attribute name. The XView attribute name remains in lowercase. XV_INSTANCE_NAME is normally used with XV_USE_DB.

```
Argument:    char *
Default:     NULL
Procs:       create, set
Usage:
                Frame      frame;
                Panel      panel;
                frame = (Frame)xv_create(NULL, FRAME,
                                XV_INSTANCE_NAME, "base_frame",
                                NULL);
                panel = (Panel)xv_create(frame, PANEL,
                                XV_INSTANCE_NAME, "panel",
                                XV_USE_DB,
                                    XV_WIDTH, 100,
                                    XV_HEIGHT, 200,
                                    NULL,
                                NULL);
```

Above, assume the name of the application is "app", the resource names constructed for lookup of the width and height of the panel are:

```
app.base_frame.panel.xv_width
app.base_frame.panel.xv_height
```

Entries in the resource manager could look like:

```
app.base_frame.panel.xv_width:400
app.base_frame.panel.xv_height:500
```

If these entries were not present in the resource manager, the width and height of the panel would take the default values of 100 and 200, respectively.

```
See Also:    22.3.2, 17.3 , XV_USE_DB
```

XV_KEY_DATA

Stores a 32-bit data value on an object. You may set multiple XV_KEY_DATA values on objects by using different keys. The key specified should be a unique number (see xv_unique_key() in Section 3, *Summary of Procedures and Macros*.)

```
Argument 1:  int
Argument 2:  XV_opaque
Default:     None
Procs:       create, get, set
Objects:     All
Usage:
                xv_create(panel, PANEL_BUTTON,
                    PANEL_BUTTON_LABEL,     "Push Me"
                    XV_KEY_DATA,            PANEL_ITEM_KEY,     "text",
                    PANEL_NOTIFY_PROC,      my_notify_proc
                NULL);
```

```
See Also:    7.19.1
```

XV_KEY_DATA_REMOVE

Causes the data associated with the specified key to be removed. If an XV_KEY_DATA_
REMOVE_PROC is defined, it will be called.

Argument: `int`
Default: None
Procs: `set`
Objects: All
See Also: 7.19.1 , XV_KEY_DATA, XV_KEY_DATA_REMOVE_PROC

XV_KEY_DATA_REMOVE_PROC

Names the function that is called whenever the object that has key data attached to it is destroyed.
This function should free the data associated with the key.

Argument 1: `int`
Argument 2: `void`(*`xv_key_data_remove_proc`) ()
Default: None
Procs: `create,get,set`
Objects   All
Callback:

```
void
xv_key_data_remove_proc(object, key, data)
        Xv_object       object;
        int             key;
        caddr_t         data;
```

See Also: 7.19.1

XV_LABEL

Specifies a frame's header label or an icon's label or simply associates a name to an object. XView
copies the strings on set.

Argument: `char *`
Default: `NULL`
Procs: `create,get,set`
Objects: All
See Also: 4.2.2

XV_LC_BASIC_LOCALE

Specifies the basic locale category, which sets the country of the user interface.This XView attribute
can only be used in xv_init (), but can be queried on any XView object which is a subclass of
window or server class via xv_get (). The value that is set using these attributes must be a valid locale name in the system. Use in situations where you want to force a program to operate in a certain
locale. For example, if a program only works in French, then the locale attribute can be set so that it
cannot be switched to another language.
Warning: This attribute should only be used for localization operations.

Argument: `char *`
Default: "C"
Procs: `xv_init(),get`
Usage:

```
xv_init(...,
        XV_LC_BASIC_LOCALE, "fr",
        XV_LC_DISPLAY_LANG, "C",
        NULL);
```

See Also: 22.1.4 , XV_LOCALE_DIR, Chapter 22, *Internationalization*

XV_LC_DISPLAY_LANG

Specifies the display language locale category, which sets the language in which labels, messages, menu items, and help text are displayed. This XView attribute can only be used in xv_init(), but can be queried on any XView object which is a subclass of window or server class via xv_get(). The value that is set using these attributes must be a valid locale name in the system. Use in situations where you want to force a program to operate in a certain locale. For example, if a program only works in French, then the locale attribute can be set so that it cannot be switched to another language.
Warning: This attribute should only be used for localization operations.

Argument:	char *
Default:	"C"
Procs:	xv_init(),get
See Also:	22.1.4 , XV_LOCALE_DIR, Chapter 22, *Internationalization*

XV_LC_INPUT_LANG

Specifies the input language locale category, which sets the language used for keyboard input. This XView attribute can only be used in xv_init(), but can be queried on any XView object which is a subclass of window or server class via xv_get(). The value that is set using these attributes must be a valid locale name in the system. Use in situations where you want to force a program to operate in a certain locale. For example, if a program only works in French, then the locale attribute can be set so that it cannot be switched to another language.
Warning: This attribute should only be used for localization operations.

Argument:	char *
Default:	"C"
Procs:	xv_init(),get
See Also:	22.1.4 , XV_LOCALE_DIR, Chapter 22, *Internationalization*

XV_LC_NUMERIC

Specifies the numeric locale category, which defines the language used to format numeric quantities. This XView attribute can only be used in xv_init(), but can be queried on any XView object which is a subclass of window or server class via xv_get(). The value that is set using these attributes must be a valid locale name in the system. Use in situations where you want to force a program to operate in a certain locale. For example, if a program only works in French, then the locale attribute can be set so that it cannot be switched to another language.
Warning: This attribute should only be used for localization operations.

Argument:	char *
Default:	"C"
Procs:	xv_init(),get
See Also:	22.1.4 , XV_LOCALE_DIR, Chapter 22, *Internationalization*

XV_LC_TIME_FORMAT

Specifies the time format locale category, which defines the language used to format time and date. This XView attribute can only be used in xv_init(), but can be queried on any XView object which is a subclass of window or server class via xv_get(). The value that is set using these attributes must be a valid locale name in the system. Use in situations where you want to force a program to operate in a certain locale. For example, if a program only works in French, then the locale attribute can be set so that it cannot be switched to another language.
Warning: This attribute should only be used for localization operations.

Argument:	char *
Default:	"C"
Procs:	xv_init(),get
See Also:	22.1.4 , XV_LOCALE_DIR, Chapter 22, *Internationalization*

XV_LEFT_MARGIN

Specifies the margin at the left of the object.

Argument: `int`
Default: Varies with object
Procs: `create, get, set`

XV_LOCALE_DIR

This attribute specifies the location of the application's locale specific files. At present, these include the `app-defaults` and `LC_MESSAGES` directories.

The directory structure referenced by `XV_LOCALE_DIR` is:

    `<XV_LOCALE_DIR>/<locale>/LC_MESSAGES`

    `<XV_LOCALE_DIR>/<locale>/app-defaults`

`<locale>` is expanded differently depending on which internationalization feature is using `XV_LOCALE_DIR`.

Argument: `char *`
Default: *$OPENWINHOME/lib/locale*
Procs: `xv_init()`
See Also: 22.3.2, 22.2.1, 22.1.2

XV_MARGIN

Specifies the offset from the border of this object.

Argument: `int`
Default: Varies with object
Procs: `create, get, set`

XV_NAME

Specifies an optional name for an object. In some cases, this attribute is used internally by packages. For instance, the SERVER package sets the display connection name using this attribute.

Argument: `char *`
Default: Varies with object
Procs: `create, get, set`
Objects: All
See Also: 15.3.1

XV_OWNER

Returns the object's owner. The object returned varies among packages.

Return Type: `Xv_opaque`
Procs: `get`
Objects: All

XV_RECT

Specifies the object's bounding box; that is, the smallest rectangle that contains the object. The `Rect *` returned points to a per-process static storage and thus should not be freed.

Argument: `Rect *`
Default: None
Procs: `create, get, set`
Objects: `Window` and its subclasses
See Also: 25.2.1

XV_RIGHT_MARGIN

Specifies the margin at the right of the object.

Argument: `int`
Default: Varies with object
Procs: `create, get, set`

XV_ROOT

Returns the root window for an object. (Object must be a window based.)

Argument: `Xv_object`
Default: Root window for default screen
Procs: `get`
Objects: `Window` and its subclasses

XV_SCREEN

Returns the screen object associated with this object.

Argument: `Xv_screen`
Default: Values for specified screen
Procs: `get`
Objects: `Window` and its subclasses
See Also: 15.2

XV_SHOW

Causes the object to be displayed or undisplayed. If object is a window, brings object to the top.

Argument: `Boolean`
Default: Varies
Procs: `create, get, set`
Objects: `Generic`
See Also: 4.3.1, `WIN_MAP`, `WIN_FRONT`

XV_TOP_MARGIN

Specifies the margin at the top of the object.

Argument: `int`
Default: Varies with object
Procs: `create, get, set`

XV_TYPE

Returns the package that belongs to an object.

Argument: `Xv_pkg *`
Default: N/A
Procs: `get`
Objects: `All`
See Also: 24.4.2

XV_USAGE_PROC

An application-defined routine that is called when an application is started with the −help option. Typically used to print a list of valid command-line options. This routine should not return. Applications that add additional command-line options to those already provided by XView should register an XV_USAGE_PROC. From within the XV_USAGE_PROC, the application should first print the application defined options and then call xv_usage() to allow XView to print the default command-line options.

Argument: void (*xv_usage_proc)()
Default: xv_usage() (XView defined usage procedure)
Procs: xv_init
Usage:

```
            application_usage_proc(name)
            char *name
            {
                printf("...");
                        xv_usage(name);
                        exit(1);
            }
            main()
            {
                xv_init(... XV_USAGE_PROC,
                            application_usage_proc, ...);
            }
```

Callback:

```
            void
            usage_proc(application_name)
                char *application_name
```

See Also: 3.2.1

XV_USE_DB

The attribute XV_USE_DB can be used to specify a set of attributes that are to be searched in the X11 resource manager database. XV_USE_DB takes a NULL-terminated list of attribute-value pairs as its values. During program execution, each attribute in this NULL-terminated list of attributes is looked up in the X11 resource manager database. If the attribute is not found in the database, then the value specified in the attribute-value pair is used as the default value.

The list of customizable attributes is shown below:

CANVAS_HEIGHT	CANVAS_MIN_PAINT_HEIGHT
CANVAS_MIN_PAINT_WIDTH	CANVAS_WIDTH
PANEL_CHOICE_NCOLS	PANEL_CHOICE_NROWS
PANEL_DROP_HEIGHT	PANEL_DROP_WIDTH
PANEL_EXTRA_PAINT_HEIGHT	PANEL_EXTRA_PAINT_WIDTH
PANEL_GAUGE_WIDTH	PANEL_ITEM_X
PANEL_ITEM_X_GAP	PANEL_ITEM_Y
PANEL_ITEM_Y_GAP	PANEL_JUMP_DELTA
PANEL_LABEL_WIDTH	PANEL_LABEL_X
PANEL_LABEL_Y	PANEL_LIST_DISPLAY_ROWS
PANEL_LIST_ROW_HEIGHT	PANEL_LIST_WIDTH
PANEL_MAX_VALUE	PANEL_MIN_VALUE
PANEL_NEXT_COL	PANEL_NEXT_ROW
PANEL_SLIDER_WIDTH	PANEL_TICKS
PANEL_VALUE_DISPLAY_LENGTH	PANEL_VALUE_DISPLAY_WIDTH

PANEL_VALUE_STORED_LENGTH	PANEL_VALUE_X
PANEL_VALUE_Y	
WIN_COLUMNS	WIN_DESIRED_HEIGHT
WIN_DESIRED_WIDTH	WIN_ROWS
XV_HEIGHT	XV_WIDTH
XV_X	XV_Y

Argument: NULL-terminated attribute-value list
Procs: create, set
Usage:

```
Frame    frame;

frame = (Frame)xv_create(NULL, FRAME,
                        XV_INSTANCE_NAME, "base_frame",
                        XV_USE_DB,
                           XV_WIDTH, 100,
                           XV_HEIGHT, 200,
                           NULL,
                        NULL);
```

In this example, the value of the attributes XV_WIDTH and XV_HEIGHT for the frame object is searched in the X11 resource manager database. If not found, XV_WIDTH and XV_HEIGHT will take the default values of 100 and 200 respectively. See XV_INSTANCE_NAME for information regarding the actual resource name used for the search.

For more detailed information, refer to the *Xlib Programming Manual*.

See Also: 22.3.2, 17.3 , XV_INSTANCE_NAME, Chapter 22, *Internationalization*

XV_USE_LOCALE

This attribute enables the internationalization features in XView. When this attribute is FALSE (default), internationalization features in XView are turned off. All internationalized applications must set this attribute to be TRUE. This attribute is only valid in the xv_init() function call. The format is as follows:

Argument: Boolean
Default: FALSE
Procs: xv_init
Usage:

```
xv_init(XV_USE_LOCALE, TRUE,...);
```

See Also: 22.1.2

XV_VISUAL

This attribute specifies the exact visual that will be used in the creation of the window or colormap segment. The value is a pointer a Visual structure that one would normally get from XMatchVisualInfo or XGetVisualInfo. This attribute applies only to WINDOW and cms objects.

Argument: Visual *
Default: Varies with server
Procs: create, get
See Also: 21.8

XV_VISUAL_CLASS

This attribute specifies the class of the visual that will be used in the creation of the window or color-map segment. The value should be one of the following:

```
StaticGray
GrayScale
StaticColor
PseudoColor
TrueColor
DirectColor
```

If the server that the window is being created with does not support the visual class that is specified by this attribute, the library will use the default visual instead. This attribute applies only to `WINDOW` and `CMS` objects.

Argument: `int`
Default: Varies with server (usually PseudoColor)
Procs: `create,get`
See Also: 21.8

XV_WIDTH

Specifies the width of the object in pixels.

Argument: `int`
Default: None
Procs: `create,get,set`
Objects: `Generic`
See Also: 15.4

XV_X

Specifies the x position of the object relative to its parent.

Argument: `int`
Default: Varies with object
Procs: `create,get,set`
See Also: 7.4.2

XV_X_ERROR_PROC

Specifies the application's Xlib error handler (different from `XV_ERROR_PROC`). This function should return `XV_OK` if the error is to be ignored by XView. Return `XV_ERROR` if XView is to process the X error and exit.

Argument: `int` (*x_error_proc) ()
Default: None
Procs: `xv_init`
Callback:

```
        int
    x_error_proc(display, event)
        Display    *display;
        XErrorEvent *event;
```

See Also: 24.3 , `XV_ERROR_PROC`

XV_XID

Returns the XID of the specified object such as the pixmap associated with a `Server_ image` or the X Window associated with a canvas paint window.

Argument:	`int`
Default:	N/A
Procs:	`get`
Objects:	`Drawable` and its subclasses
See Also:	16.1

XV_Y

Specifies the y position of the object relative to its parent.

Argument:	`int`
Default:	Varies with object
Procs:	`create, get, set`
Objects:	`Generic`
See Also:	7.4.2

3

Procedures and Macros

Section 3, Summary of Procedures and Macros, *provides alphabetically arranged descriptions of all the XView procedures and macros.*

3
Procedures and Macros

This section lists the XView procedures and macros in alphabetical order. For each procedure or macro, an explanation of its use is provided. Following each procedure is a synopsis that includes the procedure's parameters, if there are any. The parameters are described after the synopsis.

attr_create_list()

Takes an attribute-value list and converts it into an array of `Attr_attributes`, also known as an `Attr_avlist`. `ATTRIBUTE_STANDARD_SIZE`, defined in *<xview/attr.h>* defines how big an attriubte-value list can get. This is the limit on how big an attribute-value list can be created using the `ATTR_LIST` or `attr_create_list()` macros.

```
Attr_avlist
attr_create_list(attrs)
```

The return value is used as the value for the attribute `ATTR_LIST`.

CANVAS_EACH_PAINT_WINDOW()

Macro providing built-in support for iteration across all the paint windows contained in a given canvas. Allows you to perform operations on multiple paint windows for which there are no canvas attributes.

CANVAS_END_EACH

Closes the loop started by `CANVAS_EACH_PAINT_WINDOW()`. These two macros are meant to be used together.

cursor_copy()

Creates and returns a copy of `src_cursor`.

```
Xv_Cursor
cursor_copy(src_cursor)
      Xv_Cursor  src_cursor;
```

dnd_decode_drop()

This function initiates a drag and drop data transfer using the selection mechanism. The drop event is decoded in three steps: First, the selection defined within the drop event is associated with the selection object passed into dnd_decode_drop(); second, the function sends an acknowledgement to the source, informing it that the transaction has been initiated; finally, if the drop-site is valid, the drop-site item that was dropped on is returned. Otherwise, if dnd_decode_drop() fails to initiate the drag and drop transaction, XV_ERROR is returned.

```
Xv_drop_site
dnd_decode_drop(sel_object, drop_event)
    Selection_requestor    sel_object;
    Event                  *drop_event;
```

sel_object is an instantiated selection requestor object.

drop_event is a pointer to the event structure that contains the trigger event. This event is either the semantic event ACTION_DRAG_MOVE or ACTION_DRAG_COPY, indicating the type of the drag and drop: a move or a copy.

dnd_done()

This function is called by the application that is receiving the drop. It is called *after* the drop operation is completed. The function informs the toolkit that the drag and drop operation has been completed.

```
dnd_done(sel_object)
    Selection_requestor    sel_object;
```

sel_object is the Selection_requestor object that was previously passed into dnd_decode_drop().

dnd_is_forwarded()

Allows applications to detect when a drop event has been forwarded from some other drop-site. Generally this happens when the user drops on the window manager's decor window or on an icon with the attribute DROP_SITE_DEFAULT set. The corresponding preview/drop event will have the flags field set with the DND_FORWARDED flag. This is tested for by using dnd_is_forwarded(event).

In general, if the application handles previewing, it should check to see if the preview event was forwarded and not invert/highlight the drop site.

```
dnd_is_forwarded(event)
```

dnd_is_local()

Returns whether the ACTION_DRAG_COPY or ACTION_DROP_MOVE event was generated locally within the client.

```
dnd_is_local(event)
```

dnd_send_drop()

This initiates a drag. After the drag and drop object is created, an application calls dnd_send_drop(). This changes the cursor to the drag cursor, sends preview events to valid drop-sites and sends the trigger event (if a valid drop-site is dropped on). Trigger events are either ACTION_DRAG_COPY or ACTION_DRAG_MOVE.

A drag operation can be aborted by hitting the STOP key, or its equivalent. dnd_send_drop() reverts the drag cursor back to its normal state and returns DND_ABORTED when it detects the STOP key event. Application code needs to handle the DND_ABORTED after dnd_send_drop() returns. See *<xview/dragdrop.h>* for other valid return values.

```
int
dnd_send_drop(object)
    Dnd    object;
```

object is a Dnd object that describes the source data (an instance of DRAGDROP).

event_action()

Returns the semantic action from the event structure. For example, when the user selects the SELECT button, it returns ACTION_SELECT. If there is no action associated with an event, event_action() returns the value returned by event_id() for the event. The macro is passed a pointer to an Event structure.

event_alt_is_down()

Returns TRUE or FALSE, depending on the state of the Alt key. The macro is passed a pointer to an Event structure.

event_button_is_down()

Returns TRUE or FALSE, depending on the state of mouse buttons. Used in conjunction with: event_is_button(), event_left_is_down(), event_middle_is_down(), event_right_is_down(). The macro is passed a pointer to an Event structure.

event_ctrl_is_down()

Returns TRUE or FALSE, depending on the state of the Control key. Indicates the state of the Control key. The macro is passed a pointer to an Event structure.

event_id()

Returns the actual event ID, such as MS_LEFT to indicate the left mouse button. The macro is passed a pointer to an Event structure. Use of the macro event_action(), which returns the semantic action, is recommended instead of event_id().

event_is_ascii()

Returns TRUE or FALSE, depending whether or not the event is an ASCII key. The macro is passed a pointer to an Event structure.

event_is_button()

Returns TRUE or FALSE, depending whether or not the event is a button event. This is used with: event_button_is_down(), event_left_is_down(), event_middle_is_down(), and event_right_is_down(). The macro is passed a pointer to an Event structure.

event_is_down()

Returns TRUE or FALSE, depending on the state of a mouse button or keyboard key. The macro is passed a pointer to an Event structure. Also see the macro event_is_up().

event_is_iso()

Returns TRUE or FALSE, depending whether a key event is within the ISO character set. The macro is passed a pointer to an Event structure.

event_is_key_bottom()

Returns TRUE or FALSE, depending whether a key event is within the left function keys. The macro is passed a pointer to an Event structure.

event_is_key_left()

Returns TRUE or FALSE, depending whether a key event is within the left function keys. This is for function keys on keyboards that are sectioned into four sets of fifteen function keys. The macro is passed a pointer to an Event structure.

event_is_key_right()

Returns TRUE or FALSE, depending whether a key event is within the right function keys. This is for function keys on keyboards that are sectioned into four sets of fifteen function keys. The macro is passed a pointer to an Event structure.

event_is_key_top()

Returns TRUE or FALSE, depending whether a key event is within the top function keys. This is for function keys on keyboards that are sectioned into four sets of fifteen function keys. The macro is passed a pointer to an Event structure.

event_is_meta()

Returns TRUE or FALSE, and determines whether event is a Meta key. The macro is passed a pointer to an Event structure.

event_is_string()

Returns TRUE or FALSE, determines if a string is associated with the event. The macro is passed a pointer to an Event structure.

event_is_up()

Returns TRUE or FALSE, depending on the state of the mouse button or keyboard in a particular event. The macro is passed a pointer to an Event structure. Also see the macro event_is_down().

event_left_is_down()

Returns TRUE or FALSE, and determines the state of the left mouse button. Used to determine the state of particular buttons for a three button mouse. This is used in conjunction with: event_button_is_down(), event_is_button(), event_middle_is_down(), and event_right_is_down(). The macro is passed a pointer to an Event structure.

event_meta_is_down()

Indicates the state of the Meta key. The macro is passed a pointer to an Event structure.

event_middle_is_down()

Returns TRUE or FALSE, and determines the state of the middle mouse button. This is used with: event_button_is_down(), event_is_button(), event_left_is_down(), and event_right_is_down(). The macro is passed a pointer to an Event structure.

event_right_is_down()

Returns TRUE or FALSE, and determines the state of the right mouse button. This is used with: event_button_is_down(), event_is_button(), event_left_is_down(), and event_middle_is_down(). The macro is passed a pointer to an Event structure.

event_shift_is_down()

Indicates the state of the Shift key. The macro is passed a pointer to an Event structure.

event_string()

Used to determine the string value associated with the event ID. For normal ASCII event codes, event_string() returns a string value of the key. However, keys, ASCII or not, may be rebound to a string using XRebindKeysym(). The macro is passed a pointer to an Event structure.

event_time()

Returns the time field from the event structure. Used to determine the time value associated with the event. The macro is passed a pointer to an Event structure.

event_window()

Gets the window in which a particular event took place. The macro is passed a pointer to an Event structure.

event_xevent()

Returns a pointer to the X event structure associated with an XView event structure. The macro is passed a pointer to an Event structure.

event_xevent_type()

Returns the type field of the X event structure. The macro is passed a pointer to an Event structure.

frame_get_rect()

Gets the `rect` of the frame. `x,y` is the upper-left corner of the window coordinate space. Width and height attempt to include the window manager decoration.

```
void
frame_get_rect(frame, rect)
        Frame   frame;
        Rect    *rect;
```

frame_set_rect()

Sets the rect of the frame. `x,y` is the upper-left corner of the window coordinate space. Width and height attempt to include the window manager decoration.

```
void
frame_set_rect(frame, rect)
        Frame   frame;
        Rect    *rect;
```

MENUITEM_SPACE

Used to create a blank menu item.

```
menu_item = xv_create(NULL, MENUITEM_SPACE, NULL);
```

menu_return_item()

Predefined notify procedure which, if given as the value for MENU_NOTIFY_PROC, causes the `menu_done_proc()`, if any, to return the handle of the selected item.

```
Menu_item
menu_return_item(menu, menu_item)
        Menu        menu;
        Menu_item   menu_item;
```

menu_return_value()

Predefined notify procedure which, if given as the value for MENU_ NOTIFY_PROC, causes the `menu_done_proc()`, if any, to return the value of the selected item.

```
Xv_opaque
menu_return_value(menu, menu_item)
        Menu        menu;
        Menu_item   menu_item;
```

menu_show()

Displays the specified menu.

```
void
menu_show(menu, window, event, NULL)
        Menu        menu;
        Xv_Window   window;
        Event       *event;
```

`window` is the handle of the window over which the menu is displayed.
`event` is the event which causes the menu to come up. The final NULL is required for private usage.

notice_prompt()

This is an XView Version 2 compatibility procedure. If you are creating a new notice for XView Version 3, use the NOTICE package. Refer to Chapter 12, *Notices* in the *XView Programming Manual* for details. For more information on notice_prompt(), see Appendix B, *The notice_prompt Function*, in the *XView Programming Manual*.

The function displays the notice and does not return until the user pushes a button or until its trigger or the default action has been seen. It returns a value of NOTICE_FAILED if notice_prompt() fails for any reason; otherwise, it is equivalent to the ordinal value of the button which caused the return (i.e., button actually selected or default button if default action triggered return). The client_window should be the window for which the notice has been generated. This is important for fonts and positioning information. For explicit positioning of the notice, clients should specify NOTICE_FOCUS_XY. The event, if not NULL, will be completely filled in at the time the notice_prompt() returns.

The possible status values that may be returned from this function are:

- The int value passed with every NOTICE_BUTTON attribute.

- NOTICE_YES if a button created with NOTICE_BUTTON_YES is pushed.

- NOTICE_NO if a button created with NOTICE_BUTTON_NO is pushed.

- NOTICE_TRIGGERED if a trigger was used.

- NOTICE_FAILED if the notice failed to pop up.

```
int
notice_prompt(window, event, attributes)
            XV_Window        window;
            Event            *event;
            attribute-list   attributes;
```

notify_default_wait3()

Predefined function you can register with the Notifier via the notify_set_wait3_func() call. Causes the required housekeeping to be performed on the process identified by pid when it dies. See the wait(2) man page for details of the wait and rusage structures.

```
Notify_value
notify_default_wait3(client, pid, status, rusage)
    Notify_client  client;
    int            pid;
    int            *status;
    struct rusage  *rusage;
```

notify_dispatch()

Provided to allow programs which are not notification-based to run in an event-driven environment. Called regularly from within the application's main loop to allow the Notifier to go once around its internal loop and dispatch any pending events.

```
Notify_error
notify_dispatch()
```

notify_do_dispatch()

Enables "implicit dispatching," in which the Notifier dispatches events from within calls to read(2) or select(2).

```
Notify_error
notify_do_dispatch()
```

notify_enable_rpc_svc()

If you use an RPC server that also needs to work with XView, use the XView function notify_enable_rpc_svc(), and do not call svc_run(). This function takes an **int** that tells the notifier whether it should handle RPC requests.

Using this aproach, xv_main_loop() handles incoming RPC requests; dispatching them just as if svc_run() had been called.

If notify_enable_rpc_svc is enabled, the Notifier checks svc_fdset and calls svc_getreqset() if a descriptor is readable (a request is coming in). Performance is affected by the additional call to svc_getreqset().

```
void
notify_enable_rpc_svc(bool)
    int bool;
```

notify_flush_pending()

Notifier removes client and flushes requests for it.

```
void
notify_flush_pending(nclient)
    Notify_client  nclient;
```

See Also: notify_no_dispatch().

notify_interpose_destroy_func()

Interposes destroy_func() in front of client's destroy event handler.

```
Notify_error
notify_interpose_destroy_func(client, destroy_func)
    Notify_client  client;
    Notify_func    destroy_func;
```

client is the handle of the Notifier client in front of which you are interposing.
destroy_func is a notify function to be called before the client's destroy function.
The format for the destroy function is:

```
Notify_value
destroy_func(client, status)
    Notify_client   client;
    Destroy_status  status;
```

notify_interpose_event_func()

Interposes event_func() in front of client's event handler.

```
Notify_error
notify_interpose_event_func(client, event_func, type)
    Notify_client      client;
    Notify_func        event_func;
    Notify_event_type  type;
```

client is the handle of the Notifier client in front of which you are interposing.
event_func is the notify function to be called before the client's event function.
type is either NOTIFY_SAFE or NOTIFY_IMMEDIATE.
The format for the event function is:

```
Notify_value
event_func(client, event, arg, type)
    Notify_client      client;
    Notify_event       event;
    Notify_arg         arg;
    Notify_event_type  type;
```

notify_interpose_exception_func()

Interposes exception_func in front of the client's exception handler.

```
Notify_error
notify_interpose_exception_func(client, exception_func,fd)
    Notify_client  client;
    Notify_func    exception_func;
    int            fd;
```

client is the handle of the Notifier client in front of which you are interposing.
exception_func is the notify function to be called before the client's exception
function.
type is either NOTIFY_SAFE or NOTIFY_IMMEDIATE.
The format for the exception function is:

```
Notify_value
exception_func(client, fd)
    Notify_client  client;
    int            fd;
```

notify_interpose_input_func()

Interposes `input_func` in front of `client`'s Notifier.

```
Notify_error
notify_interpose_input_func(client, input_func, fd)
    Notify_client  client;
    Notify_func    input_func;
    int            fd;
```

`client` is the handle of the Notifier client in front of which you are interposing.
`input_func` is the notify function to be called before the client's input function.
The format for the input function is:

```
Notify_value
input_func(client, fd)
    Notify_client  client;
    int            fd;
```

notify_interpose_itimer_func()

Interposes the `itimer_func` in front of the `client`'s timeout event handler.

```
Notify_error
notify_interpose_itimer_func(client, itimer_func, which)
    Notify_client  client;
    Notify_func    itimer_func;
    int            which;
```

`client` is the handle of the Notifier client in front of which you are interposing.
`itimer_func` is the notify function to be called before the client's timeout handler.
`which` is either `ITIMER_REAL` or `ITIMER_VIRTUAL`.
The format for the itimer function is:

```
Notify_value
itimer_func(client, which)
    Notify_client  client;
    int            which;
```

notify_interpose_output_func()

Interposes `output_func` in front of `client`'s Notifier.

```
Notify_error
notify_interpose_output_func(client, output_func, fd)
    Notify_client  client;
    Notify_func    output_func;
    int            fd;
```

`client` is the handle of the Notifier client in front of which you are interposing.
`output_func` is the notify function to be called before the client's output function.
The format for the output function is:

```
Notify_value
output_func(client, fd)
    Notify_client  client;
    int            fd;
```

notify_interpose_signal_func()

Interposes the `signal_func()` in front of the signal event handler.

```
Notify_error
notify_interpose_signal_func(client, signal_func,
                                      signal, mode)
    Notify_client   client;
    Notify_func     signal_func;
    int             signal;
    int             mode;
```

`client` is the handle of the Notifier client in front of which you are interposing.
`signal_func` is the notify function to be called before the client's signal handler.
`signal` is the UNIX software interrupt.
`mode` is either `NOTIFY_ASYNC` or `NOTIFY_SYNC`.
The format for the signal function is:

```
Notify_value
signal_func(client, signal, mode)
    Notify_client   client;
    int             signal;
    int             mode;
```

notify_interpose_wait3_func()

Interposes the `wait3_func` in front of the Notifier.

```
Notify_error
notify_interpose_wait3_func(client, wait3_func, pid)
    Notify_client   client;
    Notify_func     wait3_func;
    int             pid;
```

`client` is the handle of the Notifier client in front of which you are interposing.
`wait3_func` is the notify function to be called before the client's wait3 function.
The format for the wait3 function on BSD-based systems is:

```
Notify_value
wait3_func(client, pid, status, rusage)
    Notify_client   client;
    int             pid;
    union wait      *status;
    struct rusage   *rusage;
```

The format for the wait3 function on SYSV-based systems is:

```
Notify_value
wait3_func(client, pid, status, rusage)
    Notify_client   client;
    int             pid;
    int             *status;
    struct rusage   *rusage;
```

notify_itimer_value()

Returns the current state of an interval timer for `client` in the structure pointed to by `value`. The `which` parameter is either `ITIMER_REAL` or `ITIMER_VIRTUAL`.

```
Notify_error
notify_itimer_value(client, which, value)
    Notify_client      client;
    int                which;
    struct itimerval   *value;
```

notify_next_destroy_func()

Calls the next destroy event handler for `client`.

```
Notify_value
notify_next_destroy_func(client, status)
    Notify_client      client;
    Destroy_status     status;
```

`status` is one of:

```
DESTROY_PROCESS_DEATH
DESTROY_CHECKING
DESTROY_CLEANUP
DESTROY_SAVE_YOURSELF
```

notify_next_event_func()

Calls the next event handler for `client`.

```
Notify_value
notify_next_event_func(client, event, arg, type)
    Notify_client      client;
    Event              *event;
    Notify_arg         arg;
    Notify_event_type  type;
```

`type` is either `NOTIFY_SAFE` or `NOTIFY_IMMEDIATE`.

notify_no_dispatch()

Prevents the Notifier from dispatching events from within the call to `read` (2) or `select` (2).

```
Notify_error
notify_no_dispatch()
```

See Also: `notify_do_dispatch()`.

notify_perror()

Analogous to the UNIX `perror` (3) system call.
`s` is printed to `stderr`, followed by a terse description of `notify_errno()`.

```
void
notify_perror(s)
    char *s;
```

notify_set_destroy_func()

Registers `destroy_func()` with the Notifier. `destroy_func()` is called when a destroy event is posted to `client` or when the process receives a `SIGTERM` signal.

```
Notify_func
notify_set_destroy_func(client, destroy_func)
    Notify_client   client;
    Notify_func     destroy_func;
```

The format for the destroy function is:

```
Notify_value
destroy_func(client, status)
    Notify_client   client;
    Destroy_status  status;
```

notify_set_event_func()

Registers the event handler `event_func()` with the Notifier.

```
Notify_error
notify_set_event_func(client, event_func, type)
    Notify_client     client;
    Notify_func       event_func;
    Notify_event_type type;
```

`type` is either `NOTIFY_SAFE` or `NOTIFY_IMMEDIATE`.

The format for the event function is:

```
Notify_value
event_func(client, event, arg, type)
    Notify_client     client;
    Notify_event      event;
    Notify_arg        arg;
    Notify_event_type type;
```

notify_set_exception_func()

Registers the exception handler `exception_func()` with the Notifier. The only known devices that generate exceptions at this time are stream-based socket connections when an out-of-band byte is available.

```
Notify_func
notify_set_exception_func(client, exception_func, fd)
    Notify_client   client;
    Notify_func     exception_func;
    int             fd;
```

The format for the exception function is:

```
Notify_value
exception_func(client, fd)
    Notify_client   client;
    int             fd;
```

notify_set_input_func()

Registers `input_func()` with the Notifier. `input_func()` will be called whenever there is input pending on `fd`.

```
Notify_func
notify_set_input_func(client, input_func, fd)
    Notify_client client;
    Notify_func   input_func;
    int           fd;
```

The format for the input function is:

```
Notify_value
exception_func(client, fd)
    Notify_client client;
    int           fd;
```

notify_set_itimer_func()

Registers the timeout event handler `itimer_func()` with the Notifier.

```
Notify_func
notify_set_itimer_func(client, itimer_func, which,
                                value, ovalue)
    Notify_client      client;
    Notify_func        itmer_func;
    int                which;
    struct itimerval   *value, *ovalue;
```

The semantics of `which`, `value`, and `ovalue` parallel the arguments to
`setitimer(2)`.

`which` is either `ITIMER_REAL` or `ITIMER_VIRTUAL`.

The format for the itimer function is:

```
Notify_value
itimer_func(client, which)
    Notify_client  client;
    int            which;
```

notify_set_output_func()

Registers `output_func()` with the Notifier. `output_func()` will be called
whenever output has been completed on `fd`.

```
Notify_func
notify_set_output_func(client, output_func, fd)
    Notify_client client;
    Notify_func   output_func;
    int           fd;
```

The format for the output function is:

```
Notify_value
exception_func(client, fd)
    Notify_client client;
    int           fd;
```

notify_set_signal_func()

Registers the signal event handler `signal_func()` with the Notifier. `signal_func()` will be called whenever `signal` is caught by the Notifier. `when` can be either `NOTIFY_SYNC` or `NOTIFY_ASYNC`.

Calling `notify_set_signal_func()` with a `NULL` in the place of the `signal_func()` turns off checking for that signal for that client.

```
Notify_func
notify_set_signal_func(client, signal_func, signal, when)
    Notify_client        client;
    Notify_func          signal_func;
    int                  signal;
    Notify_signal_mode   when;
```

The format for the `signal_func` function is:

```
Notify_value
signal_func(client, sig, mode)
    Notify_client  client;
    int            sig;
    int            mode;
```

notify_set_wait3_func()

Registers the function `wait3_func()` with the Notifier. The registered function is called after `client`'s process identified by `pid` dies. To do the minimum processing, register the predefined function `notify_default_wait3()`.

```
Notify_func
notify_set_wait3_func(client, wait3_func, pid)
    Notify_client  client;
    Notify_func    wait3_func;
    int            pid;
```

The format for the wait3 function on BSD-based systems is:

```
Notify_value
wait3_func(client, pid, status, rusage)
    Notify_client   client;
    int             pid;
    union wait      *status;
    struct rusage   *rusage;
```

The format for the wait3 function on SYSV-based systems is:

```
Notify_value
wait3_func(client, pid, status, rusage)
    Notify_client   client;
    int             pid;
    int             *status;
    struct rusage   *rusage;
```

notify_start()

Begins dispatching of events by the Notifier.

```
Notify_error
notify_start()
```

notify_stop()

Terminates dispatching of events by the Notifier.

```
Notify_error
notify_stop()
```

notify_veto_destroy()

Called from within a destroy event handler when status is DESTROY_CHECKING and the application does not want to be destroyed.

```
Notify_error
notify_veto_destroy(client)
    Notify_client client;
```

OPENWIN_EACH_VIEW()

Macro providing built-in support for iteration across all the views contained in a given openwin. Allows you to perform operations on multiple views for which there are no openwin attributes.

OPENWIN_END_EACH

Closes the loop started by the macro OPENWIN_EACH_VIEW(). These macros are meant to be used together, as in the following example:

```
OPENWIN_EACH_VIEW(openwin, view)
        Openwin         openwin;
        Openwin_item    item;
        xv_set(openwin, attributes, 0);
OPENWIN_END_EACH;
```

panel_advance_caret()

Advances the input focus to the next item that can accept input focus. If on the last input focus, rotate back to the first. Returns the new caret item or NULL if there are no input focus items.

```
Panel_item
panel_advance_caret(panel)
        Panel     panel;
```

panel_backup_caret()

Backs the caret up to the previous input focus item. If already on the first input focus item, rotate back to the last. Returns the new caret item or NULL if there are no input focus items.

```
Panel_item
panel_backup_caret(panel)
        Panel     panel;
```

PANEL_CHECK_BOX

Macro for "PANEL_TOGGLE, PANEL_FEEDBACK, PANEL_MARK." Creates non-exclusive choice item(s) with check_boxes instead of boxes.

```
xv_create(panel, PANEL_CHECK_BOX, NULL);
```

PANEL_CHECK_BOX expands to:

```
PANEL_TOGGLE,
PANEL_FEEDBACK,      PANEL_MARK
```

To use an ATTR_LIST argument, the ATTR_LIST must be the first attribute in an attribute-value list. See PANEL_CHOICE_STACK for an example.

PANEL_CHOICE_STACK

Macro for "PANEL_CHOICE, PANEL_DISPLAY_LEVEL, PANEL_CURRENT." Creates an OPEN LOOK abbreviated choice menu button.

```
xv_create(panel, PANEL_CHOICE_STACK, NULL);
```

PANEL_CHOICE_STACK expands to:

```
PANEL_CHOICE,
PANEL_DISPLAY_LEVEL,      PANEL_CURRENT
```

To use an ATTR_LIST argument, the ATTR_LIST must be the first attribute in an attribute-value list. You need to include an explicit PANEL_CHOICE, rather than the PANEL_CHOICE_STACK attribute. For example,

```
xv_create(owner, PANEL_CHOICE,
    ATTR_LIST, at,
     PANEL_DISPLAY_LEVEL,PANEL_CURRENT,
     .....,
     NULL);
```

PANEL_EACH_ITEM()

Macro to iterate over each item in a panel. The corresponding macro panel_end_each closes the loop opened by PANEL_EACH_ITEM().

```
PANEL_EACH_ITEM(panel, item)
        Panel        panel;
        Panel_item   item;
```

PANEL_END_EACH

Closes the loop started by PANEL_EACH_ITEM(). Same usage as OPENWIN_EACH_VIEW().

panel_paint()

Paints an item or an entire panel. `paint_behavior` can be either `PANEL_CLEAR`, which causes the area occupied by the panel or item to be cleared prior to painting, or `PANEL_NO_CLEAR`.

```
int
panel_paint(panel_object, paint_behavior)
        Xv_object         panel_object;
        Panel_setting     paint_behavior;
```

Note that `panel_object` may be a `PANEL` or a `PANEL_ITEM`. If `panel_object` does not exist, or `panel_paint()` is called with an invalid `paint_behavior` value, the function returns `XV_ERROR`, otherwise, it returns `XV_OK`.

panel_text_notify()

Default notify procedure for panel text items. Causes caret to advance on Return or Tab, caret to back up on Shift-Return or Shift-Tab, printable characters to be inserted into item's value, and all other characters to be discarded.

```
Panel_setting
panel_text_notify(item, event)
        Panel_item    item
        Event         *event
```

Returns `PANEL_NEXT`, `PANEL_PREVIOUS`, `PANEL_INSERT`, or `PANEL_NONE`, respectively.

PANEL_TOGGLE

Macro for "`PANEL_CHOICE, PANEL_CHOOSE_ONE, FALSE.`" Used to create non-exclusive choice item(s).

```
xv_create(panel, PANEL_TOGGLE, NULL);
```

`PANEL_TOGGLE` expands to:

```
PANEL_CHOICE,
PANEL_CHOOSE_ONE,     FALSE
```

To use an `ATTR_LIST` argument, the `ATTR_LIST` must be the first attribute in an attribute-value list. See `PANEL_CHOICE_STACK` for an example.

rect_borderadjust()

Used to adjust the borders. This macro takes a `rect` pointer and an `int`. This macro is defined as follows:

```
#define rect_borderadjust(r,m)                                    \
        { (r)->r_width+=(m)+(m); (r)->r_height+=(m)+(m); }
```

rect_bottom()

Takes a `rect` pointer and returns the position of the bottom of the `rect`. This macro is defined as follows:

```
#define   rect_bottom(rect)    ((rect)->r_top+(rect)->r_height-1)
```

rect_construct()

Constructs a `rect` based on the values specified. It takes a `rect` pointer and four `int` arguments. This macro is defined as follows:

```
#define rect_construct(r,x,y,w,h) \
    {(r)->r_left=(x);(r)->r_top=(y);(r)->r_width=(w);(r)->r_height=(h);}
```

rect_equal()

Compares two `rect` pointers and returns TRUE if all dimensions are equal. This macro is defined as follows:

```
#define rect_equal(r1,r2) \
        ((r1)->r_left=^=(r2)->r_left && (r1)->r_width=^=(r2)->r_width && \
        (r1)->r_top=^=(r2)->r_top && (r1)->r_height=^=(r2)->r_height)
```

rect_includespoint()

Returns TRUE if specified coordinates are within specified `rect`. It takes a `rect` pointer and two integers (x and y coordinates). This macro is defined as follows:

```
#define rect_includespoint(r,x,y) \
        ((x) >= (r)->r_left && (y) >= (r)->r_top && \
        (x)<(r)->r_left+(r)->r_width && (y)<(r)->r_top+(r)->r_height)
```

rect_includesrect()

Determines whether or not a specified `rect` is contained in another. It takes two `rect` pointers. This macro is defined as follows:

```
#define rect_includesrect(r1, r2) \
        ((r1)->r_left <= (r2)->r_left && (r1)->r_top <= (r2)->r_top && \
        (r1)->r_left+(r1)->r_width >= (r2)->r_left+(r2)->r_width && \
        (r1)->r_top+(r1)->r_height >= (r2)->r_top+(r2)->r_height)
```

rect_intersectsrect()

Determines whether or not one `rect` intersects another. It takes two `rect` pointers. This macro is defined as follows:

```
#define rect_intersectsrect(r1,r2) \
        ((r1)->r_left<(r2)->r_left+(r2)->r_width && \
        (r1)->r_top<(r2)->r_top+(r2)->r_height && \
        (r2)->r_left<(r1)->r_left+(r1)->r_width && \
        (r2)->r_top<(r1)->r_top+(r1)->r_height)
```

rect_isnull()

Takes a `rect` pointer and returns TRUE if either the width or the height of the rect is 0. Otherwise returns FALSE. This macro is defined as follows:

```
#define rect_isnull(r)      ((r)->r_width =^= 0 || (r)->r_height =^= 0
```

rect_marginadjust()

Adjusts the margins in a `rect`. It takes a `rect` pointer and an integer. This macro is defined as follows:

```
#define rect_marginadjust(r,m)                              \
        { (r)->r_left-=(m);(r)->r_top-=(m);                 \
          (r)->r_width+=(m)+(m);(r)->r_height+=(m)+(m);}
```

rect_passtochild()

Takes two integers (x and y coordinates) and a `rect` pointer. This macro is defined as follows:

```
#define    rect_passtochild(x,y,rect) \
      { (rect)->r_left=(rect)->r_left-(x); (rect)->r_top=(rect)->r_top-(y);}
```

rect_passtoparent()

Takes two integers (x and y coordinates) and a `rect` pointer. This macro is defined as follows:

```
#define    rect_passtoparent(x,y,rect) \
      { (rect)->r_left=(rect)->r_left+(x); (rect)->r_top=(rect)->r_top+(y);}
```

rect_print()

Takes a `rect` pointer and prints the rectangle on `stderr`.

```
#define rect_print(rect)                                    \
   (void)fprintf(stderr,"[left: %d, top: %d, width: %d, height: %d]\n",  \
        (rect)->r_left, (rect)->r_top, (rect)->r_width, (rect)->r_height)
```

rect_right()

Takes a `rect` pointer and returns the position of the right edge of the `rect`. This macro is defined as follows:

```
#define    rect_right(rect)      ((rect)->r_left+(rect)->r_width-1)
```

rect_sizes_differ()

Takes two `rect` pointers. If all dimensions are equal, it returns FALSE, if not it returns TRUE. This macro is defined as follows:

```
#define rect_sizes_differ(r1, r2) \
    ((r1)->r_width != (r2)->r_width || (r1)->r_height != (r2)->r_height)
```

SCROLLABLE_PANEL

Used to create a scrollbar panel. To add a scrollbar after creating the panel, create a scrollbar with the panel as its parent. For example:

```
panel = xv_create(frame, SCROLLABLE_PANEL, NULL);
xv_create(panel, SCROLLBAR, NULL);
```

Note: Scrollable panels are not inherently OPEN LOOK-compliant.

scrollbar_paint()

Repaints all portions of the scrollbar.

```
void
scrollbar_paint(scrollbar)
    Scrollbar    scrollbar;
```

selection_*

Appendix B, *Selection Compatibility Procedures*, describes the selection_* procedures. The selection_ procedures provide compatibility for applications using selections created prior to XView Version 3. If you are creating a new application, refer to Chapter 18, *Selections*, in the *XView Programming Manual*.

sel_convert_proc()

Default selection convert procedure provided by XView Version 3 for use with the SELECTION_OWNER Package. This procedure allows the selection owner to communicate with the selection requestor.

```
int
sel_convert_proc(sel_owner, type, data, length, format)
    Selection_owner  sel_owner;
    Atom             *type;       /* Input/Output */
    Xv_opaque        *data;
    unsigned long    *length;     /* Output */
    int              *format;
```

sel_owner is the selection owner. *type* is the form data should be converted to. *data* is a pointer to the reply buffer. *length* is a pointer to the length of the reply buffer. *format* is a pointer to an integer representing the number of bits in a single data member in reply buffer.

Returns TRUE if completed successfully, FALSE if it does not complete successfully.

sel_post_req()

This procedure is used to send a non-blocking request to the selection owner. The application's reply procedure is called by the SELECTION package when the selection owner has sent its reply.

```
int
sel_post_req( sel )
    Selection_requestor  sel;
```

sel is the selection requestor. Returns XV_OK if it successfully sends the request, otherwise it returns XV_ERROR. When no reply procedure is defined, XV_ERROR is returned (see the description for the attribute SEL_REPLY_PROC).

Procedures and Macros

textsw_add_mark()

Adds a new mark at `position`. `flags` can be either `TEXTSW_MARK_ DEFAULTS` or `TEXTSW_MARK_MOVE_AT_INSERT`.

```
Textsw_mark
textsw_add_mark(textsw, position, flags)
        Textsw              textsw;
        Textsw_index        position;
        unsigned            flags;
```

textsw_append_file_name()

Returns 0 if `textsw` is editing a file and, if so, appends the name of the file at the end of `name`.

```
int
textsw_append_file_name(textsw, name)
        Textsw              textsw;
        char                *name;
```

textsw_delete()

Returns 0 if the operation fails. Removes the span of characters beginning with `first` and ending one before `last_plus_one`.

```
Textsw_index
textsw_delete(textsw, first, last_plus_one)
        Textsw              textsw;
        Textsw_index        first, last_plus_one;
```

textsw_edit()

Returns 0 if the operation fails. Erases a character, a word or a line, depending on whether `unit` is `SELN_LEVEL_FIRST` or `SELN_LEVEL_LINE`. If `direction` is 0, characters after the insertion point are affected; otherwise, characters before the insertion point are affected. The operation will be done `count` times.

```
Textsw_index
textsw_edit(textsw, unit, count, direction)
        Textsw              textsw;
        unsigned            unit, count, direction;
```

textsw_erase()

Returns 0 if the operation fails. Equivalent to `textsw_delete()` but does not affect the global shelf.

```
Textsw_index
textsw_erase(textsw, first, last_plus_one)
        Textsw              textsw;
        Textsw_index        first, last_plus_one;
```

textsw_file_lines_visible()

Fills in `top` and `bottom` with the file line indices of the first and last file lines being displayed in `textsw`.

```
void
textsw_file_lines_visible(textsw, top, bottom)
        Textsw    textsw;
        int       *top, *bottom;
```

textsw_find_bytes()

Beginning at the position addressed by `first`, searches for the pattern specified by `buf` of length `buf_len`. Searches forward if flags is 0, else searches backward. Returns −1 if no match, else matching span placed in indices addressed by `first` and `last_plus_one`.

```
int
textsw_find_bytes(
        textsw, first, last_plus_one, buf, buf_len, flags)
                Textsw          textsw;
                Textsw_index    *first, *last_plus_one;
                char            *buf;
                unsigned        buf_len, flags;
```

textsw_find_mark()

Returns the current position of `mark`. If this operation fails, it will return `TEXTSW_INFINITY`.

```
Textsw_index
textsw_find_mark(textsw, mark)
        Textsw        textsw;
        Textsw_mark   mark;
```

textsw_first()

Returns the first `textsw` view.

```
Textsw
textsw_first(textsw)
        Textsw    textsw;
```

textsw_index_for_file_line()

Returns the character index for the first character in the line given by `line`. If this operation fails, it will return `TEXTSW_CANNOT_SET`.

```
Textsw_index
textsw_index_for_file_line(textsw, line)
        Textsw    textsw;
        int       line;
```

textsw_insert()

Inserts characters in `buf` into `textsw` at the current insertion point. The number of characters actually inserted is returned. This will equal `buf_len` unless there was a memory allocation failure. If there was a failure, it returns `NULL`.

```
Textsw_index
textsw_insert(textsw, buf, buf_len)
        Textsw    textsw;
        char      *buf;
        int       buf_len;
```

textsw_match_bytes()

Searches for a block of text in the `textsw`'s contents; ends with characters matching `end_sym`. This function places the starting index of the matching block in `first` and its ending index in `last`.

```
int
textsw_match_bytes(
        textsw, first, last_plus_one, start_sym,
        start_sym_len, end_sym, end_sym_len, field_flag)
            Textsw            textsw;
            Textsw_index      *first, *last_plus_one;
            char              *start_sym, *end_sym;
            int               start_sym_len, end_sym_len;
            unsigned          field_flag;
```

textsw_next()

Returns the next view in the set of `textsw` views.

```
Textsw
textsw_next(textsw)
        Textsw    textsw;
```

textsw_normalize_view()

Repositions the text so that the character at `position` is visible and at the top of the subwindow.

```
void
textsw_normalize_view(textsw, position)
        Textsw          textsw;
        Textsw_index    position;
```

textsw_possibly_normalize()

If the character at `position` is already visible, this function does nothing. If it is not visible, it repositions the text so that it is visible and at the top of the subwindow.

```
void
textsw_possibly_normalize(textsw, position)
        Textsw              textsw;
        Textsw_index        position;
```

textsw_remove_mark()

Removes an existing mark from `textsw`.

```
void
textsw_remove_mark(textsw, mark)
        Textsw          textsw;
        Textsw_mark     mark;
```

textsw_replace_bytes()

Replaces the character span from `first` to `last_plus_one` with the characters in `buf`. The return value is the number of bytes inserted or deleted. The number is positive if bytes are inserted, negative if bytes are deleted. (The number is also negative if the original string is longer than the one that replaces it.) If this operation fails, it will return a value of NULL.

```
Textsw_index
textsw_replace_bytes(
        textsw, first, last_plus_onebuf, buf_len)
                Textsw          textsw;
                Textsw_index    first;
                Textsw_index    last_plus_one;
                char            *buf;
                unsigned        buf_len;
```

textsw_reset()

Discards edits performed on the contents of `textsw`. If needed, a message box will be displayed at `x,y`.

```
void
textsw_reset(textsw, x, y)
        Textsw  textsw;
        int     x, y;
```

textsw_save()

Saves any edits made to the file currently loaded into `textsw`. If needed, a message box will be displayed at `x,y`.

```
unsigned
textsw_save(textsw, x, y)
        Textsw  textsw;
        int     x, y;
```

textsw_screen_line_count()

Returns the number of screen lines in `textsw`.

```
int
textsw_screen_line_count(textsw)
        Textsw      textsw;
```

textsw_scroll_lines()

Moves the text up or down by `count` lines. If `count` is positive, then the text is scrolled up on the screen. If negative, the text is scrolled down (backward in the file).

```
void
textsw_scroll_lines(textsw, count)
        Textsw   textsw;
        int      count;
```

textsw_set_selection()

Sets the selection to begin at `first` and includes all characters up to `last_plus_one`. A `type` value of 1 indicates primary selection, 2 indicates secondary selection.

```
void
textsw_set_selection(textsw, first, last_plus_one, type)
        Textsw        textsw;
        Textsw_index  first, last_plus_one;
        unsigned      type;
```

textsw_store_file()

Stores the contents of `textsw` to the file named by `filename`. If needed, a message box will be displayed at `x,y`.

```
unsigned
textsw_store_file(textsw, filename, x, y)
        Textsw   textsw;
        char     *filename;
        int      x, y;
```

ttysw_input()

Appends `len` number of characters from `buf` onto `tty`'s input queue. It returns the number of characters accepted.

```
int
ttysw_input(tty, buf, len)
        Tty    tty;
        char   *buf;
        int    len;
```

ttysw_output()

Appends `len` number of characters from `buf` onto `tty`'s output queue; it sends them through the terminal emulator to the TTY. It returns the number of characters accepted.

```
int
ttysw_output(tty, buf, len)
        Tty    tty;
        char   *buf;
        int    len;
```

window_done()

Destroys the entire hierarchy to which `win` belongs.

```
int
window_done(win)
        Xv_Window  win;
```

window_fit()

This macro causes `win` to fit its contents in the dimensions specified with `WIN_FIT_HEIGHT` and `WIN_FIT_WIDTH`. It is defined as:

```
xv_set(win, WIN_FIT_HEIGHT, WIN_FIT_WIDTH, 0, NULL)
```

window_fit_height()

Causes `win` to fit its contents in the height specified with `WIN_FIT_HEIGHT`. The macro is defined as:

```
xv_set(win, WIN_FIT_HEIGHT, 0, NULL)
```

window_fit_width()

Causes `win` to fit its contents in the width specified with `WIN_FIT_WIDTH`. The macro is defined as:

```
xv_set(win, WIN_FIT_WIDTH, 0, NULL)
```

window_read_event()

Reads the next input event for `window`. In case of error, sets the global variable `errno` and returns −1.

```
int
window_read_event(window, event)
        Xv_window  window;
        Event      *event;
```

wmgr_bottom()

This procedure is a SunView Compatibility procedure. Sets stackmode to `Below` in `XConfigureWindow`.

```
void
wmgr_bottom(frame)
        Frame    frame;
```

wmgr_changelevel()

This procedure is a SunView Compatibility procedure. Sets stackmode in `XConfigureWindow`.

```
void
wmgr_changelevel(window,parent,top)
        Xv_Window  window;
        int        parent;
        int        top;
```

wmgr_close()

Sets wmhints.initial_state to ICONICSTATE.

```
void
wmgr_close(frame)
        Frame   frame;
```

wmgr_completechangerect()

Calls XConfigureWindow with a new rect.

```
void
wmgr_completechangerect(window, rectnew, rectoriginal,
        parentprleft, parentprtop)
                Xv_window   window;
                Rect        *rectnew, *rectoriginal;
                int         parentprleft, parentprtop;
```

wmgr_open()

Sets wmhints.initial_state to NORMALSTATE.

```
void
wmgr_open(frame)
        Frame   frame;
```

wmgr_refreshwindow()

Calls XConfigureWindow repeatedly.

```
void
wmgr_refreshwindow(window)
        Xv_window   window;
```

wmgr_top()

Sets stackmode to Above in XConfigureWindow.

```
void
wmgr_top(frame)
        Frame   frame;
```

xv_col()

Returns an integer representing the number of pixels, excluding the left margin of the window. This may be used in conjunction with a panel's WIN_COL_GAG.

```
int
xv_col(window, column)
        Xv_Window   window;
        int         column;
```

xv_cols()

Returns an integer representing the number of pixels, including the left margin of the window.

```
int
xv_cols(window, columns)
        Xv_Window   window;
        int         columns;
```

xv_create()

To create *any* XView object, call the generic procedure `xv_create`. This procedure will return a handle to some XView object. It takes as parameters the owner of the object being created, the type of object to create, and a list of attributes. The attribute list must terminate with a `NULL`. In specifying the type, you must use the name of some XView package. That name must be in all capital letters to distinguish it from the corresponding data type. The package is the name of the package to which the object you wish to create belongs.

The procedure `xv_create()` returns either the handle for the new object or `XV_NULL` if the attempt at object creation fails.

```
Xv_opaque
xv_create(owner, package, attributes)
        Xv_object        owner;
        Xv_pkg          *package;
        attribute-list   attributes;
```

xv_destroy()

To destroy an XView object and any subframes owned by that object, use the procedure `xv_destroy()`. It will return either `XV_ERROR` or `XV_OK`.

```
int
xv_destroy(object)
        Xv_object   object;
```

XV_DISPLAY_FROM_WINDOW()

Macro to get at the handle of the display structure from a window object.

```
Xv_opaque
XV_DISPLAY_FROM_WINDOW(window)
        Xv_Window   window;
```

xv_error()

Is called by the XView internals in the event of an error.

```
char *
xv_error(object, attributes)
        Xv_opaque        object;
        attribute-list   attributes;
```

xv_error_format()

This function calls a pointer to a static `char *` describing the XView error that has occurred. It should be copied into your buffer if you wish to retain the value since subsequent calls overwrite the contents.

```
char *
xv_error_format(object, avlist)
        Xv_object    object;
        Attr_avlist  avlist;
```

xv_find()

To find any XView object, use the procedure `xv_find()`. If the object is not found, `xv_find` will automatically attempt to create it.

```
Xv_opaque
xv_find(owner, package, attributes)
        Xv_object              owner;
        Xv_pkg                 *package;
        attribute-list         attributes;
```

xv_get()

To get the value of any single attribute of *any* XView object, use the procedure `xv_get()`.

```
Xv_opaque
xv_get(object, attribute)
        Xv_object              object;
        attribute-list         attributes;
```

The procedure returns 0 for failure. As a result, you cannot detect errors when retrieving the values of attributes which might return 0 as a valid value. Note that, although you can supply XV_NULL as the owner when you create a new object with `xv_create`, you *must* provide the object when asking for the value of an attribute.

For example, you cannot just ask for:

```
xv_get(XV_NULL, XV_FONT)
```

to determine the default font, but you can ask for the font associated with a particular screen, as in:

```
xv_get(Screen1, XV_FONT)
```

Some attributes require a screen or server to be supplied to `xv_get()`. For such attributes, you should ask any window you think should be on the same screen what to identify as its screen or server, using the attributes XV_SCREEN and XV_SERVER.

If you know your application only runs on a single screen, you can use the global values `xv_default_server` and `xv_default_screen` or you can ask the defaults database what the server is.

xv_init()

This procedure performs many tasks including: opening the connection to the server, initializing the Notifier, and initializing the Resource Manager database (see Chapter 17, *Resources*, in the *XView Programming Manual*). By default xv_init() opens a connection to the server described by the DISPLAY environment variable. The server connections may be changed using appropriate command-line attribute-value pairs. No matter which server is used, xv_init() returns a handle to that server object. For further information concerning use with servers, see Chapter 15, *Nonvisual Objects*, in the *XView Programming Manual*.

```
int
main(argc, argv)
        int     argc;
        char    **argv:
{
/* initialization/declarations */
            .
            .
            .
    (void)xv_init(XV_INIT_ARGC_PTR_ARGV, &argc, argv, 0);
    frame = xv_create(NULL, FRAME, FRAME_LABEL, "foo", 0);
}
```

xv_row()

Returns an integer representing the number of pixels, excluding the top margin of the window. Used in conjunction with a panel's WIN_ROW_GAP.

```
int
xv_row(window, row)
        Xv_Window   window
        int         row;
```

xv_rows()

Returns an integer representing the number of pixels, including the top margin of the window.

```
int
xv_rows(window, rows)
        Xv_Window   window
        int         rows;
```

XV_SCREEN_FROM_WINDOW()

Macro to return the handle to the screen object from the window object.

```
Xv_screen
XV_SCREEN_FROM_WINDOW(window)
        Xv_Window   window;
```

xv_send_message()

Lets two separate processes communicate with each other. You can specify the addressee field either with one of the constants XV_POINTER_WINDOW or XV_FOCUS_WINDOW or with the window's XID, if known. If the addressee is XV_POINTER, then the message is sent to the window that the pointer is in. If the addressee is XV_FOCUS_WINDOW, then the message is sent to the window that currently has the focus, regardless of the pointer position. If the addressee is a window's XID, then the message is sent to the window with the corresponding ID.

```
void
xv_send_message(
        window, addressee, msg_type, format, data, len)
        Xv_object   window;
        Xv_opaque   addressee;
        char        *msg_type;
        int         format;
        Xv_opaque   *data;
        int         len;
```

msg_type is a pointer to a string specifying the property you want the Atom for.
format is the number of bits of a single data member (8,16, or 32).
data is a pointer to the data to send.
len is the number of bytes of data to send.

XV_SERVER_FROM_WINDOW()

Macro returns the handle to the server object from a window object.

```
Xv_opaque
XV_SERVER_FROM_WINDOW(window)
        Xv_Window   window;
```

xv_set()

To set the value of one or more attributes of *any* XView object, call the procedure xv_set with the handle to the object whose attributes you wish to set and a list of attribute-value pairs terminating in a NULL.

```
Xv_object
Xv_set(owner, type, attributes)
        Xv_object        owner;
        vu type          *type;
        attribute-list   attributes;
```

The procedure xv_set() returns XV_OK if it succeeds; otherwise, it returns an error code indicating that the attribute on which it ran encountered problems.

xv_super_set_avlist()

This function handles the parsing of attributes that are generic to a package's super set.

```
Xv_public     Xv_opaque
xv_super_set_avlist(object, pkg, avlist)
    register Xv_opaque   object;
    register Xv_pkg      *pkg;
    Attr_avlist          avlist;
```

xv_unique_key()

Generates a key for use with XV_KEY_DATA.

Warning: The uniqueness of any particular key is *not* guaranteed since the value returned is generated simply by incrementing a pre-defined "unique" value.

```
int
xv_unique_key()
```

xv_usage()

Prints a list of toolkit's generic command-line arguments.

```
void
xv_usage(app_name)
    char *app_name;
```

See Also: XV_USAGE_PROC

xv_window_loop()

The function `xv_window_loop()` maps the frame passed as an argument and makes other frames and windows in the application "deaf." This is similar to FRAME_BUSY except that the cursor does not change to a stopwatch and the frame header does not show the gray "busy" pattern. `xv_window_loop()` does not lock the screen.

```
Xv_opaque
xv_window_loop(frame)
    Frame       frame;
```

The frame passed into `xv_window_loop()` can have more than one subwindow of any type (this was a restriction with SunView's `window_loop()` function).

`xv_window_loop()` does not return until a call to `xv_window_return()`.

```
void
xv_window_return(return_val)
    Xv_opaque   return_val;
```

This presumably occurs in a callback originating from a button (for example) on the frame. The return value passed into `xv_window_return()` is the value returned by `xv_window_loop()`. Since the screen is *not* locked when `xv_window_loop()` is active, the user might be able to dismiss the frame using the window manager. Doing this causes the application to hang since `xv_window_return()` is not called. To avoid this behavior, you need to attach a destroy procedure to the frame. The destroy procedure should call `xv_window_return()`.

xv_window_return()

See the procedure `xv_window_loop()`.

4

Data Types

Section 4, Data Types, *lists the data types defined by XView.*

4
Data Types

The following is a list of XView data types and their descriptions.

`Canvas`	Handle to an opaque structure that describes a canvas.
`Canvas_attribute`	One of the canvas attributes (CANVAS_*).
`Xv_Cursor`	Handle to an opaque structure that describes a cursor.
`Xv_Cursor_attribute`	One of the cursor attributes (CURSOR_*).

`Destroy_status`	Enumeration:
	    DESTROY_PROCESS_DEATH
	    DESTROY_CHECKING
	    DESTROY_CLEANUP
	    DESTROY_SAVE_YOURSELF

`Dnd`	Handle to an opaque structure that describes a drag and drop object.

`DndDragType`	Enumeration:
	    DND_MOVE=0
	    DND_COPY

`Xv_drag_drop`	Handle to an opaque structure that describes a drag and drop object.
`Drop_site_item`	Handle to an opaque structure that describes a drop site.
`Xv_drop_site`	Handle to an opaque structure that describes a drop site.

Event   The structure that describes an input event. Use macros for
                               access:

```
typedef struct inputevent {
  short  ie_code;
           /* input code */
  short  ie_flags;
  short  ie_shiftmask;
           /* input code shift state */
  short  ie_locx, ie_locy;
           /* locator (usually a mouse) position */
  struct timeval ie_time;
           /* time  of event */
  short  action;
           /* keymapped version of ie_code */
  Xv_object ie_win;
           /* window the event is directed to */
  char   *ie_string;
           /* String returned from XLookupString
            * or language translation string.  */
  XEvent *ie_xevent;
           /* pointer to actual XEvent struct */
} Event;
```


Xv_Font   Pointer to an opaque structure that describes a font.

Xv_Font_attribute   One of the font attributes (FONT_*).

Frame   Pointer to an opaque structure that describes a frame.

Frame_attribute   One of the frame attributes (FRAME_*).

Fullscreen   Handle to an opaque structure that describes a fullscreen.

Fullscreen_attribute
                               One of the fullscreen attributes (FULLSCREEN_*).

Icon   Handle to an opaque structure that describes a icon.

Icon_attribute   One of the icon attributes (ICON_*).

Inputmask   Mask specifying which input events a window will receive.

Menu   Pointer to an opaque structure that describes a menu.

Menu_attribute   One of the menu attributes (MENU_*).

`Menu_generate`	Enumerated type for the `operation` parameter passed to generate procs.
`Xv_notice`	Handle to an opaque structure that describes a notice.
`Xv_Notice`	Handle to an opaque structure that describes a notice.
`Menu_item`	Pointer to an opaque structure that describes a menu item.
`Notice_attribute`	One of the notice attributes (`NOTICE_*`).
`Notify_arg`	Opaque client optional argument.

`Notify_destroy`	Enumeration:
	  `NOTIFY_SAFE`
	  `NOTIFY_IMMEDIATE`

`Notify_event`	Opaque client event.

`Notify_event_type`	Enumeration of errors for notifier functions:
	  `NOTIFY_SAFE`
	  `NOTIFY_IMMEDIATE`

`Notify_func`	Notifier function.

`Notify_signal_mode`	Enumeration:
	  `NOTIFY_SYNC`
	  `NOTIFY_ASYNC`

`Notify_value`	Enumeration of possible return values for client `notify procs`:
	  `NOTIFY_DONE`
	  `NOTIFY_IGNORED`
	  `NOTIFY_UNEXPECTED`

`Openwin_split_direction`	Enumeration:
	  `OPENWIN_SPLIT_HORIZONTAL`
	  `OPENWIN_SPLIT_VERTICAL`

`Panel`	Pointer to an opaque structure that describes a panel.
`Panel_attr`	One of the panel attributes (`PANEL_*`).
`Panel_item`	Pointer to an opaque structure that describes a panel item.

`Panel_item_type`	Enumerated type:
	  `PANEL_ABBREV_MENU_BUTTON_ITEM`
	  `PANEL_BUTTON_ITEM`
	  `PANEL_CHOICE_ITEM`
	  `PANEL_DROP_TARGET_ITE`
	  `PANEL_EXTENSION_ITEM`
	  `PANEL_GAUGE_ITEM`
	  `PANEL_ITEM`
	  `PANEL_LIST_ITEM`
	  `PANEL_MESSAGE_ITEM`

```
                          PANEL_MULTILINE_TEXT_ITEM
                          PANEL_NUMERIC_TEXT_ITEM
                          PANEL_SLIDER_ITEM
                          PANEL_TEXT_ITEM
                          PANEL_TOGGLE_ITEM
```

Panel_list_op   Enumerated type:
```
                          PANEL_LIST_OP_DELETE
                          PANEL_LIST_OP_DESELECT
                          PANEL_LIST_OP_SELECT
                          PANEL_LIST_OP_VALIDATE
```

Panel_setting   Enumerated type:
```
                          PANEL_CLEAR
                          PANEL_NO_CLEAR
                          PANEL_NONE
                          PANEL_ALL
                          PANEL_NON_PRINTABLE
                          PANEL_SPECIFIED
                          PANEL_CURRENT
                          PANEL_DONE
                          PANEL_MARKED
                          PANEL_VERTICAL
                          PANEL_HORIZONTAL
                          PANEL_INVERTED
                          PANEL_INSERT
                          PANEL_NEXT
                          PANEL_PREVIOUS
                          PANEL_NONE_DOWN
                          PANEL_LEFT_DOWN
                          PANEL_MIDDLE_DOWN
                          PANEL_RIGHT_DOWN
                          PANEL_CHORD_DOWN
```

Rect   The structure describing a rectangle:
```
                          typedef struct rect {
                                short r_left;
                                short r_top;
                                short r_width;
                                short r_height;
                          } Rect;
```

Rectlist   A list of rectangles:
```
                          typedef struct rectlist {
                                short rl_x, rl_y;
                                Rectnode *rl_head;
                                Rectnode *rl_tail;
                                Rect rl_bound;
                          } Rectlist;
```

Rectnode	One of the individual rectangles in a `rectlist`:

```
typedef struct rectnode {
        Rectnode *m_next;
        Rect      m_rect;
} Rectnode;
```

Xv_Screen	Pointer to an opaque structure that describes a screen.
Xv_Screen_attr	One of the screen attributes (SCREEN_*).
Scrollbar	The opaque handle for a scrollbar.
Scrollbar_attr	One of the scrollbar attributes (SCROLL_*).
Scrollbar_motion	Enumeration:

```
SCROLL_ABSOLUTE
SCROLL_POINT_TO_MIN
SCROLL_PAGE_FORWARD
SCROLL_LINE_FORWARD
SCROLL_MIN_TO_POINT
SCROLL_PAGE_BACKWARD
SCROLL_LINE_BACKWARD
SCROLL_TO_END
SCROLL_TO_START
SCROLL_NONE
```

Scrollbar_setting	Enumeration:

```
SCROLL_VERTICAL
SCROLL_HORIZONTAL
```

Selection_item	Handle to an opaque structure that describes the selection item.
Selection_owner	Handle to an opaque structure that describes the selection owner.
Selection_requestor	
	Handle to an opaque structure that describes the selection requestor.
Seln_attribute	One of the seln attributes.
Xv_Server	Pointer to an opaque structure that describes a server.
Server_attr	One of the server attributes.
Server_image	Pointer to an opaque structure that describes a server image.
Server_image_attribute	
	One of the Server_image attributes:

```
SERVER_IMAGE_DEPTH
SERVER_IMAGE_BITS
```

Data Types

`Xv_single_color`	Color values for a pixel. Defined in *<xview/cms.h>*.

```
typedef struct xv_singlecolor {
    u_char red, green, blue;
} Xv_singlecolor;
```

`Textsw`	Pointer to an opaque structure that describes a text subwindow.
`Textsw_action`	Enumeration of actions defined for client provided `notify_proc`:

```
TEXTSW_ACTION_CAPS_LOCK
TEXTSW_ACTION_CHANGED_DIRECTORY
TEXTSW_ACTION_EDITED_FILE
TEXTSW_ACTION_EDITED_MEMORY
TEXTSW_ACTION_FILE_IS_READONLY
TEXTSW_ACTION_LOADED_FILE
TEXTSW_ACTION_TOOL_CLOSE
TEXTSW_ACTION_TOOL_DESTROY
TEXTSW_ACTION_TOOL_QUIT
TEXTSW_ACTION_TOOL_MGR
TEXTSW_ACTION_USING_MEMORY
```

`Textsw_attribute`	One of the Textsw attributes.
`Textsw_enum`	Miscellaneous Textsw Enumerations:

```
TEXTSW_NEVER
TEXTSW_ALWAYS
TEXTSW_ONLY
TEXTSW_IF_AUTO_SCROLL
TEXTSW_CLIP
TEXTSW_WRAP_AT_CHAR
TEXTSW_WRAP_AT_WORD
TEXTSW_WRAP_AT_LINE
```

`Textsw_index`	An index for a character within a text subwindow's text stream.
`Textsw_view`	Pointer to an opaque structure that describes a text subwindow view.
`Textsw_status`	Enumeration describing the status of textsw.build and textsw.init.
`Tty`	Pointer to an opaque structure that describes a `TTY` subwindow.
`Xv_Window`	Pointer to an opaque structure that describes a window.
`Window_attr`	One of the window attributes (`WIN_*`).
`Window_scale_state`	Enumeration:

```
WIN_SCALE_SMALL
WIN_SCALE_MEDIUM
WIN_SCALE_LARGE
WIN_SCALE_EXTRALARGE
```

`Xv_error_action`	Enumeration: **XV_ERROR_CONTINUE** **XV_ERROR_RETRY** **XV_ERROR_ABORT**
`Xv_error_attr`	Enumeration: **XV_ERROR_SYSTEM** **XV_ERROR_BAD_VALUE** **XV_ERROR_CREATE_ONLY** **XV_ERROR_CANNOT_SET** **XV_BERROR_CANNOT_GET** **XV_ERROR_SERVER** **XV_ERROR_STRING** **XV_ERROR_INVALID_OBJ** **XV_ERROR_INTERNAL**
`Xv_error_severity`	Enumeration: **XV_ERROR_RECOVERABLE** **XV_ERROR_NON_RECOVERABLE**
`Xv_object`	Pointer to an opaque structure that describes an XView object.
`Xv_opaque`	Pointer to an opaque structure.
`Xv_xrectlist`	A list of rectangles returned by XView in X11 rectangle list format. Defined in *xv_xrect.h*

```
#define XV_MAX_XRECTS 32
typedef struct {
        XRectangle      rect_array[XV_MAX_XRECTS];
        int             count;
} Xv_xrectlist;
```

5

Event Codes

Section 5, Event Codes, *lists the event codes in numerical order by value.*

5
Event Codes

Table 5-1 lists the predefined event codes and their values. Table 5-2 lists the event codes for the Mouseless Model, and their values.

Table 5-1. Event Codes

Value	Event Code	Description
0	ASCII_FIRST	Marks beginning of ASCII range.
127	ASCII_LAST	Marks end of ASCII range.
128	META_FIRST	Marks beginning of META range.
255	META_LAST	Marks end of META range.
31744	ACTION_NULL_EVENT	Event was *not* translated into an action.
31745	ACTION_ERASE_CHAR_BACKWARD	Erase char to the left of caret.
31746	ACTION_ERASE_CHAR_FORWARD	Erase char to the right of caret.
31747	ACTION_ERASE_WORD_BACKWARD	Erase word to the left of caret.
31748	ACTION_ERASE_WORD_FORWARD	Erase word to the right of caret.
31749	ACTION_ERASE_LINE_BACKWARD	Erase to the beginning of the line.
31750	ACTION_ERASE_LINE_END	Erase to the end of the line.
31752	ACTION_GO_CHAR_BACKWARD	Move the caret one character to the left.
31753	ACTION_GO_CHAR_FORWARD	Move the caret one character to the right.
31754	ACTION_GO_WORD_BACKWARD	Move the caret one word to the left.
31755	ACTION_GO_WORD_FORWARD	Move the caret one word to the right.
31756	ACTION_GO_WORD_END	Move the caret to the end of the word.
31757	ACTION_GO_LINE_BACKWARD	Move the caret to the start of the line.
31758	ACTION_GO_LINE_FORWARD	Move the caret to the start of the next line.
31759	ACTION_GO_LINE_END	Move the caret to the end of the line.
31760	ACTION_GO_LINE_START	Move the caret to the beginning of the line.
31761	ACTION_GO_COLUMN_BACKWARD	Move the caret up one line, maintaining column position.
31762	ACTION_GO_COLUMN_FORWARD	Move the caret down one line, maintaining column position.
31763	ACTION_GO_DOCUMENT_START	Move the caret to the beginning of the text.
31764	ACTION_GO_DOCUMENT_END	Move the caret to the end of the text.
31765	ACTION_GO_PAGE_FORWARD	Move the caret to the next page.
31766	ACTION_GO_PAGE_BACKWARD	Move the caret to the previous page.
31767	ACTION_STOP	Stop the operation.

Table 5-1. Event Codes (continued)

Value	Event Code	Description
31768	ACTION_AGAIN	Repeat previous operation.
31769	ACTION_PROPS	Show property sheet window.
31770	ACTION_UNDO	Undo previous operation.
31771	ACTION_REDO	Repeat previous operation.
31772	ACTION_FRONT	Bring window to the front of the desktop.
31773	ACTION_BACK	Put the window at the back of the desktop.
31774	ACTION_COPY	Copy the selection to the clipboard.
31775	ACTION_OPEN	Open a window from its icon form (or close if already open).
31776	ACTION_CLOSE	Close a window to an icon.
31777	ACTION_PASTE	Copy clipboard contents to the insertion point.
31778	ACTION_FIND_BACKWARD	Find the text selection to the left of the caret.
31779	ACTION_FIND_FORWARD	Find the text selection to the right of the caret.
31780	ACTION_REPLACE	Show find and replace window.
31781	ACTION_CUT	Delete the selection and put on clipboard.
31782	ACTION_SELECT_FIELD_BACKWARD	Select the previous delimited field.
31783	ACTION_SELECT_FIELD_FORWARD	Select the next delimited field.
31784	ACTION_COPY_THEN_PASTE	Copy, then paste, text.
31785	ACTION_STORE	Store the specified selection as a new file.
31786	ACTION_LOAD	Load the specified selection as a new file.
31787	ACTION_INCLUDE_FILE	Includes the file.
31788	ACTION_GET_FILENAME	Get the selected filename.
31789	ACTION_SET_DIRECTORY	Set the directory to the selection.
31790	ACTION_DO_IT	Do the appropriate default action.
31791	ACTION_HELP	Set the directory to the selection.
31792	ACTION_INSERT	"INSERT" key. This may not be available on all keyboards.
31796	ACTION_CAPS_LOCK	Toggle caps-lock state.
31799	ACTION_SELECT	Left mouse button down or up.
31800	ACTION_ADJUST	Middle mouse button down or up.
31801	ACTION_MENU	Right mouse button down or up.
31802	ACTION_DRAG_MOVE	For moving text.
31803	ACTION_DRAG_COPY	Attempting to drag copy.
31803	ACTION_SPLIT_HORIZONTAL	Split pane horizontally.
31804	ACTION_DRAG_LOAD	Attempting to drag load.
31806	ACTION_SPLIT_VERTICAL	Split pane vertically.
31807	ACTION_SPLIT_INIT	Initialize a split pane.
31808	ACTION_SPLIT_DESTROY	Destroy a split of a pane.
31809	ACTION_RESCALE	Rescale a pane.
31810	ACTION_PININ	Pop up's OPEN LOOK pushpin in window header is in.
31811	ACTION_PINOUT	Pop up's OPEN LOOK pushpin in window header is out.
31812	ACTION_DISMISS	OPEN LOOK "dismiss" of pop-up window.
31815	ACTION_TAKE_FOCUS	Take the input focus.

Table 5-1. Event Codes (continued)

Value	Event Code	Description
31818	KBD_MAP	KeymapNotify
31819	WIN_GRAPHICS_EXPOSE	GraphicsExpose
31820	WIN_NO_EXPOSE	NoExpose
31821	WIN_VISIBILITY_NOTIFY	VisibilityNotify
31822	WIN_CREATE_NOTIFY	CreateNotify
31823	WIN_DESTROY_NOTIFY	DestroyNotify
31824	WIN_MAP_REQUEST	MapRequest
31825	WIN_REPARENT_NOTIFY	ReparentNotify
31826	WIN_GRAVITY_NOTIFY	GravityNotify
31827	WIN_RESIZE_REQUEST	ResizeRequest
31828	WIN_CONFIGURE_REQUEST	ConfigureRequest
31829	WIN_CIRCULATE_REQUEST	CirculateRequest
31830	WIN_CIRCULATE_NOTIFY	CirculateNotify
31831	WIN_PROPERTY_NOTIFY	PropertyNotify
31835	WIN_COLORMAP_NOTIFY	ColormapNotify
31836	MAPPING_NOTIFY	MappingNotify
31895	ACTION_MATCH_DELIMITER	Select text up to a matching delimiter.
31897	ACTION_QUOTE	Cause next event in the input stream to pass. untranslated by the keymapping system.
31898	ACTION_EMPTY	Empty out the object or window.
32000	PANEL_EVENT_CANCEL	The panel or panel item is no longer "current."
32001	PANEL_EVENT_MOVE_IN	The pointer enters panel or panel item with no mouse buttons down.
32256	SCROLLBAR_REQUEST	Request the scrollbar client to scroll paint window to a new view start.
32512	LOC_MOVE	MotionNotify – Pointer moves.
32513	LOC_WINENTER	EnterNotify – Pointer enters window.
32514	LOC_WINEXIT	LeaveNotify – Pointer exits window.
32515	LOC_DRAG	MotionNotify – Pointer moves while a button was down.
32516	WIN_REPAINT	Expose – Some portion of window requires repainting.
32517	WIN_RESIZE	ConfigureNotify – Window has been resized.
32518	WIN_MAP_NOTIFY	MapNotify – Notification of window being mapped.
32519	WIN_UNMAP_NOTIFY	UnmapNotify – Notification of window that is being unmapped.
32520	KBD_USE	FocusIn– Window is now the focus of keyboard input.
32521	KBD_DONE	FocusOut – Window is no longer the focus of input from keyboard.
32522	WIN_CLIENT_MESSAGE	ClientMessage – A message from another client.
32522	WIN_GRAPHICS_EXPOSE	GraphicsExpose – Source area for copy is outside of source window or obscured.
32537	SEL_CLEAR	SelectionClear
32538	SEL_REQUEST	SelectionRequest
32539	SEL_NOTIFY	SelectionNotify
32563+i-1	BUT(i)	Press pointer buttons 1–10

Table 5-1. Event Codes (continued)

Value	Event Code	Description
32563	MS_LEFT	Press left mouse button ButtonPress. or ButtonRelease.
32564	MS_MIDDLE	Press middle mouse button. ButtonPress or ButtonRelease.
32565	MS_RIGHT	Press right mouse button. ButtonPress or ButtonRelease
32573+i-1	KEY_LEFT(i)	Press left function keys 1–15KeyPress or KeyRelease.
32589+i-1	KEY_RIGHT(i)	Press right function keys 1–15 KeyPress or KeyRelease.
32605+i-1	KEY_TOP(i)	Press top function keys 1–15 KeyPress or KeyRelease.
32621+i-1	KEY_BOTTOM(i)	"BOTTOM" keys
32621	KEY_BOTTOMLEFT	
32621	KEY_BOTTOMFIRST	
32622	KEY_BOTTOMRIGHT	
32636	KEY_BOTTOMLAST	

Table 5-2. Mouseless Event Codes

Value	Event Code	Definition
31818	ACTION_ACCELERATOR	XVIEW_FIRST+74
31819	ACTION_DELETE_SELECTION	XVIEW_FIRST+75
31820	ACTION_ERASE_LINE	XVIEW_FIRST+76
31821	ACTION_HORIZONTAL_SCROLLBAR_MENU	XVIEW_FIRST+77
31822	ACTION_INPUT_FOCUS_HELP	XVIEW_FIRST+78
31823	ACTION_JUMP_DOWN	XVIEW_FIRST+79
31824	ACTION_JUMP_MOUSE_TO_INPUT_FOCUS	XVIEW_FIRST+80
31825	ACTION_JUMP_UP	XVIEW_FIRST+81
31826	ACTION_MORE_HELP	XVIEW_FIRST+82
31827	ACTION_MORE_TEXT_HELP	XVIEW_FIRST+83
31828	ACTION_NEXT_ELEMENT	XVIEW_FIRST+84
31829	ACTION_NEXT_PANE	XVIEW_FIRST+85
31830	ACTION_PANE_BACKGROUND	XVIEW_FIRST+86
31831	ACTION_PANE_LEFT	XVIEW_FIRST+87
31832	ACTION_PANE_RIGHT	XVIEW_FIRST+88
31833	ACTION_PANEL_START	XVIEW_FIRST+89
31834	ACTION_PANEL_END	XVIEW_FIRST+90
31835	ACTION_PREVIOUS_ELEMENT	XVIEW_FIRST+91
31836	ACTION_PREVIOUS_PANE	XVIEW_FIRST+92

Table 5-2. Mouseless Event Codes (continued)

Value	Event Code	Definition
31837	ACTION_QUOTE_NEXT_KEY	XVIEW_FIRST+93
31838	ACTION_RESUME_MOUSELESS	XVIEW_FIRST+94
31839	ACTION_SCROLL_DATA_END	XVIEW_FIRST+95
31840	ACTION_SCROLL_DATA_START	XVIEW_FIRST+96
31841	ACTION_SCROLL_DOWN	XVIEW_FIRST+97
31842	ACTION_SCROLL_JUMP_DOWN	XVIEW_FIRST+98
31843	ACTION_SCROLL_JUMP_LEFT	XVIEW_FIRST+99
31844	ACTION_SCROLL_JUMP_RIGHT	XVIEW_FIRST+100
31845	ACTION_SCROLL_JUMP_UP	XVIEW_FIRST+101
31846	ACTION_SCROLL_LEFT	XVIEW_FIRST+102
31847	ACTION_SCROLL_LINE_END	XVIEW_FIRST+103
31848	ACTION_SCROLL_LINE_START	XVIEW_FIRST+104
31849	ACTION_SCROLL_RIGHT	XVIEW_FIRST+105
31850	ACTION_SCROLL_PANE_DOWN	XVIEW_FIRST+106
31851	ACTION_SCROLL_PANE_LEFT	XVIEW_FIRST+107
31852	ACTION_SCROLL_PANE_RIGHT	XVIEW_FIRST+108
31853	ACTION_SCROLL_PANE_UP	XVIEW_FIRST+109
31854	ACTION_SCROLL_UP	XVIEW_FIRST+110
31855	ACTION_SELECT_ALL	XVIEW_FIRST+111
31856	ACTION_SELECT_DATA_END	XVIEW_FIRST+112
31857	ACTION_SELECT_DATA_START	XVIEW_FIRST+113
31858	ACTION_SELECT_DOWN	XVIEW_FIRST+114
31859	ACTION_SELECT_JUMP_DOWN	XVIEW_FIRST+115
31860	ACTION_SELECT_JUMP_LEFT	XVIEW_FIRST+116
31861	ACTION_SELECT_JUMP_RIGHT	XVIEW_FIRST+117
31862	ACTION_SELECT_JUMP_UP	XVIEW_FIRST+118
31863	ACTION_SELECT_LEFT	XVIEW_FIRST+119
31864	ACTION_SELECT_LINE_END	XVIEW_FIRST+120
31865	ACTION_SELECT_LINE_START	XVIEW_FIRST+121
31866	ACTION_SELECT_RIGHT	XVIEW_FIRST+122
31867	ACTION_SELECT_PANE_DOWN	XVIEW_FIRST+123
31868	ACTION_SELECT_PANE_LEFT	XVIEW_FIRST+124
31869	ACTION_SELECT_PANE_RIGHT	XVIEW_FIRST+125
31870	ACTION_SELECT_PANE_UP	XVIEW_FIRST+126
31871	ACTION_SELECT_UP	XVIEW_FIRST+127
31872	ACTION_SUSPEND_MOUSELESS	XVIEW_FIRST+128
31873	ACTION_TEXT_HELP	XVIEW_FIRST+129
31874	ACTION_TRANSLATE	XVIEW_FIRST+130
31875	ACTION_VERTICAL_SCROLLBAR_MENU	XVIEW_FIRST+131

6

Command-line Arguments
and XView Resources

Section 6, Command-line Arguments and XView Resources, *lists the XView options that can be set using command-line options. This section also lists the resources that XView uses to define certain default values when an application is initialized.*

In This Chapter:

6
Command-line Arguments and XView Resources

This section lists XView properties that can be set with command-line options or by specifying values for resources. Values for most properties can be overriden programatically using XView attributes. For example, the position and size of an application's base frame can be set using the command-line option –geometry, or by changing the value of the Window.Geometry resource. However, if the application sets its size and position by setting attributes with xv_set(), the values specified in the call to xv_set() take precedence.

This section is divided into two parts: part one, listing the properties that have an explicit command-line option, and part two, listing the properties that do not have an explicit command-line option.

XView properties may be set in a number of ways, as the following list indicates. The list shows precedence for setting property values, from highest to lowest.

1. Calling xv_set() for one or more attributes that change the value of a property.

2. Specifying a flag name plus its value, if any, on the command line.

3. Editing or adding values for resource defaults in a *˜.Xdefaults* file.

4. Calling xv_create() for an object's attributes.

5. Using the package default values for the property.

From this list, you can see that command-line options have precedence over values set during xv_create(), but that all values are overridden by an explicit call to xv_set().

The command-line options –rv (reverse), –scale, –font, –foreground_color, –background_color, and –icon_font apply to all top-level frames in the application. The remaining options apply only to the first top-level frame created by the application. Child subframes inherit properties from their parent frames. Therefore, command-line options eventually propagate to subframes unless the options are overriden programatically.

6.1 Command-line Options with Resources

–background

This option takes a single argument that is in the form of a predefined color name (lavender, gray, goldenrod, etc.) from *$OPENWINHOME/lib/rbg.txt* or a hexidecimal representation. The hexidecimal representation is of the form pound sign (#) followed by the hexidecimal representation of the red, green, and blue aspects of the color. Also see –Wb.

Short:	–bg
Type:	string (color name, or hexidecimal color specification)
Resource:	`Window.Color.Background`
Default:	white
Examples:	

        cmdtool -foreground blue -background gray

Provides a blue foreground, with a gray background.

        cmdtool -foreground #d800ff -background white

Provides a purple foreground, with a white background.

–default

This option allows the user to set resources that don't have command-line equivalents. The format is –default *resource-name value*. The XView resources without specific command-line arguments are discussed in the following section.

Short:	–Wd
Type:	string string
Resource:	Given by the first string
Default:	None
Example:	

        cmdtool -default
        OpenWindows.ScrollbarPlacement left

–depth

Specifies the window's depth.

Type:	int
Resource:	`Window.Depth`

–disable_retained

This option is useful for applications running on a monochrome display, where server memory is at a minimum. For performance reasons, monochrome windows are by default retained by the server. Using retained windows will use more memory in the X11 server; however, it also speeds up repainting when the window is covered and uncovered by other windows. When –disable_retained is set, monochrome windows are not retained, thus saving server memory.

Short:	–Wdr
Type:	Boolean
Resource:	Window.Mono.DisableRetained
Default:	Not retained on color systems. Retained on monochrome systems.

–disable_xio_error_handler

This option is useful for debugging an application. Whenever there is a fatal XIO error, the server will print an error message before exiting. XView installs an error handler to keep those messages from appearing. If you would like to see these messages, use this option.

Short:	–Wdxio
Type:	Boolean
Resource:	None
Default:	Enable xio handler. Setting this option disables the xio handler.

–display

Sets the name of the X11 server on which to connect. Host is the name or address of the machine on whose server you have permission to display. Display is a number corresponding to the server on which to display for that machine, and screen corresponds to which screen for the server. See manual page on xhost for more details on adding to permissions list.

Short:	–Wr
Type:	String of the form: host:display{.screen}
Resource:	Server.Name
Default:	Taken from the DISPLAY environment variable.
Example:	

        cmdtool –display foobar:0

Brings up a cmdtool on the default screen of the display #0 on the host foobar.

        cmdtool –display foobar:0.1

Brings up a cmdtool on screen #1 of display #0 of host foobar.

–font, –fn

Sets the name of the font used for the application (not control areas). To find out what fonts are available, use the xlsfonts command.

Short:	–Wt
Type:	string
Resource:	Font.Name
Default:	lucidasans-12
Example:	

```
cmdtool -font fixed
```

If the font you specify cannot be found, an error message is shown. For example:

```
XView warning: Cannot load font 'galant-24' (Font package)
XView warning: Attempting to load font '-
b&h-lucida-medium-r-normal-sans-*-120-
*-*-*-*-*-*' instead (Font package)
```

–foreground

This option specifies the foreground color. For example, an application's text in its textsw would take on the foreground color. Also see the –background option for information on similar functions. This option takes a single argument that is in the form of a predefined color name (lavender, gray, goldenrod, etc.) from *$OPENWINHOME/lib/rbg.txt* or a hexidecimal representation. The hexidecimal representation is of the form pound sign (#) followed by the hexidecimal representation of the red, green, and blue aspects of the color.

Short:	–fg
Type:	string
	(color name, or hexidecimal color specification)
Resource:	Window.Color.Foreground
Default:	black
Example:	

```
cmdtool -fg blue
```

Comes up with a blue foreground.

–foreground_color

This option allows the user to specify the foreground color of an application. It takes three values that should be integers between 0 and 255. They specify to the amount of red, green, and blue that is in the color.

Short:	–Wf
Type:	integer integer integer
Resource:	Window.Color.Foreground
Default:	0 0 0
Example:	

```
cmdtool -Wf 0 0 255
```

Comes up with a blue foreground.

–fullscreendebug

Enables or disables fullscreen debugging mode during which XGrabs (`XGrab-Server()`, `XGrabKeyboard()`, `XGrabPointer()`) are not done. When using the `FULLSCREEN` package, the X11 server is normally grabbed. This prevents other windows on the server from responding until the grab has been released by the one window which initiated the grab. Refer to the XView Reference Manual: *Converting SunView Applications* for further details.

Short:	`-Wfsdb`
Type:	Boolean
Resource:	`Fullscreen.Debug`
Default:	`FALSE`

–fullscreendebugkbd

Enables or disables keyboard grabbing using `XGrabKeyboard()` that is done via the `FULLSCREEN` package.

Short:	`-Wfsdbk`
Type:	Boolean
Resource:	`Fullscreen.Debugkbd`
Default:	`FALSE`

–fullscreendebugptr

Enables or disables pointer grabbing `XGrabPointer()` that is done via the `FULLSCREEN` package. Refer to Appendix F of the XView Reference Manual: *Converting SunView Applications* manual for further details.

Short:	`-Wfsdbp`
Type:	Boolean
Resource:	`Fullscreen.Debugptr`
Default:	`FALSE`

–fullscreendebugserver

Enables or disables server grabbing using `XGrabServer()` that is done with the `FULLSCREEN` package. Refer to the Appendix F in the XView Reference Manual: *Converting SunView Applications* for further details.

Short:	`-Wfsdbs`
Type:	Boolean
Resource:	`Fullscreen.Debugserver`
Default:	`FALSE`

–geometry

This sets both the size and the placement of the application's base frame. This option has priority over the `-size` and `-position` arguments. The size and placement parts of the value are optional. You can set just the size, just the position, or both. The size values are measured in pixels, and the position values use the same semantics as `-position`. However, if you use the – (minus) in front of an *x* value, it will be taken as relative to the right-hand side of the screen, instead of the left. Likewise, if you use the – (minus) with the *y* value, it will be taken relative to the bottom of the screen instead of the top.

Short:	−WG
Type:	string of the format: {WxH}{[+|-]x[+|-]y}
Resource:	Window.Geometry
Default:	Depends on the application.
Examples:	

```
cmdtool −geometry 500x600
```

Makes the base frame 500x600 pixels, with the position set by the window manager.

```
cmdtool −WG +10+20
```

Makes the base frame of the default size with the left-hand side of the frame 10 pixels from the left-hand side of the screen, and the top of the frame 20 pixels from the top of the screen.

```
cmdtool −WG −10+20
```

Makes the base frame of the default size with the right-hand side of the frame 10 pixels from the right-hand side of the screen, and the top of the frame 20 pixels from the top of the screen.

```
cmdtool −geometry 400x300−0−0
```

Makes the base frame 400x300 pixels with the right-hand side of the frame flush against the right-hand side of the screen, and the bottom of the frame flush with the bottom of the screen.

−help

Prints a description of the valid command-line arguments for the application.

Short:	−WH
Type:	None
Resource:	None
Default:	None

−icon_font

Sets the name of the font used for the application's icon. To find out what fonts are available, use xlsfonts.

Short:	−WT
Type:	string
Resource:	Icon.Font.Name
Default:	Depends on the application.
Example:	

```
cmdtool −WT '*century schoolbook*'
```

–icon_image

Sets the default filename for the icon's image. However, the application can overwrite this setting and display its own icon image. The file must be in XView icon format. The program iconedit allows you to create an image in the icon format. Several icons are available in the directory *$OPENWINHOME/include/images*. By convention, icon format files end with the suffix *.icon*.

Short: −WI
Type: string
Resource: Icon.Pixmap
Default: Depends on the application.
Example:

        cmdtool −WI /usr/include/images/stop.icon

–icon_label

Sets a default label for the base frame's icon. However, the application can overwrite this setting and display its own icon label.

Short: −WL
Type: string
Resource: Icon.Footer
Default: Depends on the application.
Example:

        cmdtool −WL "Icon Label"

–icon_position

Sets the position of the application's icon in pixels. Uses the same semantics as -position for base frames.

Short: −WP
Type: integer integer
Resource: Icon.X Icon.Y
Default: Depends on the window manager.
Example:

        cmdtool −WP 400 20

–label

Sets a default label for the base frame's header. However, the application can overwrite this setting and display its own header.

Short: −Wl
Type: string
Resource: Window.Header
Default: Depends on the application.
Example:

        cmdtool −Wl "Header Text"

–lc_basiclocale

Locale setting is the method by which the language and cultural environment of a system is set. Locale setting affects the display and manipulation of language-dependent features.

The internationalization features that XView Version 3 supports include locale setting. One of the ways locale can be set is with command-line options. See the *XView Programming Manual* for details on other methods.

The `-lc_basiclocale` option specifies the basic locale category, which sets the country of the user interface.

Type: string
Resource: `basicLocale`
Default: "C"

–lc_displaylang

Specifies the display language locale category, sets the language in which labels, messages, menu items, and help text are displayed.

Type: string
Resource: `displayLang`
Default: "C"

–lc_inputlang

Specifies the input language locale category, sets the language used for keyboard input.

Type: string
Resource: `inputLang`
Default: "C"

–lc_numeric

Specifies the numeric locale category, which defines the language used to format numeric quantities.

Type: string
Resource: `numeric`
Default: "C"

–lc_timeformat

Specifies the time format locale category, which defines the language used to format time and date.

Type: string
Resource: `timeFormat`
Default: "C"

–name

Specifies the instance name of the application. This name is used to construct the resource name used to perform lookups in the X11 Resource Manager to look for the values for customizable attributes.

Type: string
Resource: None
Default: `argv[0]`

–position

Sets the initial position of the application's base frame in pixels. The upper left corner of the screen is at position (0,0), with the x-axis increasing to the left, and the y-axis increasing downward. To determine framebuffer size, one can use the `eeprom` command on the local machine. To determine screen size for a remote display, one can use Xlib functions (see the *Xlib Programming Manual*). These values will also be generated by the "Save Workspace" option on the root menu into the *$HOME/.openwin-init* file when using the Open Look Window Manager.

Short: `-Wp`
Resource: `Window.X and Window.Y`
Type: integer integer
Default: Depends on the window manager.
Example:

        `cmdtool -Wp 100 200`

–scale

Sets the initial scale of the application (larger or smaller). Small is 10 pixels, medium is 12 pixels, large is 14 pixels and extra_large is 19 pixels. The `font.name` resource overrides the scale.

Short: `-Wx`
Type: string
Valid Values: {small, medium, large, extra_large}
Resource: `Window.Scale`
Default: "medium"
Example:

        `cmdtool -scale extra_large`

–size

Sets the width and height of the application's base frame. The values are in pixels.

Short: `-Ws`
Type   integer integer
Resource: `Window.Width and Window.Height`
Default: Depends on the application.
Example:

        `cmdtool -Ws 400 500`

–synchronous, +synchronous

These options allow you to make the connection that the application has with the X11 server either synchronous (-sync) or asynchronous (+sync).

Short:	-sync, +sync
Type:	Boolean
Resource:	Window.Synchronous
Default:	+synchronous

–title Sets a default label for the base frame's header. However, the application can overwrite this setting and display its own header.

Short:	-Wl
Type:	string
Resource:	Window.Header
Default:	Depends on the application.
Example:	

```
cmdtool -Wl "Header Text"
```

–visual

Resource specifies the visual used for the window.

Type:	Visual
Resource:	Window.visual

–Wb This option allows the user to specify the background color (i.e., the color that text is painted on) for an application. The arguments are three values that should be integers between 0 and 255. They specify to the amount of red, green, and blue that is in the color.

Type:	integer integer integer
Resource:	Window.Color.Background
Default:	0 0 0

–Wd See the –default option.

–Wdr See the –disable_retained option.

–Wdxio

See the –disable_xio_error_handler option.

–Wf See the –foreground_color option.

–Wfsdb

See the –fullscreendebug option.

–Wfsdbs

See the –fullscreendebugserver option.

–WG See the –geometry option.

–WH See the –help option.

–Wi, and +Wi

These options control how an application will come up, open or closed (iconified).

Short:
Type: Boolean
Resource: Window.Iconic
Default: +Wi
Examples:

>   cmdtool +Wi

Makes cmdtool come up open.

>   cmdtool –Wi

Makes cmdtool come up closed.

–WI (uppercase i)
See the –icon_image option.

–Wl (lowercase L)
See the –label option.

–WL See the –icon_label option.

–Wp See the –position option.

–WP See the –icon_position option.

–Wr See the –display option.

–Ws See the –size option.

–Wt See the –font option.

–WT See the –icon_font option.

–Wx See the –scale option.

–xrm This option allows the user to set resources that don't have command-line equivalents. This is similar to the `-default` option, but it takes only one argument, a string in the form of *resource-name:value*.

Type: string
Resource: given in the string
Default: None
Example:

```
cmdtool -xrm OpenWindows.ScrollbarPlacement:right
```

6.2 Additional Resources

The *Xdefaults* file stores resource settings. We recommend that you use the command-line arguments in order to change display characteristics rather than changing the *Xdefaults* file. Changing the resources in the `.Xdefaults` file modifies the behavior of the user's session. Novice users should not casually modify these settings.

Before attempting to edit the *Xdefaults* file, please read the appropriate sections of the *Xlib Programming Manual* on the file format and the specific properties you intend to change.

Note that resources documented in this section do not have command-line arguments. It is possible to change these properties without altering the *Xdefaults* file. The command-line arguments `-xrm` and `-defaults` provide instructions on how to specify values for any property. The resources that have command-line arguments are documented the previous section.

Introduction.Resources (Props)
This is an example of the format for the resources described in this section. This field contains a brief description of the resource. If the resource can be modified by the OpenWindows Property Sheet, the resource name is followed by "(Props)".

Values: Val1, Val2 (Default). This field contains the possible values for the resource. If the resource may contain any value, the default(s) are provided. Defaults are shown enclosed in parentheses following the valid values.

alarm.visible
When ringing the bell in an XView program, flash the window as well to warn the user.

Values: True, False (True)

keyboard.deleteChar
Specifies the delete character. This resource applies to text windows only and not to panel text items. This would work in either `cmdtool` or `textedit` or the compose window of `mailtool`.

Values: C (177 = octal for Delete)
                Where C is some character either typed into an editor or specified with an octal equivalent.

keyboard.deleteLine

Specifies the delete line character. This resource applies to text windows only and not to panel text items. This would work in either `cmdtool` or `textedit` or the compose window of `mailtool`.

Values: C

Where C is some character either typed into an editor or specified with an octal equivalent.

keyboard.deleteWord

Specifies the delete word character. This resource applies to text windows only and not to panel text items. This would work in either `cmdtool` or `textedit` or the compose window of `mailtool`.

Values: C (27 = octal for ^W)

Where C is some character either typed into an editor or specified with an octal equivalent.

mouse.modifier.button2

When using a mouse with less than three buttons, this resource gets an equivalent mapping for the second button which is the ADJUST button on a three button mouse. For more information on keysyms, see the `xmodmap` Reference Manual page in the Xlib documentation, or the *include* file *$OPENWINHOME/include/X11/Xkeymap.h*.

Values: Shift, Ctrl, any valid modifier keysym (Shift)

mouse.modifier.button3

When using a mouse with less than three buttons, this resource gets an equivalent mapping for the third button which is the MENU button on a three button mouse. For more information on keysyms, see the `xmodmap` reference manual page, Xlib documentation, and the *include* file *$OPENWINHOME/include/X11/Xkeymap.h*.

Values: Shift, Ctrl, any valid modifier keysym (Ctrl)

mouse.multiclick.space

Specifies the maximum number of pixels between successive mouse clicks to still have the clicks considered as a multi-click event.

Values: N (4)

Where N is an integer between 2 and 500.

notice.beepCount

Ringing the bell can consist of either an audible beep and/or a visual flash.

Values: N (1)

Where N is an integer to specify how many times to ring the bell when a notice appears.

OpenWindows.3DLook.Color

When False, do not use the 3-D look on a color or grayscale screen.

Values: True, False (True on all but monochrome screens)

OpenWindows.beep (Props)

When the value is notices, the audible bell will ring only when a notice pops up. When the value is never, the audible bell will never ring. When the value is always, the audible bell will always ring when the bell function is called by a program.

Values: never, notices, always (always)

OpenWindows.dragRightDistance (Props)

Used by menus to determine when a pullright submenu would display when dragging over the menu item near a submenu.

Values: N (100)
                        N is an integer greater than 0. A reasonable value might start at 20 and go to 200.

OpenWindows.KeyboardCommand.*

All of the OpenWindows.KeyboardCommand resource mappings may be modi-fied by users, or by specifying one of three values for OpenWindows.Keyboard-Commands: Sunview1 (which is the default), Basic, or Full. See the description for OpenWindows.KeyboardCommands and Chapter 6, *Handling Input*, in the *XView Programming Manual*, for more information.

OpenWindows.KeyboardCommand.Adjust

This mapping is loaded if KeyboardCommands is set to Full. This is a keyboard "Core Functions" resource.

Values: Insert+Alt

OpenWindows.KeyboardCommand.Again

This is a Keyboard "Core Functions" resource.

Values: a+Meta, a+Ctrl+Meta, L2

OpenWindows.KeyboardCommand.Copy

This is Keyboard "Core Functions" resource.

Values: u+Meta, L4

OpenWindows.KeyboardCommand.CopyThenPaste

This is Keyboard "Core Functions" resource. This mapping is always loaded.

Values: p+Meta

OpenWindows.KeyboardCommand.Cut

This is Keyboard "Core Functions" resource. This mapping is always loaded.

Values: x+Meta, L10

OpenWindows.KeyboardCommand.DataEnd
This mapping is always loaded. This is a keyboard "Local Navigation" command.

Default Values: End, R13, Return+Ctrl, End+Shift
Values (Basic or Full): End+Ctrl, R13+Ctrl

OpenWindows.KeyboardCommand.DataStart
Default Values: Home, R7, Return+Shift+Ctrl, Home+Shift
Values (Basic or Full): Home+Ctrl, R7+Ctrl

OpenWindows.KeyboardCommand.DefaultAction
This is Keyboard "Core Functions" resource. This mapping is always loaded.

Values: Return+Meta

OpenWindows.KeyboardCommand.Down
This mapping is always loaded. This is a keyboard "Local Navigation" command.

Default Values: n+Ctrl, P+Ctrl, Down, R14, Down+Shift
Values (Basic or Full): Down

OpenWindows.KeyboardCommand.Empty
This mapping is always loaded. This is a "Text Editing" command resource.

Values: e+Meta, e+Ctrl+Meta

OpenWindows.KeyboardCommand.EraseCharBackward
This mapping is always loaded. This is a "Text Editing" command resource.

Values: Delete, BackSpace

OpenWindows.KeyboardCommand.EraseCharForward
This mapping is always loaded. This is a "Text Editing" resource.

Values: Delete+Shift, BackSpace+Shift

OpenWindows.KeyboardCommand.EraseLine
This is a "Text Editing" resource.

Values (Basic or Full): Delete+Meta, BackSpace+Meta

OpenWindows.KeyboardCommand.EraseLineBackward
This mapping is always loaded. This is a "Text Editing" resource.

Values: u+Ctrl

OpenWindows.KeyboardCommand.EraseLineEnd
This mapping is always loaded. This is a "Text Editing" resource.

Values: U+Ctrl

OpenWindows.KeyboardCommand.EraseWordBackward
This mapping is always loaded. This is a "Text Editing" resource.

Values: w+Ctrl

OpenWindows.KeyboardCommand.EraseWordForward

This mapping is always loaded. This is a "Text Editing" resource.

Values: W+Ctrl

OpenWindows.KeyboardCommand.FindBackward

This mapping is always loaded. This is a keyboard "Core Functions" resource.

Values: F+Meta, L9+Shift

OpenWindows.KeyboardCommand.FindForward

This mapping is always loaded. This is a keyboard "Core Functions" resource.

Values: f+Meta, L9

OpenWindows.KeyboardCommand.GoLineForward

This mapping is always loaded. This is a keyboard "Local Navigation" command.

Values: apostrophe+Ctrl, R11

OpenWindows.KeyboardCommand.GoPageBackward

This mapping is always loaded. This is a keyboard "Local Navigation" command.

Values: R9

OpenWindows.KeyboardCommand.GoPageForward

This mapping is always loaded. This is a keyboard "Local Navigation" command.

Values: R15

OpenWindows.KeyboardCommand.GoWordForward

This mapping is always loaded. This is a keyboard "Local Navigation" command.

Values: slash+Ctrl, less+Ctrl

OpenWindows.KeyboardCommand.Help

This mapping is always loaded. This is a keyboard "Core Functions" resource.

Values: Help

OpenWindows.KeyboardCommand.HorizontalScrollbarMenu

This is a Full "Miscellaneous Navigation" command.

Values: h+Alt

OpenWindows.KeyboardCommand.IncludeFile

This mapping is always loaded. This is a "Text Editing" resource.

Values: i+Meta

OpenWindows.KeyboardCommand.InputFocusHelp

This mapping is loaded if KeyboardCommand is Full. This is a keyboard "Core Functions" resource.

Values: question+Ctrl

OpenWindows.KeyboardCommand.Insert

This mapping is always loaded. This is a "Text Editing" resource.

Values: Insert

OpenWindows.KeyboardCommand.JumpDown

This mapping is loaded if KeyboardCommand is Basic or Full. This is a keyboard "Local Navigation" command.

Values: Down+Ctrl

OpenWindows.KeyboardCommand.JumpLeft

This mapping is always loaded. This is a keyboard "Local Navigation" command.

Default Values: comma+Ctrl, greater+Ctrl
Values (Basic or Full): Left+Ctrl

OpenWindows.KeyboardCommand.JumpMouseToInputFocus

This mapping is loaded if KeyboardCommand is Full. This is a keyboard "Core Functions" resource.

Values: j+Alt

OpenWindows.KeyboardCommand.JumpRight

This mapping is always loaded. This is a keyboard "Local Navigation" command.

Default Values: period+Ctrl
Values (Basic or Full): Right+Ctrl

OpenWindows.KeyboardCommand.JumpUp

This mapping is loaded if KeyboardCommand is Basic or Full. This is a keyboard "Local Navigation" command.

Values: Up+Ctrl

OpenWindows.KeyboardCommand.Left

This mapping is always loaded. This is a keyboard "Local Navigation" command.

Values: b+Ctrl, F+Ctrl, Left, R10, Left+Shift
Values (Basic or Full): Left

OpenWindows.KeyboardCommand.LineEnd

This mapping is always loaded. This is a keyboard "Local Navigation" command.

Values: e+Ctrl, A+Ctrl

OpenWindows.KeyboardCommand.LineStart

This mapping is always loaded. This is a keyboard "Local Navigation" command.

Values: a+Ctrl, E+Ctrl

OpenWindows.KeyboardCommand.Load

This mapping is always loaded. This is a "Text Editing" resource.

Values: l+Meta

OpenWindows.KeyboardCommand.MatchDelimiter

This mapping is always loaded. This is a "Text Editing" resource.

Values: d+Meta

OpenWindows.KeyboardCommand.Menu

This mapping is loaded if KeyboardCommand is Full. This is a keyboard "Core Functions" resource.

Values: space+Alt

OpenWindows.KeyboardCommand.MoreHelp

This mapping is always loaded. This is a keyboard "Core Functions" resource.

Values: Help+Shift

OpenWindows.KeyboardCommand.MoreTextHelp

This mapping is always loaded. This is a keyboard "Core Functions" resource.

Values: Help+Shift+Ctrl

OpenWindows.KeyboardCommand.NextElement

This mapping is loaded if KeyboardCommand is Full. This is a "Global Navigation" command.

Values: Tab+Ctrl

OpenWindows.KeyboardCommand.NextPane

This mapping is loaded if KeyboardCommand is Full. This is a "Global Navigation" command.

Values: a+Alt

OpenWindows.KeyboardCommand.PaneBackground

This mapping is loaded if KeyboardCommand is Full. This is a Miscellaneous Navigation command.

Values: b+Alt

OpenWindows.KeyboardCommand.PaneDown

This mapping is loaded if KeyboardCommand is Basic or Full. This is a keyboard "Local Navigation" command.

Values: R15

OpenWindows.KeyboardCommand.PaneLeft

This mapping is loaded if KeyboardCommand is Basic or Full. This is a keyboard "Local Navigation" command.

Values: R9+Ctrl

OpenWindows.KeyboardCommand.PaneRight

This mapping is loaded if KeyboardCommand is Basic or Full. This is a keyboard "Local Navigation" command.

Values: R15+Ctrl

OpenWindows.KeyboardCommand.PaneUp

This mapping is loaded if KeyboardCommand is Basic or Full. This is a keyboard "Local Navigation" command.

Values: R9

OpenWindows.KeyboardCommand.PanelEnd

This mapping is loaded if KeyboardCommand is Full. This is a Miscellaneous Navigation command.

Values: bracketright+Ctrl

OpenWindows.KeyboardCommand.PanelStart

This mapping is loaded if KeyboardCommand is Full. This is a Miscellaneous Navigation command.

Values: bracketleft+Ctrl

OpenWindows.KeyboardCommand.Paste

This mapping is always loaded. This is a keyboard "Core Functions" resource.

Values: v+Meta, L8

OpenWindows.KeyboardCommand.PreviousElement

This mapping is loaded if KeyboardCommand is Full. This is a "Global Navigation" command.

Values: Tab+Shift+Ctrl

OpenWindows.KeyboardCommand.PreviousPane

This mapping is loaded if KeyboardCommand is Full. This is a "Global Navigation" command.

Values: A+Alt

OpenWindows.KeyboardCommand.Props

This mapping is always loaded. This is a keyboard "Core Functions" resource.

Values: L3

OpenWindows.KeyboardCommand.QuoteNextKey

This mapping is loaded if KeyboardCommand is Full. This is a keyboard "Core Functions" resource.

Values: q+Alt

OpenWindows.KeyboardCommand.ResumeMouseless

This mapping is loaded if KeyboardCommand is Full. This is a keyboard "Core Functions" resource.

Values: Z+Alt

OpenWindows.KeyboardCommand.Right

This mapping is always loaded. This is a keyboard "Local Navigation" command.

Default Values: f+Ctrl, B+Ctrl, Right, R12, Right+Shift
Values (Basic or Full): Right

OpenWindows.KeyboardCommand.RowEnd

This mapping is loaded if KeyboardCommand is Basic or Full. This is a keyboard "Local Navigation" command.

Values: End, R13

OpenWindows.KeyboardCommand.RowStart

This mapping is loaded if KeyboardCommand is Basic or Full. This is a keyboard "Local Navigation" command.

Values: Home, R7

OpenWindows.KeyboardCommand.ScrollDataEnd

This mapping is loaded if KeyboardCommand is Basic or Full. This is a "Text Editing" resource.

Values: End+Alt+Ctrl, R13+Alt+Ctrl

OpenWindows.KeyboardCommand.ScrollDataStart

This mapping is loaded if KeyboardCommand is Basic or Full. This is a "Text Editing" resource.

Values: Home+Alt+Ctrl, R7+Alt+Ctrl

OpenWindows.KeyboardCommand.ScrollDown

This mapping is loaded if KeyboardCommand is Basic or Full.

Values: Down+Alt This is a "Text Editing" resource.

OpenWindows.KeyboardCommand.ScrollJumpDown

This mapping is loaded if KeyboardCommand is Basic or Full. This is a "Text Editing" resource.

Values: Down+Alt+Ctrl

OpenWindows.KeyboardCommand.ScrollJumpLeft

This mapping is loaded if KeyboardCommand is Basic or Full. This is a "Text Editing" resource.

Values: Left+Alt+Ctrl

OpenWindows.KeyboardCommand.ScrollJumpRight

This mapping is loaded if KeyboardCommand is Basic or Full. This is a "Text Editing" resource.

Values: Right+Alt+Ctrl

OpenWindows.KeyboardCommand.ScrollJumpUp

This mapping is loaded if KeyboardCommand is Basic or Full. This is a "Text Editing" resource.

Values: Up+Alt+Ctrl

OpenWindows.KeyboardCommand.ScrollLeft

This mapping is loaded if KeyboardCommand is Basic or Full. This is a "Text Editing" resource.

Values: Left+Alt

OpenWindows.KeyboardCommand.ScrollPaneDown

This mapping is loaded if KeyboardCommand is Basic or Full. This is a "Text Editing" resource.

Values: R15+Alt

OpenWindows.KeyboardCommand.ScrollPaneLeft

This mapping is loaded if KeyboardCommand is Basic or Full. This is a "Text Editing" resource.

Values: R9+Alt+Ctrl

OpenWindows.KeyboardCommand.ScrollPaneRight

This mapping is loaded if KeyboardCommand is Basic or Full. This is a "Text Editing" resource.

Values: R15+Alt+Ctrl

OpenWindows.KeyboardCommand.ScrollPaneUp

This mapping is loaded if KeyboardCommand is Basic or Full. This is a "Text Editing" resource.

Values: R9+Alt

OpenWindows.KeyboardCommand.ScrollRight

This mapping is loaded if KeyboardCommand is Basic or Full. This is a "Text Editing" resource.

Values: Right+Alt

OpenWindows.KeyboardCommand.ScrollRowEnd

This mapping is loaded if KeyboardCommand is Basic or Full. This is a "Text Editing" resource.

Values: End+Alt, R13+Alt

OpenWindows.KeyboardCommand.ScrollRowStart

This mapping is loaded if KeyboardCommand is Basic or Full. This is a "Text Editing" resource.

Values: Home+Alt, R7+Alt

OpenWindows.KeyboardCommand.ScrollUp

This mapping is loaded if KeyboardCommand is Basic or Full. This is a "Text Editing" resource.

Values: Up+Alt

OpenWindows.KeyboardCommand.SelectAll

This mapping is loaded if KeyboardCommand is Basic or Full. This is a "Text Editing" resource.

Values: End+Shift+Meta

OpenWindows.KeyboardCommand.SelectDataEnd

This mapping is loaded if KeyboardCommand is Basic or Full. This is a "Text Editing" resource.

Values: End+Shift+Ctrl, R13+Shift+Ctrl

OpenWindows.KeyboardCommand.SelectDataStart

This mapping is loaded if KeyboardCommand is Basic or Full. This is a "Text Editing" resource.

Values: Home+Shift+Ctrl, R7+Shift+Ctrl

OpenWindows.KeyboardCommand.SelectDown

This mapping is loaded if KeyboardCommand is Basic or Full. This is a "Text Editing" resource.

Values: Down+Shift

OpenWindows.KeyboardCommand.SelectFieldBackward

This mapping is always loaded. This is a "Text Editing" resource.

Values: Tab+Shift+Ctrl

OpenWindows.KeyboardCommand.SelectFieldForward

This mapping is always loaded. This is a "Text Editing" resource.

Values: Tab+Ctrl

OpenWindows.KeyboardCommand.SelectJumpDown

This mapping is loaded if KeyboardCommand is Basic or Full. This is a "Text Editing" resource.

Values: Down+Shift+Ctrl

OpenWindows.KeyboardCommand.SelectJumpLeft

This mapping is loaded if KeyboardCommand is Basic or Full. This is a "Text Editing" resource.

Values: Left+Shift+Ctrl

OpenWindows.KeyboardCommand.SelectJumpRight
This mapping is loaded if KeyboardCommand is Basic or Full. This is a "Text Editing" resource.

Values: Right+Shift+Ctrl

OpenWindows.KeyboardCommand.SelectJumpUp
This mapping is loaded if KeyboardCommand is Basic or Full. This is a "Text Editing" resource.

Values: Up+Shift+Ctrl

OpenWindows.KeyboardCommand.SelectLeft
This mapping is loaded if KeyboardCommand is Basic or Full. This is a "Text Editing" resource.

Values: Left+Shift

OpenWindows.KeyboardCommand.SelectNextField
This mapping is loaded if KeyboardCommand is Basic or Full. This is a "Text Editing" resource.

Values: Tab+Meta

OpenWindows.KeyboardCommand.SelectPaneDown
This mapping is loaded if KeyboardCommand is Basic or Full. This is a "Text Editing" resource.

Values: R15+Shift

OpenWindows.KeyboardCommand.SelectPaneLeft
This mapping is loaded if KeyboardCommand is Basic or Full. This is a "Text Editing" resource.

Values: R9+Shift+Ctrl

OpenWindows.KeyboardCommand.SelectPaneRight
This mapping is loaded if KeyboardCommand is Basic or Full. This is a "Text Editing" resource.

Values: R15+Shift+Ctrl

OpenWindows.KeyboardCommand.SelectPaneUp
This mapping is loaded if KeyboardCommand is Basic or Full. This is a "Text Editing" resource.

Values: R9+Shift

OpenWindows.KeyboardCommand.SelectPreviousField
This mapping is loaded if KeyboardCommand is Basic or Full. This is a "Text Editing" resource.

Values: Tab+Shift+Meta

OpenWindows.KeyboardCommand.SelectRight

This mapping is loaded if KeyboardCommand is Basic or Full. This is a "Text Editing" resource.

Values: Right+Shift

OpenWindows.KeyboardCommand.SelectRowEnd

This mapping is loaded if KeyboardCommand is Basic or Full. This is a "Text Editing" resource.

Values: End+Shift, R13+Shift

OpenWindows.KeyboardCommand.SelectRowStart

This mapping is loaded if KeyboardCommand is Basic or Full. This is a "Text Editing" resource.

Values: Home+Shift, R7+Shift

OpenWindows.KeyboardCommand.SelectUp

This mapping is loaded if KeyboardCommand is Basic or Full. This is a "Text Editing" resource.

Values: Up+Shift

OpenWindows.KeyboardCommand.Stop

This mapping is always loaded. This is a keyboard "Core Functions" resource.

Values: L1

OpenWindows.KeyboardCommand.Store

This mapping is always loaded.

Values: s+Meta

OpenWindows.KeyboardCommand.SuspendMouseless

This mapping is loaded if KeyboardCommand is Full. This is a keyboard "Core Functions" resource.

Values: z+Alt

OpenWindows.KeyboardCommand.TextHelp

This mapping is always loaded. This is a keyboard "Core Functions" resource.

Values: Help+Ctrl

OpenWindows.KeyboardCommand.Translate

This mapping is loaded if KeyboardCommand is Basic or Full. This is a keyboard "Core Functions" resource.

Values: R2

OpenWindows.KeyboardCommand.Undo

This mapping is always loaded. This is a keyboard "Core Functions" resource.

Values: u+Meta, L4

OpenWindows.KeyboardCommand.Up

This mapping is always loaded. This is a keyboard "Local Navigation" command.

Default Values: p+Ctrl, N+Ctrl, Up, R8, Up+Shift
Values (Basic or Full): Up

OpenWindows.KeyboardCommand.VerticalScrollbarMenu

This mapping is loaded if KeyboardCommand is Full. This is a Miscellaneous Navigation command.

Values: v+Alt

OpenWindows.KeyboardCommands

All of the OpenWindows.KeyboardCommand resource mappings may be modified by users, or by specifying one of three values for OpenWindows.Keyboard-Commands: See the description for the Mouseless model in Chapter 6, *Handling Input*, in the *XView Programming Manual*.

Values: Sunview1, Basic, or Full.

OpenWindows.MouseChordMenu

Turns on the mouse chording mechanism. Mouse chording allows XView to work with two button mice. Holding the SELECT and the ADJUST buttons together will act as MENU button.

Values: Boolean (False)

OpenWindows.MouseChordTimeout

Mouse chording time-out value.

Values: Integer in microseconds (100)

OpenWindows.multiClickTimeout (Props)

Specifies a "click", which is button-down, button-up pair.

Values: N (4)
                                Where N is an integer greater than 2. Set the number of tenths of a second between clicks for a multi-click.

OpenWindows.popupJumpCursor(Props)

When False, do not warp the mouse to the notice when it appears.

Values: True, False (False)

OpenWindows.scrollbarPlacement (Props)

When set to Left, put all scrollbars on the left-hand side of the window or object.

Values: Left, Right (Right)

OpenWindows.SelectDisplaysMenu (Props)

When True, the SELECT button (usually left mouse) will display the menu as well as the MENU button (usually right mouse).

Values: True, False (False)

OpenWindows.windowColor (Props)

Specifies the base color for control areas for a 3-D look. Takes hexadecimal representation. Three other colors used for shading and highlighting are calculated based upon the value of the specified control color. The actual calculated values are done by the OLGX library to provide a consistent color calculation between XView and OLWM. The desktop properties program allows a full range of customization and previews what the chosen 3-D look will look like. Does not apply to monochrome displays.

Values: any valid X11 color specification (#cccccc — 80% gray)

OpenWindows.workspaceColor (Props)

Specifies the color for the root window and the background color for icons that blend into the desktop.

Values: any valid X11 color specification (#cccccc — 80% gray)

scrollbar.jumpCursor (Props)

When False, the scrollbar will not move the mouse pointer when scrolling.

Values: True, False (True)

scrollbar.lineInterval

Specifies the time in milliseconds between repeats of a single line scroll. This indicates how long to pause scrolling when holding down the SELECT button on the scrollbar elevator. Scrollbar sets up a timer routine for repeats.

Values: N (1)
          Where N is some integer greater than 0.

scrollbar.pageInterval

Specifies the time in milliseconds between repeats of a single page scroll.

Values: N (100)
          Where N is some integer greater than 2.

scrollbar.repeatDelay

Specifies the time in milliseconds when a click becomes a repeated action.

Values: N (100)
          Where N is some integer greater than 2.

Selection.Timeout

Selection timeout value. This value indicates the number of seconds that a requestor or a selection owner waits for a response.

Values: Integer (3)

term.alternateTtyswrc

This is only used if a *.ttyswrc* file is not found in *$HOME/.ttyswrc* and term.use-AlternateTtyswrc is True.

Values: filename (*$XVIEWHOME/lib/.ttyswrc*)
                            Where filename specifies a complete filename and absolute path of an alternate *.ttyswrc* file.

term.boldStyle

Specifies the text bolding style for a terminal-based window.

Values: None, Offset_X, Offset_Y, Offset_X_and_Y_and_XY, Off-set_XY, Offset_X_and_XY, Offset_Y_and_XY, Offset_X_and_Y, Invert (Invert)

term.enableEdit

When False, do not keep an edit log of what has been typed into the term window. This is set to False automatically when switching from a scrollable term to one that is not scrollable.

Values: True, False (True)

term.inverseStyle

Specifies the text inverting style for a terminal-based window.

Values: Enable, Disable, Same_as_bold (Enable)

term.underlineStyle

Specifies the text underlining style for a terminal-based window.

Values: Enable, Disable, Same_as_bold (Enable)

term.useAlternateTtyswrc

When True, and a *$HOME/.ttyswrc* is not found, look for an alternate *.ttyswrc* file. When False, do not look for an alternate file if one is not found in the home directory, *$HOME/.ttyswrc*.

Values: True, False (True)

text.againLimit

Number of operations the "again history" remembers for a textsw.

Values: N (1)
                            Where N is an integer between 0 and 500.

text.autoIndent

When True, begin the next line at the same indentation as the previous line as typing in text.

Values: True, False (False)

text.autoScrollBy

Specifies the number of lines to scroll when type-in moves insertion point below the view.

Values: N (1)
Where N is an integer between 0 and 100.

text.confirmOverwrite

When False, do not give user confirmation if a save will overwrite an existing file.

Values: True, False (True)

text.delimiterChars

This resource allows the user to select the delimiter characters that are used when doing word level selections in the XView package. It was added because of the needs of the international marketplace, and it allows the user to define the local delimiters for the character set that is being used with the current keyboard and Sun workstation.

The selection of delimiters will be automatically available to the user once the SunOS 4.1 becomes the default operating system environment, however this resource is used as a bridge during that period.

Note that the octal characters can be scrambled by Xrm during a rewrite of the value of `text.delimiter.Chars`. Xrm interprets the `text.delimiterChar` string when it is loaded. Specifically it will decode the backslashed portions of the string and convert them to octal representations. When this is passed to the client application, the logic will function correctly. However, this misbehavior of Xrm causes the string to be stored incorrectly if the user saves the string. The specific problem(s) that occur are the stripping of the backslash characters and the expansion of the tab character (11).

To correct this problem, one can put the text.delimiterChar entry into an *Xdefaults* file that will not be overwritten when saving the workspace properties (for example, a system-wide defaults file). Or a copy of the text.delimiterChar entry can be inserted after *Xdefaults* file saves.

Values: string
The default follows:

```
\t,.:;?!'"`*/—+=(){}[]<>\|~@#$%^&
```

text.displayControlChars

When False, use an up arrow plus a letter to display the control character instead of the character that is available for the current font.

Values: True, False (True)

text.enableScrollbar

When False, do not put a scrollbar on the text window.

Values: True, False (True)

text.extrasMenuFilename

This file is used for the text package's Extras menu. The commands specified in the extras menu are applied to the contents of the current selection in the textsw window and then it inserts the results at the current insertion point.

Values: filename (*/usr/lib/.text_extras_menu*)
                            Where filename is an absolute location to a file. Can also be set via environment variable EXTRASMENU.

text.insertMakesCaretVisible

Controls whether insertion causes repositioning to make inserted text visible.

Values: `If_auto_scroll` (Always)

text.lineBreak

Determines how the textsw treats file lines when they are too big to fit on one display line.

Values: Clip, Wrap_char, Wrap_word (Wrap_word)

text.margin.bottom

Specifies the minimum number of lines to maintain between insertion point and bottom of view. A value of −1 turns auto scrolling off.

Values: N (0)
                            Where N is an integer between −1 and 50.

text.margin.left

Specifies the margin in pixels that the text should maintain between the left-hand border of the window and the first character on each line.

Values: N (8)
                            Where N is an integer between 0 and 2000.

text.margin.right

Specifies the margin in pixels that the text should maintain between the right-hand border of the window and the last character on each line.

Values: N (0)
                            Where N is an integer between 0 and 2000.

text.margin.top

Specifies the minimum number of lines to maintain between the start of the selection and the top of the view. A value of −1 means defeat normal actions.

Values: N (2)
                            Where N is an integer between −1 and 50.

text.maxDocumentSize

Once this limit is exceeded, the text package will send a notice to the user to tell them that no more insertions are possible. If the file being edited is saved to a file, or it is a disk file being edited, then the limit does not apply.

Values: N (2000)
                           Where N specifies the bytes used in memory before a text file is saved to a file on disk.

text.retained

If True, retain text windows with server backing store.

Values: True, False (False)

text.storeChangesFile

When False, do not change the name of the current file being edited to the name of the file that is stored. The name of the current file is reflected in the titlebar of the textedit frame.

Values: True, False (True)

text.tabWidth

Specifies the width in characters of the tab character.

Values: N (8)
                           Where N is an integer between 0 and 50.

text.undoLimit

Specifies how many operations to save in the undo history log. These operations will be undone when you press the "Undo" key in the text window.

Values: N (50 maximum of 500)
                           Where N is an integer between 0 and 500.

window.synchronous, +sync -sync

Useful when debugging or tracking down a problem since the error codes emitted from Xlib will correspond to the immediate request made. Running in a synchronous mode will cause the application to run significantly slower.

Values: True, False (False)

Window.Depth

Specifies the window's depth. Use an integer.

Window.visual

Resource specifies the visual used for the window.

xview.icccmcompliant

When False, XView will set window manager hints in a way that was used before the ICCCM was adopted. Useful for window managers that are released before X11R4. Not needed with the Open Look Window Manager provided with Open Windows.

Values: True, False (True)

A

Selection Compatibility Attributes

This appendix provides the attributes for the old selection mechanism. A new selection package has been added in XView Version 3. The new selection package supports the standard XView API. The old selection mechanism is still supported in XView Version 3.

A
Selection Compatibility Attributes

This appendix lists all the Selection compatibility attributes in alphabetical order. Appendix B, *Selection Compatibility Procedures*, lists the Selection compatibility procedures. XView Version 3 supports a newer selection mechanism that implements selections using the SELECTION package. The selection mechanism that was available in older versions of XView is supported in XView Version 3; its attributes are shown in this appendix and the mechanism is described in Appendix A, *The Selection Service*, in the *XView Programming Manual*. All of these compatibility attributes use the SELN_ prefix. These attributes do *not* work with the XView SELECTION package.

Each selection attribute's description is in the format below.

INTRODUCTION
This field provides a brief description of the attribute.

Argument: This field shows the first programmer-supplied value associated with the attribute. If an attribute has multiple values, then the type of each value is shown in multiple "Argument" fields.

Default: The default field shows the default value for the attribute.

Procs: The procedures field shows the procedures that are valid for the attribute. Note: These attributes are *not* valid for Selection objects.

SELN_REQ_BYTESIZE
Specifies the number of bytes in the selection.

Argument: `int`
Default: None
Procs: `selection_ask() selection_init_request() selection_query()`

SELN_REQ_COMMIT_PENDING_DELETE
Instructs the replier to delete any secondary selection made in pending delete mode.

Argument: None
Default: None

SELN_REQ_CONTENTS_ASCII

Specifies a NULL-terminated list of 4-byte words containing the selection's ASCII contents. If the last word of the contents is not full (including NULL terminator for the string), it is NULL-padded.

Argument: `char *`
Default: None
Procs: `selection_ask() selection_init_request() selection_query()`

SELN_REQ_CONTENTS_PIECES

Specifies that the value is a NULL-terminated list of 4-byte words containing the selection's contents described in the `textsw`'s piece-table format.

Argument: `char *`
Default: None
Procs: `selection_ask() selection_init_request() selection_query()`

SELN_REQ_DELETE

Instructs the holder of the selection to delete the contents of the selection from its window (used only by text subwindows).

Argument: `void`
Default: None
Procs: `selection_ask() selection_init_request() selection_query()`

SELN_REQ_END_REQUEST

Returns an error for failed or unrecognized requests.

Argument: `void`
Default: None
Procs: `selection_ask() selection_init_request() selection_query()`

SELN_REQ_FAKE_LEVEL

Gives a level to which the selection should be expanded before processing the remainder of this request. The original level should be maintained on the display, however, and restored as the true level on completion of the request.

Argument: `int`
Default: None
Procs: `selection_ask() selection_init_request() selection_query()`

SELN_REQ_FILE_NAME

Specifies a NULL-terminated list of 4-byte words. Contains the name of the file which holds the *shelf* selection.

Argument: `char *`
Default: None
Procs: `selection_ask() selection_init_request() selection_query()`

SELN_REQ_FIRST

Gives the number of bytes that precede the first byte of the selection.

Argument: `int`
Default: None
Procs: `selection_ask() selection_init_request() selection_query()`

SELN_REQ_FIRST_UNIT

Gives the number of units of the selection's current level (line, paragraph, etc.) which precede the first unit of the selection.

Argument:	`int`
Default:	None
Procs:	`selection_ask() selection_init_request() selection_query()`

SELN_REQ_LAST

Gives the byte index of the last byte of the selection.

Argument:	`int`
Default:	None
Procs:	`selection_ask() selection_init_request() selection_query()`

SELN_REQ_LAST_UNIT

Gives the unit index of the last unit of the selection at its current level.

Argument:	`int`
Default:	None
Procs:	`selection_ask() selection_init_request() selection_query()`

SELN_REQ_LEVEL

Gives the current level of the selection.

Argument:	`int`
Default:	None
Procs:	`selection_ask() selection_init_request() selection_query()`

SELN_REQ_RESTORE

Instructs the replier to restore the selection referred to in this request, if it has maintained sufficient information to do so.

Argument:	No value
Default:	None
Procs:	`selection_ask() selection_init_request() selection_query()`

SELN_REQ_SET_LEVEL

Gives a level to which the selection should be set. This request should affect the true level.

Argument:	`int`
Default:	None
Procs:	`selection_ask() selection_init_request() selection_query()`

SELN_REQ_YIELD

Requests the holder of the selection to yield it. SELN_SUCCESS, SELN_DIDNT_HAVE, and SELN_WRONG_RANK are legitimate responses. The latter comes from a holder asked to yield the primary selection when it knows a function key is down.

Argument:	`Seln_result`
Default:	None
Procs:	`selection_ask() selection_init_request() selection_query()`

B

Selection Compatibility Procedures and Macros

This appendix provides the procedures and macros for the old selection mechanism. A new selection package has been added in XView Version 3. The new selection package supports the standard XView API. The old selection mechanism is still supported in XView Version 3.

Selection Compatibility Procedures and Macros

This section lists the XView Selection procedures and macros in alphabetical order. If you are creating new applications with XView Version 3, you should not use these functions (Refer to Chapter 18, *Selections*, in the *XView Programming Manual* for further information).

selection_acquire()

Acquires the selection of a specified rank. This is typically used internally by XView packages. It is not used to *inquire* about the current selection.

```
Seln_rank
selection_acquire(server, client, asked)
        Xv_Server      server;
        Seln_client    client;
        Seln_rank      asked;
```

client is the opaque handle returned from selection_create(). The client uses this call to become the new holder of the selection of rank asked. asked should be one of SELN_CARET, SELN_PRIMARY, SELN_SECONDARY, SELN_SHELF, or SELN_UNSPECIFIED. If successful, the rank actually acquired is returned.

If asked is SELN_UNSPECIFIED, the client indicates it wants whichever of the primary or secondary selections is appropriate given the current state of the function keys; the one acquired can be determined from the return value.

selection_ask()

`selection_ask()` is a simplified form of `selection_request()` that looks and acts very much like `seln_query()`. The only difference is that it does not use a callback `proc` and so cannot handle replies that require more than a single buffer (e.g., long text selections). If it receives a reply consisting of more than one buffer, it returns the first buffer and discards the rest. The return value is a pointer to a static buffer; in case of error, this will be a valid pointer to a NULL buffer:

```
buffer->status = SELN_FAILED
```

The call looks like this:

```
Seln_request *
selection_ask(server, holder, attributes, ..., NULL)
        Xv_Server       server;
        Seln_holder     *holder;
        Attr_union      attributes;
```

selection_clear_functions()

The server is told to forget about any function keys it thinks are down, resetting its state to all-up. If it knows of a current secondary selection, the server will tell its holder to yield.

```
void
selection_clear_functions()
```

selection_create()

The server is initialized for this client. `Client_data` is a 32-bit opaque client value which the server will pass back in callback procedures, as described above. The first two arguments are addresses of client procedures which will be called from the selection functions when client processing is required. These occasions occur when the server sees a function-key transition which may interest this client and when another process wishes to make a request concerning the selection this client holds.

```
Seln_client
selection_create(
        server, function_proc, request_proc, client_data)
                Xv_Server,      server;
                void            (*function_proc) ();
                Seln_result     (*request_proc) ();
                Xv_opaque       client_data;
```

selection_destroy()

A client created by `selection_create` is destroyed—any selection it may hold is released, and various pieces of data associated with the selection mechanism are freed. If this is the last client in this process using the Selection Service, the RPC socket is closed and its notification removed.

```
void
selection_destroy(server, client)
        Xv_Server       server;
        Seln_client     client;
```

selection_done()

Client indicates it is no longer the holder of the selection of the indicated rank. The only cause of failure is absence of the server. It is not necessary for a client to call this procedure when it has been asked by the server to yield a selection.

```
Seln_result
selection_done(server, client, rank)
        Xv_Server       server;
        Seln_client     client;
        Seln_rank       rank;
```

selection_figure_response()

Procedure to determine the correct response according to the standard user interface when `seln_inform()` returns `*buffer` or the client's `function_procs` called with it. The `addressee_rank` field in `Seln_function_buffer` will be modified to indicate the selection which should be affected by this client; `holder` will be set to point to the element of `*buffer` which should be contacted in the ensuing action, and the return value indicates what that action should be. Possible return values are `SELN_DELETE`, `SELN_FIND`, `SELN_IGNORE`, `SELN_REQUEST`, and `SELN_SHELVE`.

```
Seln_response
selection_figure_response(server, buffer, holder)
        Xv_Server                   server;
        Seln_function_buffer   *buffer;
        Seln_holder                    *holder;
```

selection_hold_file()

The server is requested to act as the holder of the specified rank, whose ASCII contents have been written to the file indicated by path. This allows a selection to persist longer than the application which made it. Most commonly, this will be done by a process which holds the shelf when it is about to terminate.

```
Seln_result
selection_hold_file(server, rank, path)
        Xv_Server       server;
        Seln_rank       rank;
        char            *path;
```

selection_inform()

Low-level, policy-independent procedure for informing the server that a function key has changed state. Most clients will prefer to use the higher-level procedure `seln_report_event`, which handles much of the standard interpretation required.

```
Seln_function_buffer
selection_inform(server, client, which, down)
        Xv_Server               server;
        Seln_client             client;
        Seln_function           which;
        int                     down;
```

selection_init_request()

Procedure used to initialize a buffer before calling `selection_request`. (It is also called internally by `selection_ask` and `seln_query`.) It takes a pointer to a request buffer, a pointer to a `struct` referring to the selection holder to which the request is to be addressed, and a list of attributes which constitute the request to be sent. The attributes are copied into `buffer->data`, and the corresponding size is stored into `buffer->buf_size`. Both elements of `requester_data` are zeroed; if the caller wants to handle long requests, consumer-procedures, and context pointers must be entered in these elements after `selection_init_request` returns.

```
void
selection_init_request(
        server, buffer, holder, attributes, ..., NULL)
                Xv_Server            server;
                Selection_request    *buffer;
                Seln_holder          *holder;
                char                 *attributes;
```

selection_inquire()

Returns a `Seln_holder` structure containing information which enables the holder of the indicated selection to be contacted. If the `rank` argument is `SELN_UNSPECIFIED`, the server will return access information for either the primary or the secondary selection holder, as warranted by the state of the function keys it knows about. The `rank` element in the returned structure will indicate which is being returned.

This procedure may be called without `selection_create()` having been called first.

```
Seln_holder
selection_inquire(server, rank)
        Xv_Server    server;
        Seln_rank    rank;
```

selection_inquire_all()

Returns a `Seln_holders_all` structure from the Selection Service; it consists of a `Seln_holder` structure for each of the four ranks.

```
Seln_holders_all
selection_inquire_all()
```

selection_query()

Transmits a request to the selection holder indicated by the `holder` argument. `consume` and `context` are used to interpret the response and are described below. The remainder of the arguments to `selection_query` constitute an attribute-value list which is the request. (The last argument should be a 0 to terminate the list.) The procedure pointed to by `reader` will be called repeatedly with a pointer to each buffer of the reply. The value of the `context` argument will be available in `buffer->requester_data.context` for each buffer. This item is not used by the selection library; it is provided for the convenience of the client. When the reply has been completely processed (or when the `consume` procedure returns something other than `SELN_SUCCESS`), `selection_query` returns.

```
Selection_result
selection_query(
        server, holder, reader, context, attributes, ...,
        NULL)
            Xv_Server           server;
            Seln_holder         *holder;
            Seln_result         (*reader)();
            char *              *context;
            A-V list            attributes;
```

selection_report_event()

High-level procedure for informing the server of a function key transition which may affect the selection. It incorporates some of the policy of the standard user interface and provides a more convenient interface to `selection_inform`.

`Seln_client_node` is the client handle returned from `selection_create`; it may be 0 if the client guarantees it will not need to respond to the function transition.

`Event` is a pointer to the structure `inputevent` which reports the transition `seln_report_event`. `selection_report_event` generates a corresponding call to `seln_inform` and, if the returned structure is not null, passes it to the client's `function_proc` callback procedure.

```
void
selection_report_event(server, client, event)
        Xv_Server           server;
        Seln_client_node    *client;
        Event               *event;
```

selection_request()

Low-level, policy-independent mechanism for retrieving information about a selection from the server. Most clients will access it only indirectly, through `selection_ask` or `selection_query`.

`selection_request` takes a pointer to a holder (as returned by `seln_inquire`) and a request constructed in `*buffer`. The request is transmitted to the indicated selection holder, and the buffer rewritten with its response. Failures in the RPC mechanism will cause a `SELN_FAILED` return; if the process of the addressed holder is no longer active, the return value will be `SELN_NON_EXIST`. Clients which call `selection_request` directly will find it most convenient to initialize the buffer by a call to `selection_init_request`.

Request attributes which are not recognized by the selection holder will be returned as the value of the attribute `SELN_UNRECOGNIZED`. Responses should be provided in the order requests were encountered.

```
Seln_result
selection_request(server, holder, buffer)
        Xv_Server       server
        Seln_holder     *holder;
        Seln_request    *buffer;
```

selection_yield_all()

Procedure that queries the holders of all selections and, for each which is held by a client in the calling process, sends a yield request to that client and a `Done` to the server. It should be called by applications which are about to exit or to undertake lengthy computations during which they will be unable to respond to requests concerning selections they hold.

```
void
selection_yield_all()
```

C

Textsw Action Attributes

This appendix provides the ACTION_* attributes that are available for use with a client supplied notify procedure. These attributes are not standard attributes and cannot be used with xv_create(), xv_get(), or xv_set().

C
Textsw Action Attributes

This appendix lists all the textsw ACTION_ attributes, in alphabetical order. When an application defines a text subwindow notify procedure and sets TEXTSW_NOTIFY_PROC, the notify procedure may handle any of the attributes shown in this appendix. These attributes are *not* valid for xv_create(), xv_get(), or xv_set(). They are provided for application (client) supplied notify procedures. For more information, see the enum Textsw_action in textsw.h. The first entry describes the format used for the attributes in this appendix.

INTRODUCTION
This field provides a brief description of the attribute.

Argument: This field shows the first programmer-supplied value associated with the attribute. If an attribute has multiple values, then the type of each value is shown in multiple "Argument" fields.

Object: This shows the object that the procedure is valid for.

TEXTSW_ACTION_CAPS_LOCK
The user pressed the Caps Lock key to change the setting of the Caps Lock (it is initially 0, meaning off).
Argument: Boolean
Objects: textsw

TEXTSW_ACTION_CHANGED_DIRECTORY
The current working directory for the process has been changed to the directory named by the provided string value.
Argument: char *
Objects: textsw

TEXTSW_ACTION_EDITED_FILE
The file named by the provided string value has been edited. Appears once per session of edits (see below).
Argument: char *
Objects: textsw

TEXTSW_ACTION_EDITED_MEMORY
Monitors whether an empty text subwindow has been edited.
Argument: No value
Objects: textsw

TEXTSW_ACTION_FILE_IS_READONLY

The file named by the provided string value does not have write permission.

Argument: char *
Objects: textsw

TEXTSW_ACTION_LOADED_FILE

The text subwindow is being used to view the file named by the provided string value.

Argument: char *
Objects: textsw

TEXTSW_ACTION_TOOL_CLOSE

The frame containing the text subwindow should become iconic.

Argument: No value
Objects: textsw

TEXTSW_ACTION_TOOL_DESTROY

The tool containing the text subwindow should exit, without checking for a veto from other subwindows. The value is the user action that caused the destroy.

Argument: Event *
Objects: textsw

TEXTSW_ACTION_TOOL_QUIT

The tool containing the text subwindow should exit normally. The value is the user action that caused the exit.

Argument: Event *
Objects: textsw

TEXTSW_ACTION_TOOL_MGR

The tool containing the text subwindow should do the window manager operation associated with the provided event value.

Argument: Event *
Objects: textsw

TEXTSW_ACTION_USING_MEMORY

The text subwindow is being used to edit a string stored in primary memory, not a file.

Argument: No value
Objects: textsw

Index

R

Index

About the Editor

Thomas van Raalte has a degree in Computer Science from the University of Vermont. He lives in Portland, Oregon and runs a consulting company, Computer Rooter, specializing in technical writing.

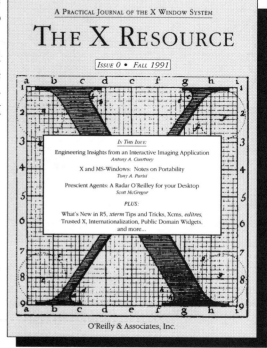

YES, send me a subscription to *The X Resource*. I understand that I will receive timely, in-depth, practical articles and documentation. (If I'm not completely satisfied, I can cancel my subscription at any time.)

❑ $65 Quarterly issues. *(Extra shipping for foreign orders: Canada/Mexico—$5; Europe/Africa—$25; Asia/Australia—$30. All foreign shipping by air.)*

❑ $90 Quarterly issues PLUS supplements: Public Review Specifications for proposed X Consortium standards and introductory explanations of the issues involved. *(Extra shipping for foreign orders: Canada/Mexico—$10; Europe/Africa—$50; Asia/Australia—$60. All foreign shipping by air.)*

Note: Foreign orders must be by credit card or in U.S. dollars drawn on a U.S. bank.
To subscribe, call (800) 338-6887 (US/Canada) or mail in this card.

NAME

ADDRESS

CITY/STATE/ZIP

COUNTRY

BILL TO MY CREDIT CARD:

❑ MASTERCARD ❑ VISA ❑ AMERICAN EXPRESS

ACCT. # — EXP. DATE

NAME AS IT APPEARS ON CARD

SIGNATURE

J21R

Books That Help People Get More Out of Computers

If you want more information about our books, or want to know where to buy them, we're happy to send it.

❑ Send me a free catalog of titles.

❑ What bookstores in my area carry your books (U.S. and Canada only)?

❑ Where can I buy your books outside the U.S. and Canada?

❑ Send me information about consulting services for documentation or programming.

❑ Send me information about bundling books with my product.

Name_____

Address_____

_____

City_____

State, ZIP_____

Country_____

Phone_____

Email Address_____

NAME _____
COMPANY_____
ADDRESS_____
CITY_____ STATE_____ ZIP _____

BUSINESS REPLY MAIL
FIRST CLASS MAIL PERMIT NO. 80 SEBASTOPOL, CA

POSTAGE WILL BE PAID BY ADDRESSEE

O'Reilly & Associates, Inc.

103 Morris Street Suite A
Sebastopol CA 95472-9902

NAME _____
COMPANY_____
ADDRESS_____
CITY_____ STATE_____ ZIP _____

BUSINESS REPLY MAIL
FIRST CLASS MAIL PERMIT NO. 80 SEBASTOPOL, CA

POSTAGE WILL BE PAID BY ADDRESSEE

O'Reilly & Associates, Inc.

103 Morris Street Suite A
Sebastopol CA 95472-9902